THE BANYAN TREE

The Banyan Tree

OVERSEAS EMIGRANTS FROM INDIA, PAKISTAN, AND BANGLADESH

HUGH TINKER

To study a banyan tree, you not only must know its main stem in its own soil, but also must trace the growth of its greatness in the further soil, for then you can know the true nature of its vitality. The civilization of India, like the banyan tree, has shed its beneficent shade away from its own birthplace. . . . India can live and grow by spreading abroad—not the political India, but the ideal India.

RABINDRANATH TAGORE

OXFORD

OXFORD UNIVERSITY PRESS

NEW YORK   DELHI   KARACHI

1977

Oxford University Press

OXFORD LONDON GLASGOW NEW YORK
TORONTO MELBOURNE WELLINGTON
CAPE TOWN IBADAN NAIROBI DAR ES SALAAM LUSAKA ADDIS ABABA
KUALA LUMPUR SINGAPORE JAKARTA HONG KONG TOKYO
DELHI BOMBAY CALCUTTA MADRAS KARACHI

ISBN 0 19 215946 1

© *Oxford University Press 1977*

*Printed in Great Britain by
Ebenezer Baylis and Son Ltd
The Trinity Press, Worcester, and London*

Dedicated
With Affection
to

DAMODAR PRASAD SINGHAL

True Son of India
and Citizen of the World

Contents

Preface

There are, broadly speaking, two ways of looking at the overseas communities from India, Pakistan, and Bangladesh. One way is that which Tagore adopts in the letter quoted on the title-page which he addressed to C. F. Andrews when contemplating a visit to Java. Tagore perceived the Indians going overseas as taking their India with them, and recreating new Indian colonies in the lands of their adoption. This view is probably the most widely held; both in the sub-continent and among foreign observers. The other approach is to see the Indians as always victims of circumstance in the lands where they settle, required to perform economic roles dictated by the structure of the colonial or metropolitan system. According to this view the capacity of the Indians to work out their own identity beyond the seas always yields to the pressures exerted upon them, which turn them into a helot or satellite group.

The present book offers a great deal of evidence that can substantiate either view: but in the last analysis it suggests that it is the dominant population—the 'Host Society' as it is sometimes misleadingly called—which determines how the Asian immigrants and their children emerge.[1] The present writer has endeavoured not to produce an explanation which is, in effect, a label: the Asians are not herein invariably depicted as victims, nor as heroes; but neither are they saddled with the stereotype of exploiters or spoilers of the lands where they settle. Least of all are they described as part of a world revolution of the oppressed; not, at any rate, in the time-scale with which this book is concerned. The book is about things as they are, not how they might be, or ought to be.

In a sense, my thinking about this subject began on a day in January 1941 when I looked down from the deck of a troopship, anchored at Durban, to see, standing on the dockside a dark,

[1] The term 'Asian' became current in East Africa in the 1950s instead of the term Indian and has been introduced elsewhere as synonymous with South Asian. It is thus employed in this book.

slender boy whose eyes were the saddest in the world: just one of
South Africa's Indians. In subsequent years, I have visited almost
every country where the Asians have sojourned: the only important exception is Fiji. The study crystallized at the Institute of Race
Relations, 1969–72, and has been brought to a conclusion while at
the Institute of Commonwealth Studies in the University of
London. Throughout all this time the study has received financial
support from the Ford Foundation, to whom my thanks are due.
I am especially grateful for the sustained support of Crauford
Goodwin. Because this subject has simmered in my mind for so
long this book owes a lot, in a disconnected way, to many friends
and colleagues. Those Indians and Pakistanis who have given me
their friendship over more than thirty years have contributed
most: it would be presumptuous to include names. On a rather
different plane, I must thank Pamela Oldroyd who is the only
typist I know who is also a skilled editor, and who has cheerfully
kept things moving.

Although I have endeavoured to substantiate all my statements
by hard, concrete evidence, some of what follows is, necessarily, a
personal assessment. It must be expected that my interpretation
will sometimes be questioned; especially, perhaps, in regard to
what has been set down about Asians in Britain, for this will be
closest to the knowledge of most readers. Anyone who has the
temerity to write about cultures other than his own (however
long he may have tried to get to know them) must expect to be
told that he has got something wrong. Race relations are not
really about getting to know other people better, but about
discovering all the gaps there are in communication.

This is a story of a tenacious, persistent people; who in all kinds
of circumstances have endured and survived. It is hoped that this
book will serve to introduce the people, originally from South
Asia, settled in one part of the world to their brothers in another
part: for I have discovered that the different overseas communities
are almost completely out of touch with each other. But my main
purpose is to get British people of all kinds to consider what it is
like to be a British or Commonwealth citizen when one's father
came from South Asia. These are my main objectives. If the book
is also considered a contribution to social science that will be
good; but it is a secondary consideration.

June 1976   H.T.

1

People on the Move

There are some societies for which emigration is a necessity. In Europe, it is difficult to imagine how either Ireland or Italy could have survived during the last hundred years without the safety-valve of mass emigration. Without emigration, these countries would have been overwhelmed by an excess of population. A hopeless decline in living standards, together with revolution, must have ensued. In the British Commonwealth there are small societies like Malta and Barbados which have also been compelled to rely upon emigration to keep them in some kind of equilibrium.

For India, Pakistan, and Bangladesh, emigration is almost an irrelevance in the struggle for economic survival and betterment. There are five or six million people throughout the world who came originally from South Asia; the combined population of the three South Asian countries in the mid-1970s is about 700 million. If the numbers of those overseas were doubled, or trebled, it would make little difference to the problems at home.

In their own perception of emigration from South Asia, Indian scholars like to dwell upon the Buddhist pilgrims of ancient times who travelled into remote corners of central and eastern Asia. Early emigrations seem to have involved only temporary visits overseas. The kingdoms of the eastern seaboard of South India—the Coromandel—built up strong connections with the islands of South-East Asia. The Palas of Bengal were in contact with the Sailendra kings of Indonesia. Then, in the eleventh century, the Cholas (Tamil princes) organized expeditions which vanquished the great Indonesian empire of Sri Vijaya.[1] Yet none of these contacts led to a distinctive Indian population overseas. Indian priests and officials married local women, and within a few generations

---

[1] Were these merely great raids, like Drake's expeditions to the Spanish Main, or did the Cholas actually subjugate Indonesia? Scholars disagree; see for example Paul Wheatley, *The Golden Khersonese* (1961), D. Devahuti, *India and Ancient Malaya* (1965), O. W. Wolters, *Early Indonesian Commerce* (1967).

were indistinguishable from local people. Even Bali, the most complete Hindu cultural colony, is no little India. Hindu culture has been transmuted into something authentically Balinese.

Trade with East Africa did lead to permanent Indian settlement. Indians were only one group among the many immigrants or invaders who created colonies along the coastline. The dominant element were the Arabs or Shirazi, who developed Mogadishu and Mombasa as great trading centres. Their dominance was challenged by the Portuguese, who seized Mombasa and erected the massive Fort Jesus, importing masons from western India to build the stonework. Their ascendancy did not last; the Arabs counter-attacked, and the Omani dynasty dominated the coastal ports, challenged by rival Arab rulers from Muscat. Slavery became the main East African commerce, and Zanzibar was its centre. Amid these adventures, the Indians laboured unobtrusively, in trade, manufacture, and the growth of cloves on Zanzibar island. They came from all along the western Indian seaboard from the Indus down to Gujarat. Most belonged to small trading communities. Some were Muslims, like the Ismailis, followers of the Aga Khan, and also the Bhoras, a Hinduized Muslim caste (from which was to come the future creator of Pakistan, M. A. Jinnah). Others, equal in numbers, were Hindus, mainly of the *banya* caste. There were also seafarers, for the Indian sailing vessel, the *khotia*, is as well-built for sea voyages as the Arab *dhow*.

How far the Indians penetrated into the interior of East Africa is a question which still awaits fuller research. A hoard of Indian gold coins, dating from the third century, has been found at Dabra Dammo, providing evidence of trade into the interior of Ethiopia. Religious influences survive in Ethiopian culture, such as the legend of an Indian prince Josaphat (a corruption of *boddhisattva*, the Buddha) and of his renunciation.[1] More controversial is the question of whether the great monuments of Zimbabwe were erected under Indian inspiration.[2] What is certain is that when the nineteenth-century European explorers like Burton first ventured into the interior they were guided on their way by

[1] Josaphat was accepted as a saint by the Greek Orthodox Church, and later by Rome. Tolstoy was moved to renounce his wife by reading the legend of Josaphat.

[2] Perhaps the pre-western cultures of Central and South America came under Indian influences? The question is considered by D. P. Singhal, *India and World Civilization*, 2 vols., Michigan, 1969.

Indian merchants. When a British official presence was established in the mid-nineteenth century, it relied upon support from British India. These Indian activities in East Africa had persisted for hundreds of years, but they were still mainly limited to the trader communities and these communities led a secluded existence—they were observed only in the market-place and the counting-house. Some maintained their wives and children back in India, journeying to see them every few years. Even those who brought their families with them, like the Ismailis, regarded India as their home, where all the important decisions affecting their community were made. Latterly, the traders of the East African coastline—whose activities extended down as far as South Africa, were referred to as 'Passenger Indians'. The meaning was that they came to Africa on their own initiative as passengers paying their own fares; and yet, the nickname seemed to have an implication that they were travellers, sojourners, not settlers or immigrants.

Surprisingly, the mercantile castes of western India continued to face west almost exclusively, building up business in South and East Africa, in Aden, and in the Persian Gulf, and only marginally moving in other directions. In the same way, Indian financial enterprise 'facing east' was concentrated in the hands of one tightly organized caste of bankers, the Chettyars or Chettis. They came mostly from Chettinad, a dry and barren place in Madras (now Tamil Nadu), and were the main bankers and traders of South India and Ceylon from medieval times. Gradually they extended their activities to Burma, Malaya, Thailand, Indonesia, and Mauritius. They were linked in a body called the Nattukkottai Chettyar Association, which decided financial policy, fixed credit terms, and assured the liquidity of its members. Despite rigidly careful business practices and a generally enlightened attitude (they endowed a new university near Madras, Annamalai University) they were the object of suspicion and even hostility outside their own ranks.[1]

The nineteenth century also witnessed the arrival in lands overseas of millions of Indians who were not passengers or independent travellers: the indentured labourers, and others press-ganged into leaving their homes. At first the labourers were recruited

---

[1] The most detailed analysis of their business methods is given by N. R. Chakravarti, *The Indian Minority in Burma; the rise and decline of an immigrant community*, London, 1971, Ch. V, 'Indian Chettyars and their Role in Burma'.

from among the floating labour-force of the Indian ports, Calcutta, Bombay, and Madras. This supply soon proved inadequate,
and more systematic recruiting was developed in certain areas
where there was a surplus of labour. An important early source of
supply was that of the aboriginal tribal people of Chota Nagpur,
who had already begun to drift down into Bengal to sell their
labour to landlords, planters, and industrialists. These folk still
relied upon a form of agriculture whereby they shifted their fields
every two or three years as the unwatered soil of their hillsides
became barren. The system, *jhoom* (sometimes described as 'Slash
and Burn'), was exhausting the soil and driving the tribal people
farther afield. The tribes of Chota Nagpur were described by the
overall name of *Dhangars* in the nineteenth century, but are now
identified separately as Shantals, Mundas, Oraons, etc. Willing,
lively, unencumbered by caste taboos, they were readily enlisted
by employers and recruiters.

In the early export of labourers to Mauritius and British Guiana
in the 1840s and the 1850s, a large proportion were from Chota
Nagpur. However, there was appalling mortality upon the emigrant ships, while a new field for employment opened up nearer
home in the tea gardens of Assam, which began to develop in the
1860s and 1870s. The recruiters had to turn elsewhere, and they
concentrated upon the rural districts of Bihar and the eastern
United Provinces (now Uttar Pradesh). The recruits were mainly
folk who had fallen on hard times, or who had never risen far
from poverty and starvation. Most spoke a form of Hindi; many,
the dialect called Bhojpuri. They came from most of the agricultural castes. In terms of hierarchy, they were about equally made
up of lower and upper castes; there were even a few Brahmins
among the recruiter's haul. Where there was an enormous disparity was among the numbers of men and of women induced to
emigrate.

Most of the labourers signed up as single men; if they were
married, they left wives and children in the care of the elders of
their joint family. Very few emigrated as a family unit, father,
mother, children. The rules laid down by the Government required the colonial recruiting agencies to send out forty women
with every hundred men. The colonial agencies constantly found
excuses for not filling the female quota, but they had to demonstrate some kind of inadequate compliance with the regulations.

In the conditions laid down by Indian custom, the woman had only one legitimate role, that of a wife. If the real wives were kept from emigrating, who would go instead?

The recruiters tried to induce widows to go; the lot of the widow—especially of the woman whose husband had died before she attained the dignity of motherhood—was one of neglect and loneliness. Many widows saw emigration as something better. The wife who had been unfaithful was even more of an outcaste; she would be glad to go, if her lover had deserted her. Then there were the prostitutes and dancers who had fallen on bad times; they were outcastes already, and the voyage overseas could not be worse than their present lot. And so the recruiter made up his female quota, supplemented by wives who were kidnapped, and women on pilgrimage to faraway shrines or otherwise vulnerable to the blandishments of the recruiter's tout. It was a sorry sisterhood who were assembled at the depot in Calcutta or Madras for embarkation. The luckier ones encountered a man in the depot who induced them to undergo a hasty marriage and embark under some kind of protection. The others set out to a life of drudgery and exploitation.

The social consequences of sexual abnormality in plantation life were to last for many decades. Whereas among immigrants arriving as families the normal process of reproduction will create a second generation, and a third generation who replace the immigrants and become inhabitants or 'belongers', the conditions of Indian labour emigration delayed that transformation of immigrants into 'belongers' for two generations or more. It was necessary to supply more recruits from India to fill the wastage. Also, a society without a normal pattern of marriage, in which women were a scarce commodity, devised crude and cruel substitutes for the connubial pattern. Indian plantation life was demoralized and debilitated for many years.

Indentured emigration ended in 1916, and thereafter the Gangetic plains no longer sent emigrants overseas.[1] Several thousand went to work in the conurbation of Calcutta and in other urban industrial centres, but the sixty or seventy years of induced emigration left no impulse to follow the routes to lands overseas.

[1] The vast migration chronicled so briefly in the last two pages is the subject of a full-length study by the present author: *A New System of Slavery: the export of Indian labour overseas, 1830–1920*, London, 1974.

The experience of South India was very different. Inland from Madras city to the south there are six enormous districts where the population has long outgrown the natural resources. Among these Trichinopoly (or Tiruchchirappalli) was the most congested district. In South India a great social gulf stretched between the caste people and those below and beyond caste, the Untouchables. Their lot was pitiful, and when a demand for labour opened up in nearby Ceylon in the 1840s, they were ready to embark upon the hazardous journey to the estates. Once the emigration cycle had commenced, they responded to demands from Burma, Ceylon, South Africa, and Fiji. When indentured emigration closed down (in 1911 for South Africa) it did not terminate the outward movement; emigration had become a necessity to the impoverished and the depressed of Tamilnad.

As the 1931 Census Report declared, 'Ceylon is no more foreign to the Trichinopoly labourer than Madras;' 'Trichinopoly district contributes to every main flow of emigration, Ceylon, Malaya, Burma, and the places in the west.'[1] This emigration reached its peak in the late 1920s; between 150,000 and 160,000 were departing from Madras every year, of whom about half came from the depressed classes, the Untouchables. However, the world slump first halted, and then reversed the flow. Mass emigration was resumed in the mid 1930s, but by now political objections were being voiced, both in India and in the receiving countries. The Government of India placed a ban upon labour emigration to Malaya in 1938 and to Ceylon in 1940. As the Japanese invasion struck Burma, Indian immigration was replaced by a massive outward movement: between 400,000 and 500,000 Indians fled before the invader and struggled back to their motherland. Indian labour emigration was never resumed to those countries. However, as a consequence of the half-century or more of labour emigration, Ceylon, Burma, and Malaya all had a large labouring population of Indian Tamils.

In East Africa, the Uganda Railway had been built largely by indentured labourers. Yet many of these men were artisans, not mere coolies, and about half the labour force was recruited in the Punjab. The Punjabis had already shown themselves enterprising people, ready to adapt to a new environment. Towards the end of the nineteenth century vast new areas of their own land, pre-

[1] *Census of India,* 1931, vol. XIV, Madras (1932), Pt. I, Report, pp. 83, 93.

viously semi-desert, were opened up by large-scale irrigation. These canal colonies were a frontier society, where the old constrictions of village life were less irksome. Many of the canal colonists—and most of those enlisted for the Uganda Railway— were Punjabi Muslims. But the community which responded most eagerly to the adventure of travel and migration were the Sikhs. Although only a relatively small community (2 per cent of the population of India, and 14 per cent in the Punjab) the Sikhs were splendid soldiers and provided about 20 per cent of the Indian army. Army service took them overseas, and in faraway fields their martial bearing and physical toughness were much admired. British administrators in colonies in Africa and Asia asked for Sikhs in their local police and militia; they even appeared as policemen in the international settlement of Shanghai.

The Sikhs were not worried by caste exclusivism; at home they were peasant farmers and artisans; they could pick up new trades and occupations where a demand appeared. In Calcutta they drove taxis; in East Africa they were carpenters and electricians; in Bangkok a special sect of Sikhs obtained a monopoly of the hardware business. One of the most remarkable of these instances of adaptation was that of the Sikhs on the Pacific coast of North America. A contingent sent to England for Queen Victoria's Jubilee celebrations were returned home via Canada. They noticed there were opportunities for hard work in British Columbia, where Chinese and Japanese workers were already coming in. Some Sikhs returned, and were employed in the felling of timber. Many were recruited to build the Canadian Pacific Railway. Others moved off south of the 49th Parallel and took up fruit farming in California. At first the Sikhs migrated as single men, but when they had established a pioneer community, they tried to bring across their wives and children to create a family life. Where they were accepted the process of adaptation went forward. Some among the next generation acquired education, and became businessmen, engineers, contractors, transport operators.

The Sikhs ventured far and wide; another group with a similar capacity for social and economic mobility, but with a more limited field of emigration were the Patidars, originally from Kaira District in Gujarat. The Patidars were farmers, with a solid reputation: 'sober, quiet, industrious, and except on such special occasions as marriage, thrifty', so a British officer described them.[1] From farming, some moved into rural trade and manufactures. Then, around 1900, Kaira District was badly hit by famine, and many Patidar families emigrated to East and South Africa. Their thrift and enterprise helped them achieve prosperity and a commanding position in the local trading economy. Among the Patidars, the Patel clan were pre-eminent (in the struggle for Indian Independence, Vallabhbhai Patel was the strong man of the Indian National Congress). From business, Patels moved into the law and other professions.

The overseas Indians are often regarded in terms of 'images' or stereotypes. The White stereotype is usually that of the impoverished labourer, the coolie.[2] The Indian self-image is that of a middle-class or professional person; and over the space of time, the reality tends to move from a proletarian to a bourgeois level.

The Indian Tamils who went in their thousands to Malaya were accompanied by clerks, doctors, teachers who also spoke their language but who were mainly drawn from Ceylon—the Jaffna Tamils, who for a time acted as brokers and spokesmen for the Indians. Similarly, the emigration of Punjabi working-men, Sikhs and Muslims, was accompanied by an emigration of literary Punjabis, most of whom were Hindus.

The professional emigration acquired a momentum of its own. Many were from the great metropolitan centres, Bombay, Calcutta, and Madras. Bengal, which supplied northern India with professional people during the nineteenth century and even later, contributed professional emigrants to all the countries where Indians settled. The small Indian community in Britain before 1939 included many who were Bengalis. Even in India, these professional people had already become different, had, in a sense, emigrated out of the traditional culture. Within carefully demarcated limits their womenfolk were emancipated; they went on to higher education, they took part openly in social gatherings, they adopted foreign fashions. Some professional men were semi-foreign even at home; they ate European food, kept dogs, smoked pipes, read the *Illustrated London News* and the *New Statesman*.

---

[1] Myron Weiner, *Party Building in a New Nation*, Chicago, 1967, p. 75. Weiner devotes some space to the role of the Patidars in political organization in western India.

[2] In South Africa, Gandhi was often referred to as 'the Coolie Lawyer'.

During the 1960s and thereafter these professional people emigrated to almost every corner of the world on the strength of their professional qualifications. The variety of their experiences illustrates that the impact of Indians as individuals is very different from their collective impact. This present-day emigration is somewhat analogous to the emigration of Brahmans and Ksatriyas in ancient times to South-East Asia and the Far East, though the earlier migrants did not, like the modern professionals, send back much-needed foreign exchange![1]

As opportunities in the former colonies dwindled, so the persistent Indians found new opportunities in the affluent metropolitan centres, in Britain, and to a lesser degree in Canada and Australia. The British working class moved out of occupations which were no longer attractive and which they were no longer compelled by necessity to follow. The Asians were drawn in. Probably this was only a temporary episode in an uneasy industrial transformation, but Western society also presented longer-term opportunities for businessmen and professionals. In business, Indians moved into the interstices left by the reconstruction of Western business into gigantic, monolithic units. Indian professional men were in demand in Britain, Canada, and Australia because before the 1950s these countries had been very slow to expand their Victorian-style institutions of higher education. In particular, the medical profession in Britain—which had attracted doctors from India for over fifty years—began to draw heavily upon this source after 1945; first to make up for gaps in training, and second to replace British doctors who were themselves emigrating overseas. A pattern of Indian integration into the British health service was established: British medical services could not function effectively without doctors from South Asia and other Third World countries; equally, the Indian medical profession could not avoid disaster without being able to syphon off surplus doctors to Britain, Canada, etc.

In 1970, 80 per cent of the doctors in India were residing in the urban areas, which contain under 20 per cent of the population; yet between 15,000 and 20,000 doctors in India were without

[1] I owe this quip to Damodar Singhal who read the manuscript and urged me to follow some of his own intellectual explorations: such as the history of the Romanies. Indeed, the banyan tree of Romany travel stretches out even farther than that of those we recognize as Indians.

employment. It is a simplification to state that those emigrating are all unemployed; many are well-placed, but resent the lack of facilities in their local hospitals. All are aware that they can earn more in the West; many are also attracted by the prospect of advanced training and practice. There is a combination of push and pull: the push of inadequate opportunity in South Asia and the pull of better prospects in the West.

Even among scarce specialists, like scientists and engineers, the same dissonance and dissatisfaction is found. In 1970, there were said to be 6,000 unemployed qualified engineers in India. At the same moment, 27,000 Indian scientists were working overseas (14,000 in America). South Asia cannot absorb all the people with advanced training; though, paradoxically, there is an acute need for these people if these countries are to attain higher living standards.

Attempts have been made to attract some well-qualified emigrants back home again. But when the Government of India approached 850 leading emigrant scientists and technologists, asking them to return, only 56 indicated that they might come back. The attractions of the home environment were not enough to outweigh the absence of career prospects. In between these counter-influences, social attitudes to migration tend to cancel each other out. Political attitudes are also, increasingly, neutral. Gandhi and Nehru had strong feelings about the Indian communities overseas and how they should be treated; and also, how they should treat those among whom they lived, especially when they lived amongst Africans. Today, both India and Pakistan continue to treat the British Asians as a live issue but they are passive concerning their compatriots in Africa, South-East Asia, and Ceylon.

Much of the discussion on communities from South Asia overseas has focused upon their total numbers. This often takes place in the context of the 'threat' posed by Asian immigration, and was evident in South Africa between 1900 and 1940, in 'White' Kenya from 1920 to 1950, and in Britain between 1960 and 1970. The Asians and their friends have replied by quoting lower totals as evidence of the truth. This 'numbers game', as it is called, is never very productive, and has affected even the most sober of professional demographers. Almost all population figures are suspect.

The total population of those who are settled throughout the world, whose origins were in South Asia, is likely to be about 5 million.[1] Other estimates have given totals as high as 6½ million.[2] Whichever figure is nearer to reality is of less importance than the conclusion that the South Asians overseas are a much smaller total than the Overseas Chinese (15 to 20 million) or the British overseas: over 50 million, *if* one uses the same basis for computation (i.e. persons of British ancestry, even if not today British or Commonwealth citizens).

It is much more relevant to observe that the Indians form the majority of the population in two island-states, Mauritius and Fiji, and in one small coastal state in Latin America—Guyana. If present demographic trends continue, there may also be an Indian majority in Trinidad before the end of this century. Apart from Trinidad—whose economy is becoming diversified—all these little countries are heavily dependent upon the export of one crop, sugar. Their economies are meshed into, and largely dependent upon the consumption of western Europe, primarily Britain.

Indians also form an important group in Malaya (or western Malaysia), Singapore, and Ceylon, where they are more than 10 per cent of the overall population, though in Malaya they are vulnerable, economically and politically, while in Ceylon (now Sri Lanka) they have been deliberately isolated and excluded from the mainstream of society and politics.

Everywhere else, the Asians are a small, sensitive group, forming less than 3 per cent of the total population. In numerical terms —which in a democracy also dictate the political terms—the Asians are marginal to the rest of the community. Accepting their political position of powerlessness, the Asians quietly pursue their occupations, preserving their family structure and family code of

[1] Answering a question in the Indian Parliament, the Lok Sabha, on 10 August 1972, the then Deputy Minister for External Affairs, Surendra Pal Singh, stated that 3,400,000 people of Indian origin were settled abroad. Even if it is assumed that this figure relates to those who came from the territories now in the Republic of India—and does not relate to the whole sub-continent—a total of 5 million seems sufficient to include the overall figure.

[2] Among the literature which followed the expulsion of the Asians from Uganda, two booklets state that there is a total of 6½ million Asians (or Indians) overseas: Douglas Tilbe, *The Ugandan Asian Crisis* (British Council of Churches), and Yash Tandon, *Problems of a Displaced Minority: the New Position of East Africa's Asians* (Minority Rights Group). Neither author gives his sources, and their figures for settlement in different countries vary strikingly.

life. Before we consider the ways in which the world views them, and treats them, let us enumerate the various communities of South Asians overseas:

Aden	2,000	Netherlands	1,500
Afghanistan	20,000	New Zealand	6,700
Australia	3,108	Nigeria	1,600
Bahrain	5,500	Philippines	2,516
Burma	250,000	Qatar	2,000
Canada	52,000	Rhodesia	10,000
Ethiopia	4,520	Saudi Arabia	1,035
Fiji	266,000	Singapore	150,000
France	1,400	Somalia	1,360
Ghana	1,750	South Africa	620,436
Grenada	9,500	Spain	1,600
Guyana	357,000	St Vincent	3,703
Hong Kong	5,000	Sri Lanka (Ceylon)	1,224,784
Indonesia	27,617	Sudan	2,550
Iran	1,000	Surinam	101,715
Iraq	12,000	Tanzania	85,000
Israel	23,000	Thailand	18,014
Jamaica	27,951	Trinidad	360,000
Japan	1,141	Trucial States	5,000
Kenya	139,593	Uganda	50,000
Kuwait	12,006	United Kingdom	750,000
Laos	1,800	United States	32,000
Madagascar	12,350	Vietnam (South)	2,000
Malawi	11,299	West Germany	4,681
Malaysia	910,000	Zaïre	3,000
Mauritius	575,123	Zambia	10,705
Muscat	4,500		

This table is intended to list all South Asians overseas, whether citizens of India, Pakistan, or Bangladesh, or citizens of other countries, or of none. It represents the position about 1970–1, the latest years for which census statistics are generally available. Since that date, the Asian population in all the East African countries has diminished, while in western Europe and North America numbers have substantially increased.[1] There are said to

[1] The table was compiled by taking information in the *Times of India Directory and Yearbook, 1970*, which was then compared and collated with other sources and substantially revised. It suffers from the defect that in some cases the figures include all persons of South Asian origin and, in others, persons from the Republic of India.

be 4–5,000 Asians in Denmark, for example, though in 1970 there was hardly an Indian in sight. These arrivals have gone unrecorded.

Externally, these communities are viewed as monolithic groups: 'the Indians', or 'the Asians', in much the same way as reference is made to 'the Jews'. In reality, these are solid communities only in the perception of the dominant population: among themselves they are separated and often fragmented.

Almost all the overseas communities have preserved the essentials of the different religions which they took with them from the sub-continent: Hindu, Muslim, and Sikh. The various castes of the Hindus are brought together in religious organizations, such as the Sanatan Dharma Maha Sabha, a conservative temple organization, and the Arya Samaj, a society of reformers with a strong missionary spirit. Other religious links are provided by the Ramakrishna Mission, dedicated to social service, and similar welfare organizations. Likewise, the Muslims have religious and cultural associations which keep Islamic values prominently before their people, such as the Anjuman-e-Islam, and the Sikhs everywhere establish their *gurudwaras*, centres for worship and fellowship. In Mauritius, the West Indies, Malaya, and other lands, the process of social and economic upliftment was often in the past accompanied by conversion to Christianity. This religious framework—which separates the Asians, though giving unity within the closed religious groups—provides the most important source of identification for the more tradition-minded among Indians overseas. For the Hindus, caste provides an extreme form of social compartmentalization which contradicts and contraverts the universalism of Hinduism.

The next significant setting is that of language. The Indian—or East Indian—communities in the Caribbean have largely discarded their mother-tongue, after three or more generations in isolation from the motherland. English and a polyglot plantation idiom, sometimes known as Creole, has replaced the various forms of Hindi which most of their ancestors spoke. For purposes of religion and festival, a few words and phrases are preserved, but not much more. In South Africa also, the pressures of the White man's world have affected the use of the mother-tongue, except among the old people.[1]

[1] The South African census, conducted within the apartheid philosophy, lists

Elsewhere the mother-tongue remains the natural medium of communication with one's fellows. Mauritius, where immigration began to dry up about 1880, still includes several Indian language groups, notably speakers of Hindi and Urdu, Tamil, and to a much smaller extent Gujarati and Marathi. The languages have survived partly because, till recently, very few Indian children went to school, and so were not exposed to a European language. Outside the home and the native language group, the Mauritius Indian finds it natural to use his own version of Creole.[1]

In Ceylon and Malaya, the majority of the local Indians speak Tamil or another South Indian language. However, in Malaya a minority—which includes some who are community-leaders—come from North India and speak Hindi or Punjabi. The Indians in Fiji are mainly Hindi-speakers, with a minority of Tamils and a few Punjabis. In East Africa, Gujarati is the most important language, though Punjabi is also heard, and the Christian Goans speak Konkani—a form of Marathi—or Portuguese.

The diversity—and to some extent division—of Asian communities overseas, emphasized by religious and linguistic differences, is accentuated by economic differentiation: the aims and interests of the prosperous, urban, middle-class Asians are quite different from those of poor workers—labourers and artisans. The first group are likely to adopt a social and political philosophy of accommodation and adjustment to Western norms; the mass of the poor, especially the rural poor, will live in conditions of isolation which can only be ameliorated by protest or even revolt.

Even in towns and suburbs, the Indians who aspire to middle-class status often live in separate areas. These 'ghettos' may be created by law (as in South Africa, Rhodesia, and colonial Kenya) or may arise out of economic and social custom, in part from the

---

about 85 per cent of the Indians as speakers of Indian languages, Tamil, Gujarati, Hindi, etc. Inquiries made by independent investigators suggest that about 70 per cent of the present generation of South African Indians communicate more easily in English than in the languages of their parents, which they speak with difficulty.

[1] The Creole of Mauritius has a French content, with many different African dialect variations and some Arab and Indian components. The Creole spoken in the Caribbean and Guyana also has a Franco-African emphasis, with Portuguese, Spanish, and Dutch as other components and some remnants of Carib speech in its derivations. But Caribbean Creole is sometimes just pidgin English with, increasingly, American overtones.

preference of the Indians for their own people and their own shop-ping and other facilities, and in part from the obstacles placed before them by others when they try to move into White or Creole areas; once again, we will often find that the 'Indian' com-munity chooses to hive off into separate residential areas for Hindus and Muslims.

In cities created in colonial times there were also different commercial areas demarcated on racial lines, as in Singapore and Rangoon. The superior European firms occupied the most presti-gious areas, and Chinese, Jews, Armenians, and Indians were all separately located. In Rangoon there was the great Sooratee (Surati) Burra Bazaar where only Indians traded; the Burmese shops were squeezed out into the suburbs where the Burmese population lived.

In almost every place where they reside—even in the Carib-bean and in Mauritius where they have now been domiciled for generations—the Indians are classified as 'different'. Theoretical analyses by social scientists also explain colonial and post-colonial society in terms of racial difference, though some argue that the line of difference should be drawn horizontally and some place it vertically. Karl Marx and Max Weber taught Europeans to view their own society in terms of class, and one school of sociologists sees race as a kind of class. Where the mass of the overseas Indians are still labourers it is possible to treat them as a class (sometimes described as the 'under class'). However, another school insists that the overriding difference is not economic but racial and cultural and conceives colonial and post-colonial society in terms of racial blocs. This is termed the 'Plural Society'.[1]

The 'race as class' interpretation seems to fit South Africa, where the legal reservation of all skilled jobs for the Whites has effectively made the White community co-extensive with the

---

[1] The concept is often ascribed to J. S. Furnivall: see his *An Introduction to the Political Economy of Burma*, Rangoon, 1931, where he declares 'Europeans, Indians, Chinese, Japanese and Burmans have no criteria in common except cheapness. All of them have in common the economic motive, the desire for gain, and in their mutual competition all other motives hamper them' (p. 165). However, Furnivall saw this as the *artificial* result of colonialism. By contrast, in the Dutch East Indies it was official policy and accepted philosophy that the 'Natives' were different from Asian immigrants (Chinese) and also from the Europeans. This deliberately-created pluralism was termed Dualistische Economie und Dualistische Samen-leving, or 'Dual Society': see J. H. Boeke, *The Structure of Netherlands Indian Economy*, New York, 1942.

middle and upper class. Only a few older, rural Afrikaners are still at the 'Poor White' level; the remainder, whether they work by hand or brain, enjoy a middle-class standard of living and privileges reserved exclusively for their race. The Africans are by law confined to the barren backlands and their only role in the industrial sector is to provide cheap labour under the migrant worker system of temporary employment. Even those who work in the offices and homes of the Whites do so on sufferance under the universal 'Pass' laws.

The Indians in South Africa are actually the racial group least identified with one class, though it can be argued that they form a 'buffer' class between White and Black. The majority do belong to the unskilled work-force, like the Africans, but a minority are businessmen, ranging from petty traders to big merchants and manufacturers, while a few are attached to the White professional elite as doctors, engineers, teachers, etc. In addition the national political philosophy has accommodated the Indians as a permanent element in the areas of White occupation, though restricting them to separate living zones, in which a wide range of housing has emerged from the slums and shanties of the poor up to the luxurious apartments of the handful of Indian millionaires. The South African Whites have a crude *class* image of the Indian as coolie and huckster, but superimposed is a very sharp *race* image of a people who are aliens, intruders, in *their* South Africa.

Emphasis on the legacy of colonialism would also enable us to view East Africa—colonial Kenya in particular—as a class system, in which the Whites occupy all the commanding heights of government and the economy, the Indians occupy the middle positions in administration and commerce, and the Africans—the latecomers in the power struggle—are confined to a proletarian role as labourers and peasants. Similarly, we might view colonial British Guiana as a class system, with the Whites inevitably in command, the Afro-Guianans as teachers, policemen, independent farmers—a kind of ex-slave middle-class—and the Indians as the plantation labourers, the undisputed working class.

If South Africa provides plausible examples of 'race as class', Malaysia offers the most convincing model of a plural society. Under British colonial rule, the Malays were largely preserved in the state in which the British found them in the 1870s, with a princely monopoly of the 'traditional' institutions of government;

the majority of the rural Malays were left as poor rice farmers and fishermen. The exploitation of rubber, tin, and other primary products was highly developed by British firms employing Chinese and Indian labour. The Chinese were also independent tin-miners, and established themselves in retail trade and small manufacturing industries. The Indians did not expand into capitalist enterprise to the same extent (though they almost monopolized the textile trade) but their adaptability and 'docility' made them the main labour-force in public employment enterprises—the post office and the railways, in particular—and this formed the basis for labour organization after the Second World War.

Thus it is possible to come up with some plausible generalizations about race and pluralism in modern Malaysia. The Malays are politically strong and economically weak. Malays dominate government and politics; they man the police and the armed forces. Yet in economic terms, they are still confined to a narrow base, and are almost wholly dependent on the rural, agricultural sector. The Chinese are at best junior, minority participants in the political process, in which they depend on Malay patronage and power. Yet in the rapidly developing economy of Malaysia, moving from the export of primary products towards manufactures, they have a virtual monopoly. In the important programmes of government-financed economic and social development, the implementation—the building of roads, schools, hospitals, etc.—largely devolves upon Chinese contractors.

The Indians have a relatively poor share in both political and economic power. Yet they have a somewhat specialized role in between, which enables them to maintain some importance. The largest trade unions are virtually Indian unions. Intellectual life has a strong Indian element: newspapers, schools, and the universities are pervasively Indian (or British-Indian). Social direction is shaped by Indian influences; doctors and lawyers include a high proportion of Indians.

Hence, in Malaysia, each of the two major communities regards the other as excluding them from power: the Malays feel excluded from economic capability, and the Chinese from political effectiveness. Each feels its own community is in reality the minority group in Malaysia. No one can argue that the Indians are in control in Malaysia; yet in certain circumstances (a railway strike, for example) the allegation is heard that the Indians have too much power.

Both explanations of societies which are racially and culturally mixed—those deriving from class and from cultural pluralism—lead to the conclusion that the different elements exist in a state of confrontation or conflict. Political leaders trying to evolve policies to defuse the pressures between communities have come up with the formula of 'the multi-racial society', designed to suggest that different races can co-exist and cooperate within the framework of the nation state. The term was especially popular in East and Central Africa in the 1950s and the 1960s when White minority regimes faced the demand to hand over power to Africans. The term has also been widely employed in Britain in the 1960s to suggest that with the arrival of people from the Caribbean and South Asia the old values and practices are no longer adequate. British society may be pluralistic in the sense that it is not so mono-cultural as (say) France, but there is no evidence that the British people are prepared to accept and absorb into their very conservative life-style the beliefs, languages, and customs of the newcomers from Asia, Africa, and the Caribbean. British society remains fundamentally British; and during the 1960s and 1970s has in no real sense become multi-racial.

The term only has meaning when applied to the city-state of Singapore. In this cosmopolitan centre of international trade, where the professional middle class live in a life-style which may be called late-colonial British, and the majority of the rest of the population live according to the style of the Nanyang Chinese, a multi-racial political programme is virtually essential, if the elite are to escape from a neo-colonial label and the masses are to be wooed from an adherence to the China of Sun Yat-sen and Chairman Mao. Hence, in the schools of Singapore a genuine multi-lingual policy is applied in order to make a reality of the multi-racial ideal.

The four languages recognized as the 'national' languages of Singapore are English, Malay, Chinese (so-called Mandarin), and Tamil. Every school is organized so that the teaching of different subjects is given in two of these languages, and all the students are required to acquire a thorough knowledge of at least one other 'national' language than their own. The application of this policy has yielded unintended results. Almost all groups are eager to acquire English, still the language of international commerce and affairs. Looking both to Malaysia in the north and to Indonesia in the south, the Singaporean sees countries larger than his own where Bahasa Malay is the language of national identity; the forward-looking student may well opt to learn this language as a form of insurance. Beyond the China Sea lies the greatest people upon the Earth; and a few students—not only would-be revolutionaries—may feel that it is important to learn Chinese.

This leaves Tamil; and who feels moved to learn Tamil? The answer, of course, is that Singapore Indians do: and by no means all of them. Short of making it compulsory for the Chinese students to learn Tamil, and for the Indians to learn Chinese, it is difficult to imagine what more the Singapore Government can do to further its multi-racial philosophy. However, the People's Action Party does press on with this policy, both at the level of the locality and at national level. It is easy to expose its inadequacy: but like the Brazilian philosophy of race relations, it does at any rate set up an ideal, even if this is not attained in reality.

In the chapters which follow we consider in greater detail how the Indians have handled the different situations which have been thrust upon them. Almost always they have demonstrated an inner strength which has enabled these persistent people to survive. The banyan tree has thrust down roots in soil which is stony, sandy, marshy—and has somehow drawn sustenance from diverse unpromising conditions. Yet the banyan tree itself has changed; its similarity to the original growth is still there, but it has changed in response to its different environment. For those who leave South Asia, in almost every case, there is no going back. The overseas Indians are no longer Indians of India; they are overseas Indians. This is what they—and their neighbours—and India (with Pakistan and Bangladesh) need to understand.

2

Permanently Second-Class Citizens

The extreme form of plural society which the Indians overseas have to accept is that of South Africa, with its *doppelgänger*, Rhodesia; but in its different way Sri Lanka (Ceylon) has imposed upon its Indian population a form of apartheid which is just as severe. It may be a coincidence that all three countries have a legal system derived directly from the old Roman-Dutch law, obsolete in the Netherlands since the French Revolution.[1] Certainly, Roman-Dutch law has shaped their system of land-tenure, and in other respects it introduces an authoritarian tinge to civil rights.

A more immediate common feature of the three countries is that between 1946 and 1950, the rights of the Indians were reduced and 'frozen'. During the following quarter of a century, they have had to accept the status then imposed upon them, of being perpetual outsiders, perpetual non-belongers. Each country would like to resolve its 'Indian problem' by exporting the problem, by repatriating all the Indians to their ancestral motherland. However, none of these governments has taken steps to introduce compulsory repatriation. There is enough respect for fundamental legal rights to exclude this solution, so freely applied in the twentieth century. The Indians remain; unwanted, unregarded, but still around.

In terms of population, the Indian communities in the three countries are of strikingly different proportions. In Sri Lanka, they form about 10 per cent of the total population; in South Africa they constitute 3 per cent; and in Rhodesia they are only an insignificant fraction (under ·2 per cent). The total population of Sri Lanka (1971) is about 12,711,000, and the Indians number 1,224,784. The main community is formed by the Sinhalese language-speakers, comprising 9,146,679 altogether. Though

---

[1] British Guiana was also stranded in this legal backwater until 1917, when Roman-Dutch law was replaced by the English Common Law.

divided somewhat in their culture and economic status, as between the Low-Country Sinhalese and the Kandyans, all (except a minority of Christians) are Buddhists; they form 67 per cent of total population and they regard themselves as the legitimate Sons of the Soil. Most of the Indian community are Tamil-speakers, and are known as Tamils; however, they form only half of the Tamil-speakers—the remainder, the Ceylon Tamils, are accepted as an indigenous community; indeed, they have inhabited the island for as long as the Sinhalese. Besides these two Tamil communities, predominantly Hindu by religion, with a combined population of over 2,500,000 (18 per cent of the total), there are 850,000 Muslims who also speak Tamil. Yet the three groups have little in common, culturally, politically, geographically, or economically. Whereas the Ceylon Tamils include many whose standard of living is better than average (and the average is low) the Indians are a very poor group, among the poorest on the earth. The Indians are concentrated in the central, upland districts, the tea-growing area. The small but still important Indian trading community lives mainly in Colombo: they form about 7 per cent of its 562,000 population.

The South African population totalled 21,448,169 at the 1971 Census. The Africans formed over 70 per cent of the total (15,057,952); the Whites were the next largest group, more than 17 per cent (3,751,328); the Coloureds followed with 9 per cent (2,018,453); and the Asians numbered 620,436 altogether. However, 80 per cent of the Indians (500,000) live in Natal, where the total population is 2,140,000: hence in Natal they form a very important group, especially in Durban, where they outnumber the Whites.[1] By comparison, in Rhodesia the Indians are nowhere significant in number, though they are concentrated in the larger towns and cities. The total population of Rhodesia at the 1969 Census was 5,070,000 but the rate of increase is high, and later estimates put the figure at 5,600,000 of whom about 5,310,000 are African. The Whites are less than 250,000; the Indians number 10,000, while about 17,000 are in the category 'Coloured', which in Rhodesia includes some Black immigrants from South Africa. In 1971 the city of Salisbury had a population of 463,000, with

---

[1] Population of Durban municipal area, 1971: 990,235. African, 38 per cent; Indian, 32 per cent; White, 26 per cent; Coloured, 4 per cent. Until 1960 the Indians were the largest community in Durban, outnumbering the Africans.

340,000 Africans, 113,000 Whites, and 10,000 Asians and Coloureds; Bulawayo with a total population of 284,000 included 220,000 Africans, 55,000 Whites, and 9,000 Asians and Coloureds.[1]

Before the 1960s, South Africa dominated the consciousness of the peoples—and especially the leaders—of the sub-continent, as the test-case in the struggle for racial equality. For most of them the issue of racial equality hinged upon the treatment of the Indians by the Whites in South Africa. Only for a few (such as Nehru) was the South African issue one of overall discrimination against all non-Whites, whether Black or Brown.

The controversy went back to the years before 1914 when Gandhi launched his first mass campaign of non-violent protest against Smuts and the South African Government. What seemed like a new relationship was created by the Cape Town Agreement of 1927. This was concluded by the South African Government, headed by Hertzog and Malan, and by a deputation from the Government of India led by V. S. Srinivasa Sastri. The Agreement appeared to provide three assurances. The first was that anti-Indian legislation, restricting their settlement and economic development, was withdrawn. The second—more vaguely—bound White South Africa to undertake the 'upliftment' of the Indians, so as to bring them to the same level of 'civilization' as the Whites. The third component—and the reason why the South African Government signed the Agreement—was an undertaking on behalf of the Indian Government to give a helping hand in voluntary repatriation from South Africa to India.

A new deal, it seemed, but the Agreement disguised the fundamentally different attitudes of both sides. To White South Africans, the Indians were only transients. They had come to work on the sugar plantations under five-year agreements; their labour completed, they ought to have returned to India, and they should be assisted to go back. The Indians regarded themselves as settlers who had made their home in the country. Indian immigration had been stopped in 1911; thereafter, only the tiniest trickle of professional people and dependants were allowed in. By 1930, two-thirds of the Indian community were South African born.

[1] The Rhodesian Asians have protested vehemently at the Government's policy of assigning them to the same category as the Coloureds for zoning and other purposes.

Hence, the repatriation aspect of the Cape Town Agreement was never fully accepted by the domiciled Indian community.

One of the reasons why the domiciled Indians did not appear to speak clearly on the issue was that their community organizations were divided, and indeed in conflict. Gandhi had helped to found an umbrella organization, the South African Indian Congress, but this was never really active, and the provincial organizations of Natal and the Transvaal were the main forums of argument. Even they were torn by divisions between moderates and militants. Hence, the Government of India had made an undertaking on their behalf without the community's endorsement.

Sastri arrived from India as Agent, or representative of the Indian Government. Under his direction, small attempts were made to promote the 'upliftment' policy, mainly by better educational facilities. New Indian secondary schools were founded, taking only Indians, for South African education was as divided as the society which produced it.

The South African Government judged the situation wholly by the success of the repatriation scheme. Because of the world depression there was much unemployment and there were some small financial inducements to go, yet few availed themselves of the scheme. In 1927-33, 12,451 Indians were repatriated, and during the next six years (to 1939) only 3,758 returned to India. The scheme was manifestly a failure, and in 1939 the Smuts Government tabled fresh restrictive legislation. Urgent pleading from Delhi and Whitehall caused Smuts to stay his hand. The onset of war meant that bigger issues took precedence. Yet it was during the Second World War that White intransigence came to a head.

Natal was loyal, British, in sentiment; support for the war effort was largely concentrated in this province. White Natalians enlisted in the forces to take part in the battles in North Africa. The Indians were encouraged to enlist—and special Indian units were formed—but the response was half-hearted. Because South African policy restricted the fighting element—infantry, artillery, armour—to the Whites, the Indians could only join ancillary formations. Maybe this discouraged recruitment. A minority of the Durban Indians were making their own contribution to the war effort, to their own benefit. As the troop-carrying convoys put into Durban docks, they were replenished by ships' chandlers who were often Indian. A small group among the Durban Indians grew rich: and they invested their profits in house-property. A judicial inquiry revealed that property valued at more than £600,000 had been transferred from White to Indian ownership during 1941–2.[1] The White Natalians responded with a shrill demand for stringent limitation upon Indian settlement.

The Smuts Government quickly passed a new 'Pegging Act', defining areas in which Indians could neither reside nor buy property. A few Indians defied the act, notably P. R. Pather, who refused to vacate his newly bought house. He was fined and threatened with jail. Eventually he vacated the house, as a gesture towards reconciliation. Within India, the voice of protest was muffled because the Congress leaders were in jail: even so, the Indian central legislature enacted a measure, the Reciprocity Act, which enabled the Government of India to take counter-measures against any country in which discrimination against Indians was practised.

In this atmosphere of mutual hostility, an attempt was made to find a compromise, and this resulted in what was called the Pretoria Agreement of April 1944. The Pretoria conference was significant because, for the first time, the South African Government negotiated with South African Indian leaders—if not as equals, at any rate as recognized and responsible members of the community.[2] At this time the Indians in Natal were substantially united behind A. I. Kajee, a Durban Muslim businessman. Kajee was a moderate (in the race relations world of the 1970s he would inevitably be labelled an Uncle Tom). He knew that the Indians could not hope for equality for many years, if ever; but he was prepared to compromise only if they did obtain some concessions in return for their moderation. The Pretoria Agreement appeared to have ensured that the Pegging Act would be withdrawn, though in return the Indians agreed to a 'voluntary' system of zoning and separate settlement.

However, the Pretoria Agreement led nowhere, for its terms were repudiated by the Natal Whites, who introduced legislation

[1] *Report of the Second Indian Penetration Commission (Durban)*, 1943, conducted by Mr. Justice Broome.

[2] It might be argued that the famous Smuts–Gandhi agreement of 1914 was the first such direct negotiation. But this was accompanied by much behind-the-scenes activity by a representative of the Indian Government, Sir Benjamin Robertson, and much anxious communication from Whitehall.

in their provincial Council to enforce a policy of segregation in all the urban areas of Natal. The Afrikaner Nationalists watched with grim satisfaction as loyal, British, Natal demonstrated that on an issue of racial equality involving their own interests they were as South African as the best Nationalist. From thence onward, despite efforts in Delhi, London, and Pretoria to find some acceptable compromise, events seemed to move inexorably towards a parting of the ways.

First, Kajee and the moderates lost control of their political base. The Natal Congress was taken over by leaders who wanted a policy of confrontation: the president was Dr. G. M. Naicker and the joint secretaries M. D. Naidoo and A. B. Maharaj. These men belonged to a younger generation, and they were the descendants of the indentured coolies, not members of the business community; most of them were also Tamil, not Gujarati by origin. They demanded the franchise on the basis of a common electoral roll, which in South Africa was like crying for the moon. They were still constitutionalists, and the label of 'extremist' which was pinned upon them was wide of the mark. However, the only Indians the South African leaders wanted to deal with were those who would play the political game *their* way. Smuts decided to make a gesture which might have appeased the erstwhile Kajee group. He planned to give the Indians their own representation in the Union Parliament, in the provincial Councils and in municipalities. The first proposal was for three elected Indian members in the Natal Council and one in the Transvaal. White opposition whittled down these concessions. The provincial representation which was eventually conceded, in 1946, was for two *White* representatives of the Indians in Natal only. Their representation in the Union Parliament, on the lines of 'native' (African) representation was also through White members, elected by a separate Indian vote. The other side of this concession was the reinforcement of the 'Pegging' provisions throughout Natal and the Transvaal. Inevitably, all South African Indians rejected this deal, condemning the new representation as bogus and meaningless.

India was now moving into the last phase of urgent debate and demand for self-government and independence, but the South African issue was not lost to sight. Every shade of political opinion was united in condemning Smuts' new discriminatory legislation.

In March 1946, India's trade agreement with South Africa was terminated by the Viceroy, Lord Wavell, and his Council. In April, it was announced that if the Land and Franchise Bill (discussed in the preceding paragraph) became law in South Africa, India would take the issue of discrimination to the forum of the United Nations. When the bill became law, the Indian Government informed the Secretary-General of the U.N. that it was intended to raise the issue in December 1946.

Before this could happen, as soon as the Land and Franchise Act was passed, the South African Indians launched a mass campaign of *satyagraha*—non-violent resistance. They defied the 'Ghetto Act', as they termed it, by illegal occupations of property in White areas. According to the Indian Passive Resistance Council, 1,286 satyagrahis were sentenced in the first four months. However, the Government merely handed out fines, being anxious for the campaign to exhaust itself without undue publicity.

The Government of India anticipated that publicity was one of its major weapons. The debate at the U.N. was one of the first arraignments of colonialism and racialism in that organization. By December 1946, the Congress was in power (though India was still not independent) and Nehru's sister, Mrs. Vijaya Lakshmi Pandit, led the delegation. The Indians based their case on right and equity; the South Africans upon a strict interpretation of law. After protracted debate, in committee and in the full assembly, a two-thirds majority was obtained for a resolution calling upon India and South Africa to resolve their dispute and report back to the U.N.[1]

The vote caused anger in White South Africa. Even Smuts, who had written the preamble to the U.N. Charter, denounced the resolution. The Natal Whites organized a boycott of Indian shops. When a referendum was held to determine whether the Indians should be admitted to a separate municipal franchise, the White electors turned this down by 15,066 to 1,639 votes. The politics of adjustment and adaptation was finished. Kajee reported to Smuts: 'I fear that the moderate policy which I and those with me have pursued is being undermined by an extremist group,

[1] The voting was on lines which reflected the growing cold war, though there was some cross-voting. *For the resolution*: 32 votes; viz: African and Asian states 12, Communist 6, Latin Americans 11, West Europeans 3. *Against the resolution*: 15 votes; viz: White Commonwealth 4, West Europeans 4, U.S.A. and Latin Americans 7. *Abstentions*: 7.

openly backed by the Communist Party.' Smuts did not reply, and Kajee died in January 1948.

When India again brought the issue to the U.N., the country was fully independent. Yet, paradoxically, the result was less satisfactory. The 1947 Indian resolution did not receive the required two-thirds majority, and in subsequent years the stalemate continued. The South African Indians joined the Palestinians and the Kashmiris in a United Nations limbo; they were not forgotten, yet action never followed.

The defeat of Smuts and the victory of Dr. Malan and his Nationalist Party in 1949 is often regarded as the end of the road for the South African Indians. Like most observers, they had expected another instalment of government by Smuts and the United Party. Psychologically, they were even less prepared to adapt to Afrikaner, Nationalist politicians than to Smuts.[1] Malan indicated that he was prepared to talk to the moderates of the Natal Indian Organization; he was even ready to discuss setting up a round table conference. But his basic strategy was draconian: to deprive the Indians of their recently acquired representation, and to abolish the token representation of Africans also, while taking the Coloureds off the Cape common roll. He was going to consolidate power without bothering over constitutional niceties. For the more militant Indians, there were warnings: they were forbidden to leave South Africa, and they were forbidden to contribute to U.N. discussions.

The Indian cause received a heavy blow with the Durban riots of January 1949. Increasingly, both Indians and Africans were becoming urban workers, competing for scarce jobs and scarcer accommodation. The Durban riots began with African assaults upon Indian shops and homes; the White sections of the city were not much involved. The death toll totalled 50 Indians and 87 Africans (mostly shot by the police), while a thousand were severely injured. Over a thousand buildings were damaged by fire and looting, and a factory and 58 shops were destroyed. The official inquiry attributed the riot to African resentment at Indian competition in the labour market, and to Indian commercial

[1] Bridglal Pachai, in *The International Aspects of the South African Indian Question, 1860–1971* (Cape Town, 1971), observes (p. 194): 'Had the leaders who opposed the limited franchise measures [of 1946] . . . foreseen the debacle of the United Party in 1948 the counsels might have been different'. It is difficult to imagine that any different strategy would have had any important effect.

exploitation.[1] Community leaders replied that the combustion was the result of social deprivation and political repression. The South African Indian Congress (revived again, under activist control) made a link-up with the African National Congress and planned joint action.

One last attempt to reach a joint settlement was made: another international conference was opened at Cape Town in February 1950, with distinguished leaders from India (Pandit H. N. Kunzru), Pakistan (Dr. Mahmoud Hussain), and South Africa (Dr. T. E. Dönges). As though thirty years had not intervened since the first Cape Town conference, the South Africans put repatriation on the agenda, and India and Pakistan proposed 'opportunities for fullest development' of the South African Indians. The February meeting was intended to be the overture for a plenary meeting later in the year, but meanwhile the Nationalists introduced and passed the Group Areas Act 1950. This measure completed and systematized the whole segregation policy of the previous half-century. In protest, India and Pakistan broke off negotiations. They were not to be resumed.

The Group Areas Act was to become the cornerstone of apartheid. It prohibited the Indians from moving out of their province of domicile.[2] The great majority were restricted to Natal, with a minority in the Transvaal, virtually no one in the Orange Free State, and a few hundred in the Cape. Within their own province, they were required to live in strictly defined locations, and the Government was empowered to reclassify an area of Indian (or African, or Coloured) settlement for White occupation at any time. Under this provision, the suburb of Durban known as Riverside, an area originally given to Indian smallholdings, but nicely situated near the seashore, was re-zoned as a White area. The Indians were removed to a raw, new township, Chatsworth. Similarly, in Johannesburg, although 39,000 Asians remain in the restricted, central municipal area (compared to 483,000 Whites, 804,000 Africans, and 83,000 Coloureds), many were removed to a satellite township, Lenasia, about twenty miles outside the city.

---

[1] *Report of the Commission of Enquiry into Riots in Durban*, 1949, Chairman Mr. Justice van der Heever.
[2] Indians had to obtain a permit to pay a visit to another province. The rules were relaxed in 1975.

All Indian economic activity had to be deployed in the Indian zones; no factory could be located elsewhere.

Finally, the Group Areas Act controlled business and industry on a racial basis. The Indians (and other non-Whites) were required to obtain licences to carry on trades and manufactures, and such licences were periodically reviewed and were revoked if they impinged upon White interests. From 1950 to 1973, 1,061 traders' licences in Natal were cancelled. The smaller trading community in the Transvaal lost 2,407 licences, and 1,078 were revoked in the Cape province.[1] In most cases, these traders were thrown out of business. Only 457 were permitted to open up their business elsewhere. The great majority found themselves compelled to start again as employees, having once been employers.

The one positive consequence of the Group Areas Act was to unite all the non-White opposition forces in the realization that apartheid was directed against them all. A National Action Committee was founded in 1952 to fight the Group Areas Act. Its demands were ignored by the Government and, in April 1952, mass protest demonstrations began. During the next two years, over 8,500 demonstrators were arrested, but of these only 246 were arrested in Natal. The Indian share in the campaign was comparatively small compared to the African contribution. In 1960 the Government banned the Natal Indian Congress, and all overt political activity came to a halt.

At the United Nations, the indictment was also broadened to cover the whole impact of apartheid, but the South African Government persisted in the defence advanced by Smuts in 1946, that the U.N. was trying to interfere in the internal affairs of the Union. Though there were few active supporters of the South African case, the number of abstentions showed that readiness to intervene was largely restricted to spokesmen of the Third World and the Communist bloc.[2] Denunciation continued through the years; but as no proposal to put teeth into the U.N. declarations was ever accepted, South Africa ignored the clamour and turned its back upon the U.N.

[1] *Survey of Race Relations in South Africa, 1973,* Johannesburg, 1974.

[2] At the 1952 meeting of the U.N. General Assembly, a resolution calling on South Africa to bring its policy on race into conformity with the U.N. Charter of Human Rights was passed by 24 votes to one (South Africa). But 34 member countries abstained; some indicated that they considered the resolution out of order. For the further debate at the U.N., see Bridglal Pachai, op. cit.

In all these exchanges, India and Pakistan were the most persistent lobbyists. But they had discovered that as independent
countries they had no more power and influence than before.
They had to be content with gestures. The Indian representative
had not returned to South Africa when the 1946 legislation was
enacted; but India had still maintained a small office in Durban.
Finally, in 1954, this office was closed, and all communication
between South Asia and South Africa ceased.

An opportunity to re-open the issue came in 1960, when the
South African Whites, by a small majority, voted to adopt a
republican constitution. Like India, South Africa was required to
bring the question of becoming a republic before a conference of
Commonwealth Prime Ministers. The 'new' Commonwealth
members—and also Canada—made it clear that continued
membership could not be approved unless South Africa revised
its racial policies. Abdul Rahman of Malaya and Ayub Khan of
Pakistan were both strongly critical of the South African premier,
H. F. Verwoerd; but the strongest stand was taken by Nehru who
insisted that South African racial policies were 'inconsistent' with
Commonwealth membership. He indicated that he was prepared
to put the question to the vote of the assembled premiers.
Conscious that he could not win, Verwoerd withdrew his application for continuing Commonwealth membership.

All were aware that this was a hollow victory for the forces
opposing racialism. Nehru told the Indian Parliament, the Lok
Sabha, that because of South Africa's enforced withdrawal, 'The
question of racial equality has been put on the highest level, in the
world context.' But, he added, apartheid had not been weakened:
'The evil continues and will continue in an aggravated form.'[1]

Verwoerd and his successor, Vorster, pursued policies which
were harsh but not unsophisticated. They might have placed
White South Africans in jeopardy if through the enforcement of
apartheid they had goaded all the non-Whites—83 per cent of the
total population—into combined resistance. Instead, they employed the classic imperial technique of *divide et impera*. To the
Africans they offered 'homelands' or 'Bantustans' where, in the
barren backlands, the leaders of the great tribal groupings might
enjoy the outward trappings of sovereignty. For the Coloureds

[1] Text quoted by Nicholas Mansergh, *Documents and Speeches on Commonwealth
Affairs, 1952–1962*, London, 1963.

and Indians there could be no prospect of separate homelands, but they were offered the outward dignity of their own institutions.

A Department of Indian Affairs was set up in 1961, hived out of the Department of the Interior. The Minister responsible, the departmental Secretary, and all the senior officials were White; but it did provide an umbrella organization to promote Indian interests.[1] In 1964, an advisory council was created, which in 1965 became the South African Indian Council (S.A.I.C.). This body was entirely nominated, in contrast to the Coloured Persons' Representative Council, which has twenty members nominated by the Government, but also forty elected by the community. In November 1974 it was announced that the S.A.I.C. would be expanded in membership to thirty, and that half the members would be elected. However, unlike the Coloured Persons' Council, whose elected members were chosen by a reasonably democratic vote, the Indian elections were confined to an 'Electoral College' of four hundred selected nominees. Some former members of the S.A.I.C. refused to stand for election, on the grounds that it was a sham. H. E. Joosub, the former Chairman of the Council, declared, 'It cannot be representative of the Indian community' and withdrew.[2] Elections for the Coloured Persons' Council have been won by politicians avowedly opposed to the policy of the Nationalists. The S.A.I.C. has continued to be made up of professional and middle-class Indians who have accepted the role of clients to their Nationalist patrons. Several well-known Indians have accepted nomination, including P. R. Pather, the former militant, who became Chairman of the Executive Committee till his death in 1970, and A. S. Kajee, brother of A. I. Kajee.

The role of the S.A.I.C. is to mediate between Government departments and local authorities on one side and the Indian community on the other. It is a buffer institution, appearing as apologist for Government policy as much as the voice of the Indians (for it is prevented from being their champion). Attempts to ameliorate the pressures of the Group Areas Act have achieved

[1] Whereas in 1961 only 27·5 per cent of the departmental staff were Indian, by 1970, 75·7 per cent were Indians, though all senior posts were still held by Whites. See Kogila A. Moodley, 'South African Indians; the Wavering Minority' in *Change in Contemporary South Africa*, eds. Leonard Thompson and Jeffrey Butler, California, 1975, p. 268.
[2] *Leader*, 1 November 1974.

only the smallest success. The Council cannot oppose Government policy and practice; it can only maximize the small concessions which the Government is prepared to offer.

The biggest development is the emergence of local authorities, controlled and staffed exclusively by Indians. The first to emerge was the municipality of Verulam in Natal. This is no longer an area of White residence, and therefore the Indians have been given a free hand, finally acquiring the dignity of their own mayor, town clerk, and municipality. Elsewhere, parallel municipal organizations are being created, where White and Indian communities reside in adjacent neighbourhoods. The plan is for White and Indian councils to function 'in tandem', with a substantial amount of consultation and coordination.

Professional and middle-class Indians have taken up this opportunity to acquire recognition and prominence with a rather surprising alacrity. In part this is because the relentless drive of apartheid, over nearly thirty years, has left them little alternative. With the banning of the African National Congress in 1960, Black and Brown cooperation had to stop, and with the passage of the Prohibition of Political Interference Act, 1968, inter-racial political activity of any kind became illegal. The former Indian political associations therefore lapsed and expired: and the S.A.I.C. and the municipalities became the main field for lawful political activity. The Natal Indian Congress re-emerged in October 1971, but could not decide whether to participate in the S.A.I.C. A People's Party was also founded in Durban, calling for 'Indostans', but made little impact. Indian political frustration was directed against the S.A.I.C. rather than against the Government: one observer concluded that 'Indians still emphasize cultural superiority in their quest for identity and use it as a bulwark against political deprivation.'[1]

The alternative is the politics of mendicancy (in Gandhi's phrase). Although there may be no hope of stopping the broad implementation of the Group Areas Act a few concessions may be won. Thus, the removal of Indian business from the Grey Street areas of Durban has not been pressed, while in Johannesburg the Indians have been permitted to have their shops in the Fordsburg district of the city.

While a minority of the more affluent Indians have been co-

[1] Kogila A. Moodley, op. cit., p. 278.

opted by the South African White establishment, the majority are still excluded from all the benefits of White society. Surveys have shown that 60 per cent of the Indian community are living below the 'poverty datum line level', as it is calculated in South Africa, while about 25 per cent are barely above the poverty line, about 12 per cent are moderately comfortable, and only a tiny proportion are affluent.[1]

The community is being transformed from the rural-based group of labourers and market-gardeners of fifty years ago into a group which today is 85 per cent urban. Urbanization may not mean prosperity. Most Indians live in shanty-towns, or run-down suburbs, while ever-growing numbers have been removed to the new locations where all are housed in row after row of identical concrete boxes. Even so, Indian incomes are improving. Whereas until recently the Coloureds stood second in line, after the Whites, the evidence now is that the Indians have pulled ahead of the Coloureds in many occupations.[2] The heavy incidence of unemployment, formerly endemic, has shrunk during the boom years of South African expansion, and less than 2,000 Indians are registered as unemployed. However, Indian urban workers are a small proportion of the whole: 8,688,000 persons are classified as urban workers in South Africa, and of these only 197,000 (2·3 per cent) are Indians.

The relative increment of the different races varies considerably according to occupation. In mining, Whites earn twelve times as much as the Africans and four times the pay of Indians; in the construction industry, a White worker earns five times as much as an African, twice as much as an Asian. In the retail trades, Whites earn three times as much as Africans, 75 per cent more than Asians; and in the transport business the ratio is about the same.[3] Most Asians work for White companies, but to an

---

[1] These estimates have been revised from figures issued in the late 1960s (e.g. Institute of Race Relations, *The Indian South African*, Johannesburg, 1968) and assume that there has been a small but distinct improvement in overall living standards.

[2] According to a recent estimate, the Whites—17·5 per cent of the population—command 73·4 per cent of South Africa's income; the Coloureds form 9·4 per cent of the population and receive 5·4 per cent of the income; the Indians with 2·9 per cent of the population have 2·4 per cent of income; while the Africans—70·2 per cent of the population—get 19·8 per cent of the income.

[3] Based on figures in *Survey of Race Relations in South Africa, 1973*, Johannesburg, 1974. The differentials are greater according to other estimates.

increasing extent there is an Asian sector of business—largely catering for the Asians, though also producing goods for Africans. By 1970, about one-sixth of the firms in Natal were Indian firms, employing Indian workers, and operating in such lines as clothing and textiles, laundries, garages, food processing, timber. Almost all these enterprises come within the definition of 'pariah' capitalism; they exist because they do not compete with the big multinational companies who dominate the South African market. The Indians operate within the interstices of the economy, and it would seem that there are definite limits to their scale of expansion.

Part of the improvement in Indian conditions must be attributed to the rapid development of their educational facilities. As long as education was a provincial and municipal responsibility, it was consistently neglected. Durban municipality had a specially bad record. The efforts by a few Indian social reformers to persuade the business leaders of their community to fill the gap were not encouraging. The Department of Indian Affairs has now taken over all primary and secondary schools, and although facilities remain sparse, compared to White standards, far more Indian children now attend school. Since the take-over, the school population has increased from 27,000 to about 170,000 and education is now compulsory up to fourteen years of age in almost all urban areas. There has also emerged a new separate Indian university in Durban-Westville, with an enrolment of 1,650 students in 1970. The teaching staff number 151, of whom 34 are Indians. Even more than the White English-speaking universities, Durban-Westville is blanketed by police surveillance.[1]

Some Indians still participate in the underground resistance, though numbers are now much smaller. The non-violent methods of yesterday are largely discredited, and today the goal is armed revolt. Those who fall into police hands suffer the same harsh treatment as the Africans; at least two have died under interrogation. When Nelson Mandela and his comrades were sentenced for conspiracy, an Indian, Billy Nair, was given twenty years in jail.

In general, a mood of resignation echoes through the Indian community. There are few alternatives. As they contemplate the

---

[1] Some Indian students are members of S.A.S.O. (South African Students' Organization) which is mainly drawn from the 'English' universities and is increasingly militant.

ancestral motherland, they are very conscious that their own economic gains, uneven and inadequate though they are, compare very favourably with the gains and losses of similar classes or groups in India and Pakistan. For a handful, there is the prospect of escape to Britain or America; for the rest, there can be no escape, and Central and Southern Africa (Mozambique, Malawi, Zambia) look no more welcoming than East Africa. So they concentrate upon the short-term possibilities within South Africa; for the long-term may not be easy, when at last the White hegemony declines. Will they then be regarded as the running-dogs of the Whites? Or will their earlier deeds as the front-runners of resistance be remembered by the new African elite? Few South African Indians want to grapple with these terrible questions. The legend of Gandhi and satyagraha, and the reality of day-to-day economic survival are enough to be going on with.

Rhodesia—formerly Southern Rhodesia—has probably the most isolated and introverted Indian community anywhere. Most of the progenitors of present-day Rhodesian Indians entered the country before about 1920, indeed many arrived before 1900. The first crude census of 1901 showed a population of 11,032 Whites and 1,093 Indians; today there are still only about 10,000 Indians though the European population was replenished by massive new immigration (especially after the Second World War) to reach over 250,000 at its peak. Thus, while the Indian population has just increased tenfold over seventy years, the Europeans are more than twenty times as numerous as in 1900.

The first Indians arrived from two directions. Some came up from the Transvaal, and these included shoemakers, tailors, washermen, market-gardeners, and others providing services. The rest arrived direct from the east coast of Africa, via Nyasa country. These immigrants were mainly Gujaratis, including many of the Patidar caste, the Patels, especially. The first restriction on Indian immigration was imposed in 1904, when the technique used to keep Australia White—the loaded literacy test—was introduced. From 1914, there was an ordinance on South African lines, designed to exclude all Indians; though in deference to Colonial Office advice, instead of all Indians being declared prohibited immigrants (as in South Africa) each individual Indian application was rejected individually.

Originally, under the literacy test, a tiny minority of Indians qualified for the franchise. By 1922, when the White population had risen to 33,000, Winston Churchill offered them the option to decide by referendum whether Southern Rhodesia should become a province of South Africa or remain separate, with an instalment of self-government just short of independence. There were 5,989 votes for joining South Africa, and 8,774 to go it alone. Among the 14,826 voters who had this fateful decision to make, 35 were said to be Africans and about 130 Indians.

Under the new regime, entry was even more restricted. Yet the Southern Rhodesian Government never applied its regulations with the mindless rigidity employed by South Africa. Wives of domiciled Indians, and children under sixteen were allowed to enter, while Indian teachers and priests were admitted on a temporary permit which was usually extended.

Southern Rhodesia remained the preserve of the English middle and upper class, and prejudice was overtly expressed against Afrikaners, and even more against the poor Jews from Eastern Europe, together with Greeks and Cypriots, who made up a sizeable proportion of the immigrants. The Jews and the Greeks were in direct competition with the Indians in the rural stores which sprang up everywhere catering for tribal Africans. Contrary to White belief, the Indians were not a homogeneous, tightly organized community; the Jewish community was much more dedicated to support for fellow-Jews. The Indians were basically divided between those pioneers who had arrived as single men, taking African or Coloured wives, and having Afro-Asian progeny, and those—especially the Gujaratis—who married in accordance with caste and had 'legitimate' families.

Before and after the Second World War, the Indian community remained insignificant (2,180 were registered in 1936 and 2,547 in 1944) and the Government classified them with the Coloureds for official purposes. The Southern Rhodesian Indian Association protested to the Government of India at thus being categorized. They were gradually moving on and up from rural trading into urban commerce. Their rivals, the Jews and Greeks, moved in the same direction, but whereas the former gradually obtained acceptance from the English ascendancy (so that the Polish Jew, Roy Welensky, became Prime Minister), the Indians were never accepted into White society. However, they prospered; and in the 1940s about 240 were registered as voters, with 60 on the municipal electoral roll of Salisbury. The city municipality provided educational and sports facilities for the Indians which compared favourably with those in South Africa.

The creation of Federation in 1954 brought certain changes. Freedom of movement was extended to all Indians of Northern and Southern Rhodesia and Nyasaland; at the same time, the onerous 'South African' restrictions upon Indian immigration were imposed upon the two former Colonial Office territories. Many 'colonial' Indians moved into Southern Rhodesia, where opportunities were better. The Government of India sent a High Commissioner to Salisbury during the Federation period, and efforts were made to encourage the local Indians to cooperate with the Africans in political demands.

The dissolution of the Federation on 31 December 1963 separated the Rhodesian Indians from those of Zambia and Malawi, and the declaration of U.D.I. two years later sealed them off, effectively, from the rest of the world. The community adopted a low political posture. While hundreds of African nationalists were interned for years without trial, only two young Indians joined them. The few Indians who were qualified to vote under the property and income franchise continue to exercise their rights, and this remains the extent of their participation in Rhodesian politics. Their educational facilities are closer to those enjoyed by Europeans than to the meagre openings for the Africans. They have fully exploited the opportunities offered by the multi-racial University of Salisbury: in 1970, among the 850 students, 460 were White, 310 were African, and most of the remainder (80) were Indian.

The Rhodesian Indians are accepted as citizens of the country (providing they remain silent, passive citizens) and can obtain passports with little difficulty. Their problem is that, as citizens of an illegal regime, they have only a limited acceptance outside Rhodesia. Unlike African activists, they cannot claim entry into Britain as political exiles. They have nowhere to go. Even more than the middle-class South African Indians, they can see no alternative to living, from year to year, within the unequal society which circumstances have made their own. Meanwhile, their affluence has increased, even under U.D.I. and they are permitted some privileges as Brown Europeans. When—as at last appears certain—the Africans win majority rule, the Indians are likely to find themselves more vulnerable than White Rhodesians.

The 'problem' of the Ceylon Indians emerged when the island became the first colonial territory in the British Empire to obtain universal suffrage in 1929. When the new reform (known as the Donoughmore constitution) was debated, the main Sinhalese attack was upon including the domiciled Indians among the electors. Don S. Senanayake—who was to become the first Prime Minister after Independence—declared: 'We were told that if anyone of us went to England it would not be difficult for him to get the vote. But I wonder what the people of England will say if every year hundreds of thousands of people were recruited from abroad into their island.' Through the India Office, the Government of India was able to resist Sinhalese objections. A veiled threat to stop labour emigration to Ceylon drew from the Colonial Office an assurance that the industrial and other regulations protecting Indian labourers would always be preserved.

Following the world slump, there was increased pressure to eliminate Indians, especially from the menial grades of the public services. The Indian National Congress asked Jawaharlal Nehru to visit Ceylon as 'an ambassador of peace'. As the champion of nationalism, he received a warm welcome (he stayed with Kotela-wala, a future Prime Minister), but he obtained no concessions for Indian workers. In an effort to outbid the Congress, the Government of India announced that from 1 August 1939 the emigration of unskilled workers from India to Ceylon would be prohibited. The ban caused much resentment.

Retaliation against the Indians in Ceylon included a campaign to deprive them of their votes by a much more rigorous interpretation of the electoral regulations. There were 141,899 Indian names on the voting registers in January 1941. All were required to prove their right to vote by means of documentary evidence which most could not provide, for they were illiterate estate workers. Less than 20,000 were successful in establishing their qualification to vote. At the same time, the numbers of Sinhalese voters dramatically increased. This was a grim warning of what a nationalist government might do: for this purge happened while a British Governor still had the last word in any constitutional controversy.

The differences between the two countries were almost resolved in September 1941 when a package deal was negotiated, giving all Indians with seven years' residence in Ceylon the status of permanent settlers with the right to vote, though all admitted thereafter would be treated as temporary residents. However, the agreement was never ratified, owing to India's reservations.

While the Indian Congress leaders tried to utilize the pressures which developed after Japan's entry into the war to make the British 'Quit India', the politicians in Ceylon—led by Don Senanayake—played an active part in the war effort. As victory came nearer, they insisted that the British Government ought to reward 'loyal' Ceylon by a substantial move forward to independence. The British response was at first hesitant. Late in 1944, a commission headed by Lord Soulbury reached the island, and conducted a lengthy investigation. Regarding the Indians, they reported hopefully that the Senanayake Government 'already has the desire to assimilate the Indian community and to make it part and parcel of a single nation'. Perhaps in reaction against what was happening in India—where the division between the Congress and the Muslim League blocked any agreed formula for constitutional advance—the Soulbury Commission steadily ignored all minority pressures and concentrated upon working towards unification. No safeguards were recommended: it was expected that if the Indians and other minorities retained the vote they would be strong enough to protect themselves.[1]

Elections were held under the new Soulbury constitution in 1947. Despite the de-registration of thousands of Indian voters, there were seven constituencies in which Indian M.P.s were elected. These were all planting districts, and the seats were taken by the Ceylon Indian Congress. With 12 per cent of the population, the Indians obtained under 8 per cent of the representation. In addition, it was calculated that in twenty other constituencies the Indian vote was decisive in electing opposition, mostly Marxist candidates.

Perhaps the Indians might have been permitted to retain their modest share of power if only Senanayake's electoral position had not been so uncertain. His newly formed United National Party

[1] Lord Soulbury later conceded 'I now think it is a pity that the Commission did not also recommend the entrenchment in the constitution of guarantees of fundamental rights'; see his Foreword to B. H. Farmer, *Ceylon; a Divided Nation*, London, 1963.

was 41 strong in Parliament, out of a total of 95 elected members. He could also count on support from most of the 26 Independents, and he could ensure that the six nominated members (representing small minorities) were friendly. But the Left had made a strong challenge, with 18 seats, and the Tamil Congress, controlling seven seats, needed watching. There was a strong temptation to grab the seats in the central highlands now controlled by the Indian Congress, a move likely to be popular with his rural Sinhalese supporters.

However, the first move was towards conciliation. On the eve of his country's Independence, Senanayake met Nehru in Delhi. They devised a six-point formula based upon the unratified agreement of 1941. This would have granted citizenship to all Indians who had been living in Ceylon 'for a prescribed number of years', but over the question of duration the whole arrangement broke down. Senanayake was prepared to reckon seven years' continuous residence for married persons, and ten years' residence for single persons, to count for citizenship: in either case, to be counted before 31 December 1945. This would have allowed more Indians to qualify than under the 1941 provisions, but Nehru held out for a qualification of eight years for all, married and single, with 1 January 1948 as the qualifying date. This small difference was enough to kill the agreement.[1]

The problem was then put into liquidation by the unilateral action of the Ceylon Government. There were three draconian measures. The Citizenship Act of 1948 limited the status of a national of Ceylon to persons who could claim it by descent or by registration. The conditions for acquisition under the latter procedure were defined in the Indian and Pakistani Residents (Citizenship) Act of 1949, which required continuous residence since 1946, and before that seven years for married, and ten years for unmarried persons (the Senanayake terms). The applicant had to produce documents to establish citizenship, which most estate labourers did not possess and could not obtain.[2] Finally, the

---

[1] Nehru was never prepared to bargain or compromise; his political decisions were always based upon his own (sometimes rather peculiar) conclusions as to what was just and right. A more detailed account of these and later negotiations is given by S. U. Kodikara, *Indo-Ceylon Relations since Independence*, Colombo, 1965, presented from a Ceylonese point of view.

[2] The whole registration procedure was qualified by fixing an annual quota of 25 persons who could obtain citizenship by ministerial discretion.

Ceylon (Parliamentary Elections) Amendment Act of 1949 removed the voters of Indian origin from the electoral roll. The effect of these changes was to render the great majority of the Indians in Ceylon stateless. After these measures no Ceylon Indian was elected to Parliament.

Whether or not the political history of the South African Indians was frozen when the Nationalists came to power in 1949, the history of the Ceylon Indians was certainly put into a kind of deep-freeze in 1949. Consequent efforts to revive them, as a people with a voice and a future, have come to nothing.

At the time of Independence, the leaders of Ceylon professed their unease about the possibility that the new India might enforce a military solution to the Ceylon 'Indian problem'. This was an important element in the decision to conclude a defence agreement with Great Britain, under which R.A.F. personnel remained in full control of the principal military airport while the Royal Navy had full facilities in the great harbour of Trincomalee. However, it very soon became obvious that Nehru attached far too much importance to non-alignment and India's role as the champion of international reconciliation to contemplate using military threats against Ceylon. India could not exert economic pressure, for almost all her products were in competition with Ceylon's exports; and for Ceylon it was possible to obtain the main food import, rice, from Burma once again. The tea-planters had ceased to ask for labour from India; there was now a plentiful domestic supply. Hence, India was not in a strong position to persuade Ceylon to come to terms over the local Indian population.

Quite rapidly, the long-term policy of the Ceylon Government emerged as that of mass repatriation. This was not inhumane in its intention. It was proposed that the Indian head of a family might continue working until he reached the age of retirement. He would then return to India, taking his savings, and a small Government gratuity, but he must also take all the members of his family with him. The proposal did not receive a warm reception.

The next important discussion of the issue came when Nehru met the second Prime Minister of Ceylon, Dudley Senanayake (son of the first premier) at a Commonwealth conference in London in 1953. Dudley Senanayake introduced a triple formula which was to provide the essence of all subsequent negotiations.

He distinguished three categories of Indians. The first were qualified to be registered as Ceylon citizens; the second were not qualified for citizenship, but would be given permanent residence permits, subject to future review; and the third category were designated as Indian citizens, who would be gradually—but compulsorily—repatriated to India. As in 1947, there was agreement in principle, but disagreement over implementation. Senanayake was prepared to acknowledge 400,000 Indians as belonging to Ceylon; he calculated that 250,000 should be eligible for permanent residence short of citizenship; and 300,000 should be accepted by India in a phased repatriation.

The response of Nehru on this occasion was both unyielding and unreal. He asked that the third category be reduced from 300,000 to 250,000 and Senanayake refused to budge. Even some of the Indian newspapers now declared that Nehru was responsible for the failure of these negotiations.[1]

Perhaps Jawaharlal Nehru realized that he had miscalculated, for in January 1954 a definite agreement was concluded with a new premier of Ceylon, Sir John Kotelawala. This endorsed the 1953 'three categories' formula. In addition, action was to be taken to check illegal immigration into Ceylon, for traffic by small craft across the narrow waters between the continent and the island was continuous. Those Indians accepted as voters were to be placed on a separate register: they would still be excluded from the central highlands constituencies they had once dominated. Four additional M.P.s would be elected by the 'Indian and Pakistani district'. However, the 1954 agreement broke down because of mutual suspicions. India considered that Ceylon was not fulfilling its obligations. When the Indian High Commissioner, C. C. Desai, met a deputation of British tea-planters (who now wanted to dispose of surplus labour) they reported to the tea companies 'Mr. Desai informed us categorically that he would not register a single estate worker as an Indian unless he or she was already registered and in possession of an Indian passport.' As the labourers were not able to fulfil these requirements they were not accepted, even if they did wish to return to India.[2]

---

[1] See *Hindu* (Madras), 19 December 1953. It was alleged that Nehru had even refused to agree to the repatriation of persons with Indian passports.

[2] *The Times*, 13 October 1964, 'Ceylon's Hope of Repatriating Indian Immigrants'.

Thereafter, the whole issue languished. The United National Party came under pressure from a new political force, deliberately exploiting the chauvinistic feelings of the Sinhalese that Ceylon was *their* country, and theirs alone. S. W. R. D. Bandaranaike who led the new forces—the Sri Lanka Freedom Party (S.L.F.P.)—demanded (October 1955): 'What about the Indian labourers, whose return to India is now just fading away into the dim and distant future?' His strictures against all who were not Sinhalese—Ceylon Tamils, as well as Indian Tamils—paid off an electoral dividend: he stormed into power in the general election of April 1956 at the head of a coalition determined to wrest Ceylon from the hands of foreigners and minority interests and restore the Sinhala language and the Buddhist religion.

The Ceylon Tamils had not shown solidarity with their brethren of Indian origin. When the overall number of Tamil M.P.s was cut from 20 to 13 by the 1949 legislation they did not at first see that they were threatened. Now, Bandaranaike turned upon the Ceylon Tamils, and elevated Sinhala to be the one national language. Belatedly, the Ceylon Tamils linked up with the dispossessed Indian Tamils. The politics of Sinhalese versus Tamils became the dominant mode. The Ceylon Tamils closed ranks behind the hardline Federal Party who won 15 of the 18 Tamil seats in the 1960 elections. They called for the creation of linguistic states in Ceylon. But this still did not offer any outlet to the tea-estate workers.

Death took away the national leaders, both in India and Ceylon. Nehru died, worn out from twenty years of unremitting labour as premier; Bandaranaike was assassinated. Their successors, Lal Bahadur Sastri of India and Mrs. Sirima Bandaranaike, again tried to solve the question which had so long defied solution. In October 1964 they agreed to another variation on the triple-numbers game. By now there were almost a million stateless Ceylon Indians to be considered. It was agreed that 525,000 would be treated as Indian citizens and repatriated over a fifteen-year period, while over the same time-span 300,000 persons would be granted Ceylon citizenship. There remained over 150,000 persons whose status would be settled by further negotiation. Mrs. Bandaranaike invited Parliament to endorse the agreement by accepting the Governor-General's formal address in December 1964 (the only other subject mentioned was that of the status of

Buddhism). By one vote Parliament refused to accept the address, and Sirima Bandaranaike was compelled to go.

The next general election brought Dudley Senanayake and the U.N.P. back into office (for Ceylon has adhered to the classical Westminster politics of 'our turn' and 'your turn'), but they proved cautious, both in considering the demands of the Ceylon Tamils and the unresolved Indian question.[1] The Indo-Ceylon Agreement (Implementation) Act of 1968 removed the fears held by many of compulsory repatriation of those who became Indian citizens. However, by 1969 only 1,208 Ceylon Indians had been granted Ceylon citizenship, compared to 41,877 granted Indian citizenship. Also, 24,806 Indians left Ceylon for India in 1964–9. After Mrs. Bandaranaike returned to power in 1970 she enacted a new republican constitution in 1972. This recognized Sinhala as the single, official language of government and acknowledged the 'foremost place' of Buddhism in the nation's culture. By elimination, the non-Sinhalese, non-Buddhists are accorded minority status, at best. Mrs. Bandaranaike ran into a host of troubles (the greatest being a radical revolt, suppressed by punitive force) but she found time to consult with Mrs. Gandhi, who paid a three-day visit to the island in April 1973. Their talks covered a wide range of issues—including international and regional questions, on which they agreed to cooperate—and paved the way for a revision of the Sirima–Sastri agreement, which was finalized in January 1974.

The Sirima–Indira Pact (as it is inevitably described) endorsed the triple formula, and concluded that the 150,000 persons over whom agreement was not reached in 1964 should be accepted as the equal responsibility of the two countries (75,000 for Sri Lanka, 75,000 for India); thus, 600,000 Indians would be registered for repatriation, while 375,000 would receive the citizenship of Sri Lanka.[2]

[1] The U.N.P. return to power was helped by Indian support. Senanayake reached an understanding with the leader of the (Indian) Ceylon Workers Congress, S. Thondaman, to ameliorate the conditions of the agreement of October 1964, but this proved a political embarrassment to the U.N.P. See A. Jeyaratnam Wilson, *Electoral Politics in an Emergent State; the Ceylon General Election of May 1970*, Cambridge, 1975, pp. 31–2, 132–3.

[2] As the total Indian population of Ceylon had now reached about 1,230,000, the Sirima–Indira Pact did not close the issue; there remained 250,000 Indians outside the Pact. Under the decennial re-negotiation approach, whereby discussions are based on the last set of figures, there can never be finality.

However, the formal agreement did nothing towards resolving the question of who would go and who would stay. For the whole Indian population on the island, Ceylon is the place where they have spent the greater part of their lives (apart from the illegal immigrants of recent years) while for most it is the land where they were born. By the end of 1974, over 700,000 had applied for the citizenship of Sri Lanka, though only 140,000 had succeeded in establishing their right to registration. Indian policy has again been geared to keeping in time with Sri Lanka; hence, when 400,000 Indians had applied for the citizenship of their ancestral land, the Indian High Commissioner closed the lists. It looks as though the whole question will drag on and on, for the Sri Lanka authorities keep a sharp observance on what India is actually doing, rather than abiding by the formal commitment.

The dilemma of the estate workers is made much worse by the rapid deterioration of the economic climate in both countries. In India, the inland districts of Tamil Nadu already support a heavy concentration of population. The obvious area in which to settle the repatriated estate workers would be in the Nilgiri Hills, where there are well-established tea, coffee, and rubber estates. But these areas already have a work-force whose members are ill-paid and are agitating for better conditions. Within Sri Lanka, there has been a steady economic decline for over a decade. Inflation is running at a higher rate than in India, and a cumbersome network of exchange controls prevents any movement of funds. If the repatriation of Indian workers is based upon the assumption that they can return to India with their savings, only a tiny minority of the foremen, *kanganis*, will have managed to accumulate any savings because of inflation, while the working of exchange controls will prevent even this minority from exporting their money.

Most of the estate Indians have no prospect of even this kind of future. During the 1960s their living standards, formerly somewhat higher than those of their Sinhalese peasant neighbours, have sharply declined.[1] While prices of all necessities, including food, rose steeply, wages remained static, until in 1974 a long-overdue increase of 30 per cent was granted. Present rates of pay are still badly depressed. Most estate families are all members of the work-

[1] For a different interpretation, see *Equality of Opportunity in Employment in Asia: Problems and Policies*, International Labour Office, Geneva, 1970; paper by E. S. Appadurai of Ceylon.

force. The women pick the leaf from the bushes, the men transport the leaf to the factory and carry out all the processes in the factory, while youngsters of twelve years and upward are employed on weeding, sweeping, and other odd jobs. The rates of pay vary quite considerably from one estate to another, but men will earn about Rs.60 a month, women Rs.45–50, and juveniles Rs.20–25. This means that the combined income of a man, his wife, and one working youngster totals about £6·50 a month, though each person is also paid in kind, the weekly ration being 2 lb. of rice, 3½ lb. flour, 3 ounces sugar. These wages are, of course, earned only when the workers are actually employed, but for many weeks in the year they are laid off, and then their only support from the estate is the right to live in the estate lines.

The workers are supposed to receive certain other benefits, such as medical care and education for their children. These obligations are partially discharged on the better-run estates and are virtually ignored on the backward estates. Whereas until Independence all the estates were headed by a European manager, usually with a European assistant, and were owned by a big Western company, there has been a steady reduction of European participation as Government controls have made the export of profits almost impossible and taxation has gnawed away at these profits. The old system was paternalistic, and often despotic, but there was continuity, and a certain sense of responsibility for the estate workers. Today, increasingly, the estates are run-down and are managed solely for short-term profits. The workers' accommodation, the 'lines' —which may consist of units in a long barrack, but are most often hutments set in line—are almost all forty, or fifty, or sixty years old. They have no proper services, no water-pipes, no electricity, and worst of all, no proper sanitation.

The workers are still subject to the 'insanitary' diseases which afflicted their forbears—dysentery and hookworm (anchylostomiasis), with occasional outbreaks of cholera. In addition to endemic disease, they are now suffering from chronic malnutrition, owing to inadequate diet, which at times amounts to starvation (in periods of lay-off, they are actually limited to drinking tea and boiling up roots).

This state of things has largely flowed from the political disagreement about which country is responsible for these poor people. Before the Second World War, and immediately after, the Government of India maintained an Agent, accredited to the Ceylon Government, with authority to watch over the conditions of the estate workers. The Agent resided permanently at Kandy and was able to negotiate with the tea-estate companies, as well as with the authorities. Because India no longer regards the estate workers as Indian citizens, they have withdrawn their Agent.

Similarly, the Ceylon Government has a Labour Department, and in former days Labour Officers kept a close eye upon the estates and were able to ensure that the tea companies discharged their obligations, defined at length in laws and regulations. Today, the political leadership of Sri Lanka does not consider the estate workers to be their responsibility. Their main objective is to promote cooperative agriculture for the rural Sinhalese. The labour code is a dead letter. The Minimum Wages code, for example, which is enforced for all other workers, is ignored on the tea estates.

Under the old regulations, estates were required to provide schools for the children of the workers. In theory, the Ceylon Government took over this responsibility under the 1951 Education Act. In reality, there are no schools for the majority of the Indian children. The total number of schools has fallen steadily and is now about 800 altogether, accepting about 75,000 children out of a total of over 300,000. The pupil-teacher ratio is one to 63.[1] Because the stateless children are not included when a calculation is made for the purpose of determining in which language primary education shall be given, almost all the estate schools in the central highlands use Sinhalese as the language of instruction.[2]

There are signs that the neglect which the estate workers have suffered for so long is, in the 1970s, reaching disaster-point. Infant mortality, and mortality generally, run at much worse levels than for the rest of the population. There are sporadic protests—strikes, and rowdy scenes—on individual estates, but the workers are

[1] See paper by S. Thondaman in *Equality of Opportunity in Employment in Asia*, previously cited. His paper provides a strong alternative argument to that of Appadurai.

[2] An estate school might have 100 Indians, 10 Ceylon Tamils, and 30 Sinhalese children on its roll. The 100 Indians would not be counted, therefore education would be given in Sinhalese. The same policy is adapted to the calculation of constituency boundaries: the Indians are regarded as present but invisible. The rural Kandyan constituencies (the S.L.F.P. strongholds) are calculated on a *total* population which includes the Indian workers, though they have no vote. Hence the Kandyan highlands are substantially over-represented in Parliament.

without any effective organized trade union power.[1] Some of the
estate Indians drift away in desperation. Many are beggars in
Kandy and Colombo, and some have been reduced to selling
their children into bondage.

From time to time, the *Hindu*, and other Indian newspapers,
have run features on the plight of the Ceylon Indians. The story
has been picked up in the West, and the misery has been plainly
revealed on the Independent Television programme 'World in
Action' and has been reported in the *Guardian* and the *Observer*.
The response, both in India and Britain, has been ambivalent.
Even when British firms have featured in these exposures, there
has been only apology, and no action. Indeed, the publicity has
actually backfired. Brooke Bond, one of the British firms involved, decided in May 1975 that rather than institute expensive
reforms it would hand over its tea estates to the Government of
Sri Lanka, virtually as a gift. The result will be that the estates
will be made over to Sinhalese cooperatives, and the present
Indian workers will have to search for non-existent alternative
employment.

Anti-Indian discrimination is not confined to the estates. Since
1956, three important parts of the private sector have been
nationalized: the port of Colombo, the bus services, and life
insurance. The port of Colombo previously employed large
numbers of Indian Tamil dockers. These have almost all been
replaced by Sinhalese. There are other examples of discrimination
by Government policy. The Estate Bazaar Act 1958, allows the
Government to acquire an estate bazaar, and when this happens,
stateless stallholders are expropriated.

It is perhaps not surprising that the professional and middle-
class Indian population, largely concentrated in Colombo, do not
involve themselves in the miseries of other Indians. Indian doctors,
lawyers, and teachers are still working, as individuals, among their
Sinhalese counterparts. Indian businessmen, including the Chettyars, are still important in trade and credit operations, though
much ingenuity is required to operate in and out of the network
of regulations. These professional and middle-class people form a
high proportion of those who have succeeded in registering their
citizenship applications, or are high on the list for registration.

---

[1] The president of one of the biggest estate trade unions—who is a descendant
of a *kangani*—is himself the owner of a big tea estate.

Naturally they do not intend to get involved in protests which could so easily do damage to their citizenship claims.[1]

In an effort to increase their political effectiveness, the main Indian organization, the Ceylon Workers' Congress, merged with all the main Ceylon Tamil parties in May 1972 into one body, the Tamil United Front, led by the veteran chief of Tamil politics, S. J. V. Chelvanayakam, to assert 'the freedom, dignity and rights of the Tamil people'; the Front launched a non-cooperation campaign in October 1972, but without avail. In 1976 the Ceylon Workers' Congress withdrew from the coalition, and renounced the common demand for a separate Tamil state.

Some see the best prospect for the 'under class' of the Ceylon Indians in a physical move into the northern province of the island, the Tamil stronghold. The hard-liners of the Tamil United Front[2] advocate this as part of their campaign for a separate Tamil state. Some of their spokesmen openly observe that more pressures are needed on the estate-Indians so as to start a mass exodus. The expectation is, presumably, that if the Ceylon Tamils and Indian Tamils congregate together they will be numerically twice as strong, and can demand a much bigger 'Tamil-stan'. However, the implications of a divided island have not been thought out, even in outline. The northern provinces have few natural resources, and Tamils are almost inextricably mixed up in the economy of the non-Tamil areas.

There is no encouragement for such a move from India; indeed, there is clear discouragement. Within Tamil Nadu there is a strong cultural movement, reaching out to Malaysia and Ceylon. At the popular level this is manifested in Indian Tamil films and pop songs, and at a more intellectual level in literary clubs and congresses. But cultural imperialism is a very different phenomenon from political imperialism. Enough excitement is generated, however, to give the more chauvinist Sinhalese politicians a reason for declaring that they are threatened by a 'Greater Tamil Nadu', and to call for stronger counter-measures against all the Tamils in Ceylon. Hence, the separatist movement seems effective only in being counter-productive.

[1] Their future may be threatened by educational extinction. In 1953 Indians amounted to 1·4 per cent of the university students in Ceylon. By 1967 they were less than 0·1 per cent.

[2] Later the Tamil United Front was re-named the Tamil Liberation Front, with Thondaman as co-president.

In their powerless condition, the Ceylon Indians cannot see much hope in any direction. Their circumstances are fashioned for them by others. This is the factor that links together the otherwise dissimilar Indian communities of these three countries. Their role has been created for them by the ideology of the dominant group: the Whites in Southern Africa, and the Sinhalese in Sri Lanka. This ideology has sought to restrict them to the political and cultural status of an outsider—for all time, that of an Indian from India. They are compelled to assume a ghetto identity, and the only escape offered is that of a return to the ancestral motherland. Yet their long sojourn in these inhospitable lands has largely detached them from that motherland; when they do return they are strangers in India.

3

Independent—But Still Colonized

In the era of decolonization in the 1950s and 1960s, Trinidad was well up with the small, island-states while Guyana, Mauritius, and Fiji lagged behind in the independence race. All but Trinidad are predominantly sugar-producing colonies with a clear majority of the population who are Indian in origin. Mauritius is the nearest to India and the island most deeply affected by Indian immigration. In 1971 the total population was 830,606 of whom 575,123 (69 per cent) are regarded as Indians, though the major immigration took place before 1880. Among the other peoples of the island, those originally from China amount to 24,996 (3 per cent) and the White *Franco-Mauriciens* are some 17,000 (2 per cent). The remainder, 213,487 (26 per cent) are the descendants of the slaves imported from Madagascar and Africa (East and West). Many of them have the blood of other continents in their veins, and the term Creole can cover those who are White, through to those who are Black.[1]

The total population of Guyana in 1970 was 714,233. The Indians (or East Indians) account for 51 per cent, the Afro-Guyanese form nearly 31 per cent, while 5 per cent are Amerindians, 1 per cent Portuguese, and 0·6 per cent Chinese. The remainder (about 11 per cent) are classed as 'mixed', with a strong African element among them. The population of Fiji was estimated at 531,000 for 1971, and the Indian section forms

[1] The accepted attitude to the population-mix may be understood by reference to a colonial report, selected at random, *Mauritius: Report for 1928*, p. 34: 'The population of the island is divided into two groups, the general population, which includes Africans and Chinese, and the Indian population. The estimated total population on the 31st December 1928 was 404,802 (general population, 123,777, Indian population, 281,025).' We note that ratios have not changed over nearly fifty years, neither has the attitude which relegates the majority community to a special category, and regards the minorities as the 'general population'. See *Encyclopaedia Britannica*, (1974) vol 11, p. 715: 'The largest ethnic group is Indian, comprising both Hindus and Muslims, followed by a general group composed of those who are either European, African, or Malagasy or who are of mixed parentage. All are Christians.' The author is *Franco-Mauricien*.

50·8 per cent of the total population. The Melanesian Fijians are just under 43 per cent, persons of European and Eurasian stock form nearly 3 per cent, and the remainder are other Pacific Islanders and Chinese.

Trinidad and Tobago is different from most other states in that all its peoples are minorities (if we choose to regard them in that way). The total population in 1970 numbered 945,210, and was composed of 43·3 per cent Blacks, 36·4 per cent East Indians, 2 per cent Whites, 1 per cent Chinese, and 16·3 per cent in the category 'mixed' (in Trinidad the mixture includes Spanish as well as French and African elements).[1]

In all four states, the Indians (and the Blacks) form the base of the economic pyramid. They provide the labour force required in the plantation industries in which human labour is still reckoned cheap, and investment in plant and technology is geared to cheap labour. Most of the producing corporations are based in metropolitan countries: for Fiji, till recently, in Australia, for Mauritius, mainly Britain, and for Trinidad and Guyana the metropolitan overlords are British, Canadian, and American. The top levels of management in these four states are metropolitan also, though for Mauritius there is an important difference. In Fiji, Trinidad, and Guyana British, Australian, or North American managers are transients; they come for periods which are increasingly brief, and then the firm sends them somewhere else. In Mauritius the White managers have been in their Île de France since the eighteenth century, and they have no intention of allowing the formalities of Independence to disturb them. The pre-eminence of this Francophone elite has made an enormous cultural difference—and, till the mid-1960s, a considerable political difference.

All four states are examples of J. S. Furnivall's 'industrial agriculture'.[2] The fronds of the sugar-palm waving in the sea-breeze have undeniable beauty; but there is something uncanny about the rural landscape in which, for mile after mile, the sugar-cane stands in regimented ranks. Perhaps because the tea-

[1] These proportions do appear to represent the reality of the situation, though delays in releasing the latest Trinidad census statistics have been widely interpreted as an indication that actually the East Indian community is now greater than the Black community. A similar delay in publishing the results of the last census in Malaysia was likewise interpreted as indicating that Chinese had overtaken the Malays as the largest group, but later this was disproved.

[2] *Political Economy of Burma*, p. 44.

gardens are always in the highlands, with towering peaks above, the monotony of bush after bush, all pruned to the same size and shape, is less overwhelming. Most oppressive of all are plantations of rubber. As one drives down a road between the rubber groves, and line after line of darkly looming rubber trees stretch out endlessly, the effect is completely opposite to that of a natural forest. It appears sinister and sterile.

At the centre of cultivation stands the factory—where the sugar-cane is crushed and the crystals are manufactured, or the tea is dried and packaged, or the rubber is transformed from latex into sheets. The factory might be in a New England town like Manchester or in Birmingham, England. It is the 'dark satanic mill' where man is the necessary adjunct to the machine. Somewhere on the plantation, beyond the factory, we shall find the dwelling-places of the workers. They may live in regulated lines on the estate, or they may have settled in a straggling village beyond its boundaries. Even the best labourers' dwellings have a woebegone, bedraggled air about them. They may have been standing for seventy years, but they seem to have a temporary appearance.[1] Why do people live here? Because they work on the estate. The connection between the place where you work, and the place where you spend your remaining hours, is just as stark as in a Western industrial company-town.

In these conditions, the workers cannot create a community of their own. The contrast between a shabby, rootless plantation village and a village in India—just as poor, or maybe poorer—is complete. The Indian village seems always to have been there —the temple, the banyan trees, the narrow lanes and clustered dwellings all speak of permanence, continuity. The Indian village is India; the Indian village in the sugar colony can only be a shabby extension of the estate.

Yet glimpses of India are seen in Mauritius, and even in Fiji and the Caribbean. By a river-bank, the women are washing their clothes, pounding them on flat stones and laying them out to dry—the spread-out saris making a patchwork of colour, just as in India. At the market, there are mounds of fruit and

---

[1] As it happens, the West Indies and Mauritius both lie in the track of hurricanes. Early in 1975, Mauritius was devastated by one of the worst hurricanes in its history. Under these conditions there is some advantage in a 'temporary' house: when the hurricane blows it over, it is not difficult to put it up again.

vegetables, heaped sacks of spices, woven baskets and other handi-
crafts, and there are apprehensive-looking fowls and ducks, just
as in India. The women draw their water—not from a well, but
from a stand-pipe, but with the same undulant grace. A boy
drives the goats back from the grazing-ground at sunset. Oil-
lamps are lit, and offerings of marigolds are laid before a crude
little shrine under a sacred tree, just as in India.

To an extraordinary extent, the estate Indians have survived
their exposure to being anonymous units in an industrial system,
and have preserved their own identity. The urban Indians have
accepted a much greater degree of 'acculturation' towards
Western norms. The Indianness of the estate workers has survived not so much by deliberate efforts at preservation as by
external neglect. Missionaries from the Arya Samaj, and others
sent out by religious and social movements from India, have
done something to revive Indian customs and festivals and to
encourage the use of Hindi; but they have been isolated individuals, having an effect only in limited localities. The main reason
for the survival of Indian traits—and particularly Indian languages
—has been the lack of access to education and the absence of
exposure to urban life. In 1941 H. N. Kunzru of the Servants of
India Society told the Government of India that the proportion
of children of Indian origin attending school in Fiji came to 31
per cent. Considered by sexes, 39 per cent of boys and 22 per
cent of girls were at school. Of the total number at school, 70
per cent of the Indians were less than eleven years old, and most
were in the lowest four classes. In Guiana, 44 per cent of the
Indians were literate (1946 Census). In Trinidad literacy was
higher (50 per cent); in Mauritius it was lower: between 1923
and 1938 the proportion of Indian children at school actually
decreased by 5 per cent.

Down to the Second World War, the White plantocracy
was dominant, and almost unchallenged in its dominance; the
'Coloureds'—the lighter-skinned African Creoles—formed the
middle class, and the Indians were effectively excluded from
power. This political stratification was at its most extreme in
Mauritius, where the eccentric Irish Governor, Pope Hennessy,
had introduced an elective system in 1885. This created a legislative council of 27 members, with a non-official majority, 10
members being elected. The franchise was so narrow that the

vote was confined to the planters and the business community (by 1939 there were only 8,000 electors in a total population of 450,000). All elected members belonged to the tiny *Franco-Mauricien* elite, though the Governor used his power of nomination to include one or two Indian members—selected from the urban middle class. Amazingly, the 1885 constitution lasted unchanged until 1947.

The political history of Fiji and British Guiana showed more constitutional activity, in terms of despatches from Whitehall and discussions in the local legislatures; but in effect the British officials and the White bosses of the sugar industry retained complete control. In Fiji political development was inhibited by the steadfast insistence of the Sons of the Soil, the Fijians—as represented by their chiefs—that they wished to continue under the protection of the British Crown, and hence did not desire elections. The Indians were permitted to elect representatives to the legislature from 1929 onwards, but on a franchise separate from the rest of the voters. In 1935 the Governor of Fiji proposed that the elective system be abolished, and he even received support from some Indian legislators—speaking for Muslim and Sikh groups. The Governor's proposal was modified: but the elected membership was actually reduced.[1] This 1937 constitution remained the framework of government in Fiji until 1965.

Guiana's stormy political coming-of-age was preceded by a long inert adolescence. The Court of Policy, inherited from the Dutch in Napoleonic times, lasted until 1928, when British Guiana was given a regulation Crown Colony constitution. This provided a legislature numbering 30 members, of whom 14 were elected on a narrow franchise (less than 3 per cent of the population). Black, middle-class Guianese could now enter politics, but not the Indians, who had to rely upon the Governor's nomination. Despite modifications, the elective element remained unchanged until the Waddington Constitution was announced in 1952.

Trinidad forms an exception to this story of unchanging colonialism for, following Jamaica, it was a pioneer in small-island democracy. At the end of the Second World War, universal

[1] From 1937, the Legislative Council of Fiji contained 16 British officials, and 15 non-officials, split equally to represent Europeans, Indians, and Fijians. For the Europeans and Indians there were 3 elected and 2 nominated members, and the Fijians were represented by (appointed) chiefs. Hence, in a legislature of 31, 6 were elected.

3

adult suffrage was introduced, in which the Indians had parity
with the Blacks, though this came about only after an attempt to
restrict the franchise to English-speakers was dropped.[1] The constitutional advance of Trinidad was linked to its more advanced
economy. The rise of the oil industry, followed by the establishment of the American military base in 1941, provided industrial
alternatives to plantation agriculture. The trade union movement
was active and assertive, and raised political as well as industrial
demands. Although the Oil Workers Union had a predominantly
Black membership, its first organizer and leader was an Indian—
Krishna Deonarain—who called himself Cola Rienzi. The wave of
strikes which swept Trinidad in 1937, entailing the deployment of
British troops, was first a protest against the depression of wages
(while the oil company's profits soared) and secondly a rejection
of the White racial dominance of the oil management staff, many
of whom were South Africans. The solidarity of the oil-field
workers demonstrated that it was no longer possible to govern
a quiescent proletariat through an official machine responsive
only to the pressures of the metropolitan companies; the price
of industrial peace was to be political representation. So Trinidad
moved ahead of colonies dependent on sugar.

On the sugar estates the long aftermath of slavery persisted—
both in the Caribbean and in the Mascarenes—for a hundred
years after emancipation. Whereas the monthly wage of an
indentured coolie in Mauritius in the 1830s and 1840s, on first
recruitment, was Rs.5 (together with rations) rising to Rs.7 or 8
for an experienced hand, in the 1930s Mauritius sugar workers
were still being paid Rs.10, with their rations. Meanwhile, the
value of the rupee had fallen from 2s. to 1s.6d., while the price
of all essential commodities had doubled. In Trinidad, where
wages were better, the Indians were paid 1s. per task (i.e. one
day's work) when they first arrived in the 1840s; in the 1930s
the rate for a task was 35 cents—1s.6d.—or 7s.6d. for a full week.
Somehow the discontent seethed ineffectually for a hundred years
below the surface, until in the late 1930s it at last boiled to the
top and became visible. The world slump created the climate in
which the latent protest became active.

The explosion was more or less spontaneous, for the powerful

[1] Yogendra K. Malik, *East Indians in Trinidad; a Study in Minority Politics*,
London, 1971, p. 75.

trade unions which provide the thrust that almost automatically boosts strike action in Britain were lacking. Lord Passfield (Sidney Webb), as a Socialist Colonial Secretary issued a despatch in September 1930 to encourage the formation of trade unions. Except in Trinidad and Jamaica it was a waste of paper, for nothing happened. From 1919, there was a nominal trade union in Guiana, called the British Guiana Labour Union. By the mid-1930s the B.G.L.U. had less than 500 members (under ·3 per cent of the labour force). Neither Mauritius nor Fiji had introduced legislation to enable trade unions to be registered and operate as recognized negotiating bodies.

As a result, when strike action was taken by the sugar workers it was invariably on an individual estate, in response to some local grievance. Nevertheless, the strikes were bitter; as in the days of slavery, the managers called in armed police to break the strikes for them, and bloody clashes could end in shooting and killing. In Guiana and Trinidad, though the strikers were almost always Indians, the police were almost invariably Black. After each wave of violence, the colonial Government usually appointed a commission of inquiry. The workers were never represented, and the reports all ended up in the files. Finally, in the wake of the strike epidemic of the 1930s, and under some pressure from the British T.U.C. the Colonial Office appointed a high-powered commission under Lord Moyne to investigate conditions throughout the Caribbean. Their disclosures were considered too shocking to be published in wartime, and the Moyne Report was not released until 1945.

The Government of India had only the vaguest notion of what conditions were like in the sugar colonies. When the Moyne Commission was announced, the Indian Government despatched an official, J. D. Tyson, to collect information and give evidence before the commission. His report was illuminating. In Guiana, there was a quasi-political organization, the East Indian Association, hopelessly split between activists and those who favoured 'cotton-wool methods'. A new, mainly Indian trade union had superseded the ineffective B.G.L.U.; it was called the Man-Power Citizens Association, and had recruited 10,000 members, but its demands were brushed aside by the firms. Most sugar workers still lived in barrack-like 'ranges' almost dating back to slavery. There were two Indian members among the 14 elected legislative council members, but they were largely excluded from the public services. The police force, numbering 805, included only 42 Indians.

Tyson's account of Trinidad was more promising. Three of the seven elected members of the legislature (total, 25) were Indians. Indians were penetrating into the professional and commercial class, though in this process they shed their ancient religions, Hinduism and Islam, for Christianity—the medium of education and advancement. Concerning the whole area, Tyson concluded: 'If the Indian is now becoming race-conscious, the blame is not his; . . . [it was] forced on him by a realisation of the very definite prejudices existing against him.'[1]

Mauritius, isolated from almost all external influences, also experienced the first rumblings of industrial protest in the late 1930s. An attempt was made to start a political movement, a 'Labour Party', Parti Travailliste. The founder was Dr. Maurice Curé, a French Creole, and his associates included other Creoles, such as Emmanuel Anquetil, and also Indians, like R. Jomadar. Their London representative was a Mauritian Indian doctor, Seewoosagur Ramgoolam, who was also active in the London branch of the Indian National Congress. Apart from establishing contacts with sympathizers in the British Labour Party, such as Arthur Creech Jones and Henry Polak, all this activity achieved little, for the Mauritius Government dismissed them all as 'agitators'.

The labour unrest in Mauritius in 1938 and 1939 did lead to the introduction of a law permitting trade unions, and about 30 unions were registered. Within four years all but two had expired. During the war years the growing disparity between the rapid rise in prices and the sluggish rise in wages created widespread labour unrest. These culminated in marches upon Port Louis, riots, and repression by the police, in which strikers were fired on and killed.

The usual commission of inquiry was appointed, headed by the island's Colonial Secretary. This attempted to probe a little more deeply than was usual into the nature of the problem. They discovered that though there was a Department of Labour, all the estates on which trouble had erupted were paying the workers

[1] *Report on the Condition of Indians in Jamaica, British Guiana and Trinidad*, New Delhi, 1939.

less than the legal minimum wage. They found that the police, sent to quell the disturbances, were unable to communicate in the language of the strikers. The commission concluded:

Laws may be passed, administrative machinery may be created, money may be spent [by Government] and the situation may nevertheless remain unchanged. This is particularly true of Mauritius. The situation as it exists today is the end product of an historical process, which should be reckoned in generations. . . . The trend of development of an organism cannot be suddenly altered. . . . The organisation has run down to such an extent as to breed a general pessimism which tends to apathy and a disbelief in the possibility of improvement.[1]

This portrait of a sugar colony in which ideas and methods had remained unchanged for a century was given confirmation by the way in which it was received: for nothing was done to implement its recommendations, and Mauritius went its old way, prolonging the 'historical process, which should be reckoned in generations'.

The war years in Fiji produced a similar story of indifference on the part of Government and sugar barons to the plight of the rural workers, squeezed between inflation of the cost of living and the rejection of their own demands for betterment. As in Trinidad, the cultivation of the cane had passed from the big plantations to individual plots, leased by Indian peasant farmers. However, the Indians were not really more independent than before, when they were field-hands. When sugar-cane is harvested, it has to be transported to the factory and processed within one or two days, otherwise the sugar-content falls and the yield is down. The farmers were therefore still largely in the hands of the big companies, for they had little bargaining power when they were compelled to bring in their cane for processing, on terms more or less dictated by the companies.

In 1943 the price received was the same as in 1939—30s. per ton—though living costs had increased by 60 per cent. A social worker, Swami Rudranand of the Ramakrishna Mission, launched a campaign to persuade the farmers not to cut their cane until a new price was negotiated. A Government appointed commission recommended no further increase in price; the farmers withheld

---

[1] *Report of the Commission of Enquiry into the Disturbances . . . in 1943*, Mauritius [1944].

their cane; neither side gave way, and most of the 1943 crop was ploughed back into the soil or left to rot. Next year the Indian farmers were too impoverished to keep up the fight, and the 1944 crop was sold at the 1939 price. This long-drawn-out conflict left a bitter taste. The Whites accused the Indians of 'disloyalty' in time of war, while the Indians in turn felt an even greater absence of identification with the lands to which their fathers had come.

The feeling of separate identity was reinforced after the transfer of power in India in 1947. There, the new, independent Government sought to re-establish links with these far-off lands where Indians had emigrated, and application was made for quasi-diplomatic representatives to be assigned to these territories and others. The Colonial Office assented only reluctantly; Creech Jones, the Colonial Secretary observed (30 June 1947), 'Since Indians in all our colonies share in the common life, and all political and social rights of other inhabitants, such protection by an outside authority is not called for.' The new Indian Commissioners (as they were called) arrived in the West Indies (Trinidad), Mauritius, and Fiji during 1948. There was a stirring of local Indian pride, and a certain amount of flexing of Indian muscles. The Whites and other non-Indians reacted to the situation with much consternation. Somehow, it was believed that independent India would powerfully reinforce these local communities, who would make a bid to take over the colonies as limbs of Greater India. One response was to tighten up immigration controls, and to urge the need to promote emigration, or otherwise restrict the growth of the Indian population.

The feeling was perhaps strongest in Fiji where, about 1945, the Fijian Indians became the largest ethnic group.[1] Under the Immigration Ordinance 1947, entry was governed by a 'reciprocity' provision, and the acquisition of a right to permanent residence became more difficult for new arrivals. The number of new Indian immigrants was now limited to a few hundred every year (by 1956 only about 150 Indians were admitted annually). But this restriction did not satisfy the critics—whose

[1] *1936 Census*: Fijians 97,651, Indians 85,002, total population 198,379. *1946 Census*: Fijians 118,070, Indians 120,414, total population 259,638. The Indians did not actually constitute an absolute majority of the population until twenty years later. *1966 Census*: Fijians 202,176, Indians 240,960, total population 476,727.

spokesmen were mainly Whites. They demanded that the Indians be sent elsewhere—to Hawaii, or the Marquesas Islands. These proposals came to nothing, but they led to a greatly increased demand for an effective birth control service to restrict further growth of the Indian population. The *Fiji Times* (17 December 1952) warned against the 'swamping of the indigenous Fijians and the immigrant Europeans by the immigrant representatives of Asia'. An outstanding Fijian leader, Ratu Sir Lala Sukuna, advised the Indians: 'Study your birth rate and do not allow it to damage social relations.'[1] These warnings were accepted by some of the Fijian Indian leaders, and a family planning programme was implemented. However, even in the 1970s, the subject still remains explosive.

For Mauritius also, during the 1950s and even into the 1960s, experts suggested a subsidized emigration policy, looking to such unlikely places as Borneo, Brazil, and Honduras as receptacles for Mauritian emigrants. These plans got nowhere. In the West Indies, the possibility of exporting the surplus Black population of islands like Barbados to Guiana was recommended by a British Government commission. This would serve to balance the increase in the East Indian population, now becoming the majority community.[2] The East Indians reacted unfavourably, as they did in Trinidad, when immigration of Blacks from the islands became a strong probability under the Federation plan.

However, it was only in Fiji that the shifting ethnic proportions occasioned an open and acrimonious political debate, and it was only in Fiji, during the early years after the Second World War, that politics were explicitly shaped by racial considerations. In the Caribbean, and in Mauritius, these years in which the demand for popular government and the ending of colonialism acquired strength and momentum were largely a continuation of the ferment of the 1930s, with a new political force based upon mass support challenging the old forms of political control representing metropolitan capitalism. In the 1940s and 1950s, parties and movements were still at an embryonic stage. The popular leaders—who were almost all middle class, though anti-colonial in sentiment—

[1] *The Politics of Family Planning*, ed. T. E. Smith, London, 1973, Ch. 6: 'Fiji: a Study of Ethnic Plurality and Family Planning', by Terence and Valerie Hull.

[2] *Commission to Report on the Possibility of Settlement in British Guiana and British Honduras*, Cmd. 7533, 1947, the 'Evans Report'. At the 1946 Guiana Census, the East Indians numbered 163,434, the Blacks 143,385, and the rest 68,685.

made their appeal in terms of socialism and democracy. They minimized the race factor in their appeal. The more conservative politicians, linked to big business, needed to discover an alternative appeal to a popular audience. Some evoked the bogy of Communism, so popular in the 1940s and 1950s, and thus labelled their opponents. Sometimes they also evoked the argument that the threat to the electors did not come from their governors and bosses but came from those among them who were different— different in race or religion—and the threat was emphasized whether the different people were actually a majority or a minority.

Almost without wanting to become so involved, the popular leaders were also drawn into the politics of separatism and communalism, where gut reactions are so quickly aroused. In Guiana, Trinidad, and Mauritius, what started out as 'worker' movements with a mixed leadership and following, both Creole and Indian, were compelled by force of circumstances to become parties based upon the support of one community only. In Guiana the popular leadership was given the label 'Communist', and thereby the Black section of its following was syphoned away to support the 'non-Communist' party. In Mauritius, the attempt to brand the Labour movement as Extremist did not come off; though non-Indian working-class supporters were enticed away. In Trinidad, the one-time popular leadership became identified with capitalist control, and willy-nilly acquired a reactionary label. In each case, politicians who began as popular national leaders ended up as sectional leaders.

In each of these three countries there appears to be a contrasting pattern between the initial 'breakthrough to independence' phase, and the 'consolidation' phase which follows. The 'breakthrough' phase was relatively brief in Trinidad, but long-drawn-out in Guiana and Mauritius. In all three countries, the breakthrough was not achieved without laying bare the raw nerves of racial suspicion and rivalry. In all three countries, strenuous efforts were made in the course of consolidation to get away from confrontation between races, so destructive to nation-building.[1] These efforts by the major parties were only partially successful; and

[1] A commonly heard slogan uttered by Caribbean Government leaders is 'Out of Many Peoples, One Nation'. An admirable sentiment, not often fulfilled in practice.

signs appeared that it was from the extreme Left that the bid to capture broad proletarian support, irrespective of race, might arouse most response.

For Trinidad, the approach to independence followed the Ghana pattern: a people with some political experience declared their acceptance of a strong national leader at the polling booth, and with this backing he successfully demanded an early transfer of power from Britain. During the 1940s and early 1950s, Trinidad politics were in the hands of wheeler-dealer politicians whose appeals to the multitude revealed no very clear policy or programme, and who made alliances and dissolved them with alarming frequency.[1] Among them, Bhadase Sagan Maraj was the leading Indian contender. Maraj (1919–71), the son of an immigrant, became one of the richest men in Trinidad. He combined business interests with the leadership of the All-Trinidad Sugar Estates and Factories Workers Trades Union, whose membership included virtually all the Indian sugar workers. He was a conspicuous philanthropist and promoter of Indian religious festivals. In 1952 he founded the Sanatan Dharma Maha Sabha as the religious organization of the Hindus, and in 1953 launched the People's Democratic Party (P.D.P.).

In response to demands from the political leaders, the Colonial Office conceded a considerable measure of self-government whereby after elections in 1956 the functions of government would be transferred to a Chief Minister who must have the confidence of the legislature. The 1956 elections were contested by Maraj's P.D.P., and by all the political old guard, but the front-runner emerged as a man new to Trinidad politics, Dr. Eric Williams, author of *Capitalism and Slavery*. Williams came forward with a new party, the People's National Movement (P.N.M.) appealing to all the have-nots as Trinidadians, not as Indians or Blacks or Whites. Williams chose a team of candidates representing the different communities, though the outstanding men, such as Learie Constantine, were all Black. Williams

---

[1] An authentic and hilarious picture of this era in Trinidad politics is portrayed by V. S. Naipaul in *The Suffrage of Elvira* (1969). Naipaul is out of favour with many Trinidadians and other overseas Indian communities because his characters are so often unprincipled, opportunistic, irresponsible. His world has much the same existential relationship to the real world as, say, the novels of Anthony Powell or Evelyn Waugh do to actual English society—and Naipaul is perhaps the greater novelist.

lambasted Maraj and the P.D.P. He tried to detach them from the Indian masses by labelling the P.D.P. as the party of Brahmins and Maharajas. He quoted Jawaharlal Nehru's denunciations of the Hindu Maha Sabha in India as reactionary and communalistically-minded, and he applied Nehru's strictures to the Trinidad Maha Sabha.

Williams and the P.N.M. won a clear victory, capturing 13 of the 24 seats in the legislature, and taking 39 per cent of the vote —almost double the votes cast for the P.D.P., the next largest party, which gained only five seats in the legislature. Despite this breakthrough, Williams did not manage to win support in the rural constituencies of the sugar belt, where the East Indian labourers voted solidly for the P.D.P. Williams obtained massive support from the predominantly Black population of Port of Spain, and other towns, and picked up some Indian votes in marginal, peri-urban areas.

Williams now became Chief Minister, and rapidly got a grip on the civil service and the police, predominantly Black, as well as over sections of the Press and business. His style of government was brisk and sometimes tough. The opposition was given the opportunity to challenge his dominance when, in 1958, elections were mounted for the legislature of the West Indies Federation. Alliances were made between different Caribbean political groups, and Alexander Bustamente of Jamaica fixed up deals with almost all the Trinidad opposition leaders. As a result, Maraj and the P.D.P. joined an alliance called the Democratic Labour Party (D.L.P.), and a slate of candidates was picked with care to 'fit' the ethnic and class character of all the different constituencies. In consequence, the D.L.P. won six of the ten seats in the Federal legislature assigned to Trinidad; the P.N.M. won the remaining four seats.

The 1958 election was treated as a defeat for the P.N.M. by everybody concerned. Yet immediately afterwards, the East Indian leadership revealed its Achilles' heel: it was able to mobilize the East Indian mass-vote at election time, and it was capable of making skilful deals with discontented Black politicians—but it had no ongoing political strategy. Williams counter-attacked in two directions. He aroused the Black voters to the danger (real or imaginary) of an Indian takeover, and won back those who had switched support to his Black opponents, labelled as Indian stooges. Then he carefully overhauled the machinery of elections. The boundaries of constituencies were revised, additional seats were created (increased from 24 to 30), and as a result Indian seats became marginal, and marginal P.N.M. seats were made safe. Williams also consulted American market research specialists and on their advice imported voting machines, instead of the traditional British ballot boxes. His opponents claimed the machines were fixed.

When the five-year period after 1956 elapsed, Williams was ready. The D.L.P. remained the main opposition force, with a new leader, Dr. R. N. Capildeo, a Lecturer of London University. His elder brother, S. N. Capildeo, was an established politician, but the new leader had virtually no political experience, either in Trinidad or in England. The D.L.P. leaders reasoned that in order to confront the charisma of Williams, the 'Doctah', they must produce a similar intellectual with a record of metropolitan academic honours. The choice was unhappy. Lacking experience, Capildeo went overboard in a campaign of verbal violence. The P.N.M. replied in kind, denouncing Capildeo's pretensions to be the 'Coolie Prime Minister'. On election day, the P.N.M. won 20 of the total of 30 seats in the legislature; the D.L.P. won the other ten. The D.L.P. included Black candidates on its list; those who won—M. A. Forrester and Peter Farquhar—were returned in constituencies where the Indians were heavily in the majority. The two Black D.L.P. victories were scored over East Indian P.N.M. candidates. The lesson drawn by observers was that the Indian population now identified with a communal party to an extent that overrode any appeal by Indians standing as multi-racial candidates.

Fortified by a clear majority vote and supported by an overwhelming legislative majority, Williams presented a demand for independence. The usual constitutional conference assembled at Lancaster House; the Trinidad members included the majority and minority parties, P.N.M. and D.L.P., and also representatives of other bodies, including the Indian National Association. Whereas the D.L.P. had to maintain a multi-racial stance at the conference, the Indian Association was free to speak purely for the Indians of Trinidad. They put forward a demand for elections to be changed to the proportional representation system; they also demanded that recruitment to the public services be based upon quotas, so that Indians could achieve parity in the civil service and the police with the Blacks. Reginald Maudling as Colonial Secretary refused to consider the proportional representation (P.R.) demand. Thereupon, the Indian Association asked that as a condition of independence Trinidad be partitioned into two states representing the Black and Indian majority areas. This demand was, predictably, turned down flat.

When it appeared as though the conference had reached deadlock, Williams had a private discussion with Capildeo, which was followed by a public announcement that he was ready to make concessions. These amounted to undertaking that the agreed constitution should not be altered except by the vote of three-quarters of the legislature. The 'entrenched provisions' covered important subjects, such as the procedure for revising constituency boundaries. This seemed to be a major concession, and Dr. Capildeo hailed it as such. Time was to demonstrate that Williams conceded nothing of substance.[1] With this breakthrough, the more extreme communal demands faded out of the discussion. In August 1962 Trinidad achieved formal Independence.[2]

In neighbouring British Guiana, the pathway to decolonization was infinitely more rugged, and the road was opened and closed many times before the final stretch was reached. The future was to be disputed between two men—the Indian, Cheddi Jagan, and the Black, Forbes Burnham. In the late 1940s both returned from abroad—Jagan from America, and Burnham from England —and they became associates, determined to liquidate the old politics of race. Burnham told a fellow Black, Robert Hart, of the League of Coloured Peoples: 'The political situation in B.G. is still far from good, complicated as it is by the racial issue. . . . The Negro section of the Labour Party are in favour of building up their own political organization in the form of the League of Coloured Peoples, the Indians want to concentrate on the East Indian Association, while Cheddi is thinking in terms of

---

[1] One consequence was that the Head of State in Trinidad remains the Governor-General; there was no move to a presidential system, as in Guyana, until in 1976 a Bill was brought forward to make the Head of State a President with strong executive powers.

[2] For a more detailed, analytical examination of this subject, see Selwyn D. Ryan, *Race and Nationalism in Trinidad and Tobago: a Study of Decolonisation in a Multiracial Society*, Toronto, 1972.

forming a People's Party' (14 April 1949). The Waddington Constitution, introducing universal suffrage and a ministerial system, provided their opening.

Elections were held in April 1953, and the newly formed People's Progressive Party (P.P.P.) obtained 51 per cent of the popular vote, winning 18 of the 24 elected seats in the legislature. This was an amazing success for a new party, lacking funds and organization. At this stage, the P.P.P. could not be given a communal label. Its support had come overwhelmingly from the rural labour force, both Indian and Black. Their rivals were strong only in urban, mainly middle-class areas. The P.P.P. leaders, beside Jagan and Burnham, included Janet Jagan (American), Sidney King, Rory Westmaas, Fred Bowman (Black), Edward Behary, Lachman Singh, Nazruddeen (Indian). Most were trade union organizers, who had acquired their reputation as spokesmen of the sugar workers.

The P.P.P. took office, with six Ministers in charge of the main departments; three Ministers were appointed from the civil service. The P.P.P. ministry lasted only 133 days. In October 1953, backed by a massive deployment of military might (including two naval cruisers and the Argyll and Sutherland Highlanders), the Governor dismissed the P.P.P. Ministers. The *New York Times* (7 October 1953) greeted this exercise with the headline: 'British Rush Force to Guiana to Block Communist Coup'. This was to be the theme of all explanations for attacks on the P.P.P., and was taken up by the more cautious Caribbean leaders. Grantley Adams, the Federal Prime Minister, wrote to a friend in the British Labour Party to warn them against 'backing the wrong horse' in Guiana; Jagan was 'a menace', Adams concluded.[1]

The Governor of British Guiana followed up his action against the P.P.P. by interning several of the leaders, and when Jagan and Burnham tried to leave the country to put their case before world opinion they discovered that no air line would (or could) fly them out. When they did get away, they rapidly made for India.

In Delhi, their arrival was a major event. The leader of the Maha Sabha group in Parliament demanded that India take the issue of Guiana to the Trusteeship Council of the U.N. Although

[1] *The Times*, 23 October 1953.

Nehru affirmed his support publicly at a cordial meeting with Jagan and Burnham, declaring that India had the question of a reference to the U.N. 'under consideration', nothing happened. Nehru told Parliament that sympathy for Jagan and Guiana was not sufficient cause for intervening when there were 'legal and constitutional difficulties'.[1] It was a sign that the mantle of Independent India could not be cast over the overseas Indians even when they were suffering repression. Some of the illusions of former days now had to be discarded in the harsh light of international power politics. When Jagan signified that he would like to make Ceylon the next stopover on his journey, he was sharply told that he would be banned from entry.

Having dismissed the P.P.P. and interned many of its members, the Governor of British Guiana seemed uncertain what to do next. In a broadcast, the Governor named four of the former P.P.P. Ministers as Communists; he also suggested that they were 'racial extremists'. Among the wilder stories was the allegation that the P.P.P. had planned to burn down Georgetown. One consequence of the uncertainty was that some Indians applied for assisted passages back to India, and 243 actually departed in October 1955, the last of the descendants of the indentured labourers to return home.

For four years there was deadlock in British Guiana. Jagan continued to be viewed as an extremist by British and American standards (he had been jailed in 1954), but Burnham was increasingly regarded as a sound man, though when he attempted to gain the leadership of the P.P.P. in 1955 he failed to oust his rival. Jagan was re-elected Chairman, with Fred Bowman as Vice-Chairman.

At last, elections were announced for August 1957. A constitution less democratic than the Waddington Constitution would be imposed, but the elections were, as before, based on universal suffrage. Only 14 constituencies were demarcated for the 1957 contest. The atmosphere was uncertain, and many voters were reluctant to come forward; only 60 per cent actually polled. Once again, Jagan headed the P.P.P. candidates. Burnham came forward as the leader of a reform group in the P.P.P., and there were new parties, including the National Labour Front (N.L.F.), led by Lionel Luckhoo, the Indian mayor of Georgetown. The

[1] *Hindu* (Madras), 24 November 1953.

campaign was rough, even violent. When the votes were counted, Jagan had received nearly 48 per cent of the vote, winning nine seats; Burnham obtained 25·5 per cent of the vote and won only three seats; the N.L.F. with 11·5 per cent of the vote gained one seat, and the last seat went to the U.D.P. (this was an Amerindian constituency in the remote interior).

The Jaganite P.P.P. which won again in 1957 was less broadly representative of all the working people: its nine M.P.s included six Indians, two Blacks, and Mrs. Jagan. It went into a legislature in which, beside the 14 elected M.P.s, six were nominated by the Governor (including a representative of Booker's, the sugar monopoly), and three were officials. Jagan did not have a majority; nevertheless, the Governor accepted five P.P.P. members as Ministers, along with three ministerial officials. Jagan at once demanded a new constitution, transferring 'real power'. There followed three years of intermittent negotiation with the Colonial Office. Jagan put forward many suggestions; he proposed that representatives of India and Ghana should act as 'adjudicators'; he proposed a second chamber, where minorities and other interests might have the power of review. These suggestions were brushed aside, and when in 1961 the Colonial Office unveiled their own constitutional proposals these fell far short of independence.

Meanwhile, Castro had staged a revolution in Cuba, and the United States was exceedingly worried about the spread of Communism in the Americas. Calls for action against Jagan were sounded in the U.S. Senate, and were not dispelled by an open letter from Jagan to the Organization of American States. He declared, 'I wish to state here categorically that I and my party will adhere to the principles of parliamentary democracy.'[1]

The new constitution provided for 35 single-member seats. Once again, the election was a bitter contest, with Jagan fighting hard to kill the twin charges of Communism and racialism voiced by his opponents. Burnham launched a new party, the People's National Congress (P.N.C.). The poll was exceptionally high: nearly 90 per cent of the electorate. The P.P.P. received 43 per cent, the P.N.C. gained 41 per cent, and the middle-class urban party, the United Front (U.F.), headed by the wealthy Portuguese industrialist, Peter d'Aguiar, obtained 17 per cent of

[1] *New York Times*, 18 August 1961.

the vote. The 'first past the post' electoral system gave the P.P.P. a much larger share of the seats—20, compared to 11 for the P.N.C., and 4 to the U.F. Thus the P.P.P. received 57 per cent of the parliamentary seats and the P.N.C. only 31 per cent, despite a difference of only 2 per cent in the popular vote. The opponents of the P.P.P. now began to demand proportional representation.[1]

After the election, Jagan at once travelled to London to ask the Colonial Secretary for independence in 1962; in this he was following exactly the same tactic as Eric Williams had done a few months before, and he could claim almost as much electoral and parliamentary backing as Williams had enjoyed. Reginald Maudling had said 'Yes' to Williams; to Jagan he gave a categorical 'No'.

By now, John F. Kennedy was President of the United States and at his inauguration he enunciated a doctrine of world-wide confrontation with Communism. Jagan visited Washington, to ask for American economic aid, but Kennedy and his adviser, Arthur Schlesinger, found him 'romantic' and 'naïve'. Subsequently, Forbes Burnham called on the President, and made a much better impression. Schlesinger advised Kennedy that 'an independent British Guiana under Burnham . . . would cause us many fewer problems than an independent British Guiana under Jagan.' 'And the way was open to bring this about,' wrote Schlesinger; 'An obvious solution would be to establish a system of proportional representation.'[2]

The suspicion that the Big Powers were preparing to back Burnham against Jagan began to permeate Guiana politics. A trickle of prominent P.P.P. men defected from his camp. Sidney King had quit before the 1961 election; now Fred Bowman departed, while Balram Singh Rai, one of Jagan's Ministers, was expelled from the P.P.P. There was unrest and some violence in Georgetown; once again there were officially inspired hints of a Jagan coup, but an inquiry by the British judge, Wynn-Parry, said the troubles were only evidence of 'spontaneous combustion'. At length, in October 1962, a constitutional con-

---

[1] According to Cheddi Jagan (*The West on Trial*) the suggestion was first put forward by Anthony Tasker, the Booker's representative on the Legislative Council.

[2] Arthur M. Schlesinger, *A Thousand Days*, New York, 1965, p. 713.

ference was convened in London. Burnham demanded proportional representation. After two weeks they adjourned with nothing decided. Jagan reminded the British Government that it had turned down P.R. (proportional representation) for Trinidad: why, then, impose P.R. on Guiana? He accused the British Government of deliberately allowing the talks to break down.

During 1963, the unrest continued. A Labour Relations Bill to introduce elections in the trade unions led to an 80-day strike. A 'State of Emergency' was proclaimed by the Governor in May. Dean Rusk, American Secretary of State, publicly urged Britain to liquidate the constitution and return to direct rule.[1] In the American Congress, Senators declared that a Communist takeover in Guiana was 'imminent'.[2] At length, the Colonial Secretary, now Duncan Sandys, produced his plan. Before any further move to independence, there must be fresh elections under P.R. based on a new register of electors. The Labour spokesman on the colonies, Arthur Bottomley, observed that it 'Looks far too much like manipulation, with the blatant purpose of ousting Dr. Jagan' (1 November 1963). But the Sandys plan went ahead.

Before elections were held, Labour took over from the Conservatives in Britain, and Jagan flew to London to see the new Colonial Secretary, Anthony Greenwood. He discovered that bipartisanship was the policy at the Colonial Office: there was to be no change.

The 1964 election actually showed a strengthening of the P.P.P.'s hold over the rural workers: almost 97 per cent of the electors cast their votes, and 46 per cent of the voters supported the P.P.P. The P.N.C., now bolstered by the adherence of former rivals, like Carter and Luckhoo, slipped to 40 per cent. D'Aguiar's United Force received just 12 per cent support, a distinct drop from the 1961 result, and 2 per cent of the vote was divided among minor parties. However, under P.R.—which was worked on the Continental 'list' basis, instead of the single transferable vote, the system later applied to Northern Ireland—the

---

[1] *The Times*, 10 July 1963.

[2] *New York Times*, 27 September 1963. The reality seems to have been that the C.I.A. and the American confederation of trade unions had moved in to topple Jagan, allegedly providing over $1 million to his opponents. See S. Meisler, 'Dubious Role of AFL–CIO Meddling in Latin America', *Nation*, 10 February 1964.

P.P.P. was allocated only 24 seats, the P.N.C. was awarded 22 seats, and the U.F. received 7 seats. Jagan announced that he would stay in office, but Burnham told the Governor that he was able to call on the support of the United Front (although the two parties were far apart in their ideology). Jagan was dismissed by the Governor. Next it was necessary to break the constitutional rules, which laid down a maximum of 10 Cabinet Ministers; for d'Aguiar demanded his reward, and Burnham was compelled to give him three seats in a Cabinet of 14.

So Burnham was Chief Minister; and now independence could be agreed with the British Government. Jagan launched a general strike on the sugar estates. To this, Burnham replied ominously: 'If it comes to a showdown, the East Indians must remember that we could do more killing than they could.'[1] He soon proved his point. In areas where the Indians were in a minority, they were assaulted and their homes were burned. From the industrial town of Mackenzie, up river, 1,300 Indians had to be evacuated after being terrorized out of their homes by the Black majority. The police (all Blacks) made no attempt to interfere. Altogether, 160 were killed in the 1964 disorders, the majority being Indians. Many called for the partition of Guiana into Indian and Black zones, with a 'free' zone centred on Georgetown, open to all who wanted to live there. This demand was, predictably, ignored.

The International Commission of Jurists was invited to investigate inter-racial relations. They reported that within the security forces, under 20 per cent of personnel were Indians, while in the civil service the proportion was one-third. Indians provided about 40 per cent of the school-teachers of Guiana. By this time (1965), the Indian population formed over 50 per cent of the peoples of Guiana. The International Commission recommended that before Independence the proportion of Indians in the police force ought to be increased to afford them a greater sense of security.[2] Burnham made some attempt to provide reassurance by recruiting more Indians into the civil service (mainly from

[1] *Daily Telegraph*, 1 May 1964. The escalation of inter-communal tension to this level is ascribed to American cold war phobias by J. B. Landis, 'Racial Polarization and Political Conflict in Guyana', in *Ethnicity and Nation-Building; Comparative, International and Historical Perspectives*, Beverly Hills, California, 1974.
[2] International Commission of Jurists: *Report of the British Guiana Commission of Enquiry into Racial Problems in the Public Service*, Geneva, 1965.

supporters of the P.N.C.). The police remained solidly Black; and a new military force raised to provide defence, after the British withdrawal, was almost entirely Black. Backed by these forces, and backed by the business community, Burnham brought Guyana to Independence in May 1966.[1]

The road to independence for Mauritius was not so sensational in its ups and downs; but it stretched out even longer, for Mauritius had to cover more ground in the shift from an oligarchy to a democracy. In the first constitutional proposal made in 1946, the Governor quoted one of his White *Mauricien* friends in his Despatch to the Colonial Secretary as observing that: 'If the Asiatic element is allowed to obtain the upper hand, over the Mauritian Christian element, the effect on the populations in Ceylon and Kenya will be disastrous.' This was an oblique declaration of solidarity with other White planters. In 1946 it seemed persuasive; but two years later the Governor had to concede that these proposals were 'not acceptable'; he now suggested that the vote should go to all who could pass a simple literacy test—as well as to all who had served in the armed forces. The legislature would contain 19 elected members, 12 nominated non-officials, three officials, and the Governor as president.[2]

The first elections, held in 1948, took place with an electorate of 71,230 (out of a total population of about 500,000). There was no real party organization, though Curé's Labour Party put up candidates, and among their leaders elected were Dr. Ramgoolam and Guy Rozemont, a radical Creole, regarded as the party's popular hero. Inevitably, the conservative Creoles called Rozemont a Communist, but it was difficult to pin this label upon Ramgoolam, who was obviously moderate and reasonable. There was no great change, either in the government or legislature; a Colonial Office Report in 1949 stated that 'Indian divides against

[1] This account of Guyana's turbulent approach to Independence has been based largely upon contemporary newspaper sources, as no serious, objective account of the period was available at the time of writing. A vigorous, persuasive, partisan account is given by Cheddi Jagan, *The West on Trial*, London, 1966. See also B. A. Ince, *Decolonization and Conflict in the United Nations; Guyana's Struggle for Independence*, Cambridge, Mass., 1974.

[2] *Revision of the Constitution of Mauritius*, Cmd. 7228, 1947. One who observed these events closely describes Governor Kennedy as 'An administrator of the old school trained in the tradition of rigid orthodoxy'; K. Hazareesingh, *History of Indians in Mauritius*, London, 1975, p. 127.

Indian, and Coloured against Coloured'. The White *Mauriciens*, the 'Francos', still, effectively, ruled.

At the next election in 1953, Labour candidates were in a majority of those elected (14 out of 19) and in 1955 they succeeded in getting a resolution through the Legislative Council asking for a further extension of the franchise. There followed consultations in London, and in February 1956 the Colonial Office offered a new constitution. The elected members of the legislature would be increased from 19 to 25. At the next elections—due in 1958—there would be a universal franchise, but on a basis of P.R. Also, the Governor's Executive Council would include seven out of 12 members from the legislature; these would be chosen by the legislators, voting by P.R. The Labour Party replied with a boycott of the Executive Council.

Anxiously, Dr. Ramgoolam wrote to Creech Jones, now in opposition. The new proposals had been received 'in dead silence' by the Legislative Council, he related; the P.R. system was designed to 'strike a blow at the [Mauritius] Labour Party' (14 March 1956). Other Indian Labour M.P.s wrote to British Labour leaders, in a spirit of fraternal expectation. J. N. Roy told Creech Jones: 'The danger in a multi-racial community is that the [Labour] Party will break up on the system of preferences in which each section would wish to tick off its candidate as No.1. Proportional representation would mean the end of socialism in the colonies. It may, as a reaction, lead to communism.'

These protests were successful: P.R. was dropped, and a 'first past the post' election with 40 single-member seats was instituted under universal suffrage. The 1959 elections were fought upon a regular party basis. From among the Indian community there emerged two new parties: the Independent Forward Bloc (I.F.B.), launched by Bissoondayal as a Hindu communalist party, and the Muslim Committee of Action (M.C.A.) founded by Abdool Razack Mohammad. These defections from the Labour Party seemed likely to split the Indian rural vote. Meanwhile, the White *Mauriciens* recognized that they must mobilize all the non-Indian elements in the population, and the Parti Mauricien Social Démocrate (P.M.S.D.) emerged, heavily financed by the sugar planters, and led by Jules Koenig, a dignified, loquacious White conservative.

Despite the new parties, Labour scored its best-ever success in 1959, gaining 24 of the 40 seats. The I.F.B. won six, and the

M.C.A. won five. For Koenig and his P.M.S.D. it was a disaster: they picked up three seats only, the last two seats going to Independents.

Throughout the 1950s, the attitude of the Colonial Office was that Mauritius had so many problems and so many social divisions that full self-government was impossible. There was a policy to send a series of eminent British social scientists to the island, to diagnose its social diseases and devise suitable remedies. Most of the big names in social administration, sociology, and political science were appended to reports on the social services, family planning, local government, and other desirable reforms.[1] The former policy of holding inquiries and pigeon-holing their proposals still enabled administrators and big business to play for time, leaving things as they had always been. Apart from small-scale reforms—a community development and family planning programme being the showpiece—nothing changed in the 1950s; yet the administration was able to sidetrack the demand for self-government by the fashionable cry of 'development'.

Now that Ramgoolam and Labour had such a formidable mandate from the electors it was no longer possible to postpone the constitutional question indefinitely.[2] A conference was convened in London in June 1961, and attended by representatives of all the parties. While accepting ultimate self-government as 'inevitable', the conference report emphasized the heterogeneous composition of the population and the need for proper safeguards. The leader of the Labour Party, Ramgoolam, would now become Chief Minister, but before any further instalment of reform there must be another general election.

[1] There were few socialist and liberal social scientists who did not spend an agreeable fortnight or so in the Mauritius sunshine, telling the islanders what to do: the roll-call includes Richard Titmuss, Brian Abel-Smith, Brian Keith-Lucas, Thomas Balogh, Stanley de Smith, Margaret Read, Burton Benedict, James Meade, and Sir Robert Birley. A few European experts also turned up, like Stanislas de Lestapis, Professor of Sociology (Paris).

[2] Ramgoolam was backed by 60 per cent of the elected M.P.s. When Eric Williams made his successful bid for independence in 1962, he had the backing of 66 per cent of the Trinidad M.P.s. When Jagan also demanded independence in London in 1962, he had 57 per cent of Guiana's M.P.s behind him: he was turned down. When Burnham asked for independence in 1965 he was supported by 52·7 per cent of Guiana's M.P.s, and he was successful. It is impossible to find a pattern in all this, but the Colonial Office rule of thumb appears to have been to make it much harder for an Indian leader to claim independence than a Black leader.

The next election was due in 1964, but Ramgoolam advanced the date to 1963. This time, he went before the electors as the man responsible for the Government—and by association, the economy. Moreover, the P.M.S.D. had acquired a new personality, Gaëtan Duval, a Creole lawyer of light colour, a dynamic personality, who was able to attract people of very different classes and creeds. Ramgoolam was getting older (he was now in his sixties) and the popular Guy Rozemont was dead. The 1963 election was a setback for Labour. Although it still remained the trusted party of the Indian sugar workers, Labour won 19 seats—just short of a majority; the P.M.S.D. captured eight seats, the I.F.B. won seven seats, the M.C.A. won four, and there were two Independents. Following the election, Ramgoolam brought together an all-party Ministry (including Duval) but its unity was very fragile, and when they all returned to London to meet the Colonial Secretary (Greenwood) in 1965, they spoke with different voices. Labour—and also the I.F.B. and M.C.A.—called for independence. The P.M.S.D. and the representatives of the Europeans, and other small minorities, asked for 'associated status' with Britain. This would leave Britain responsible for defence, external affairs, and certain constitutional provisions. The P.M.S.D. also demanded that, before any decision was taken, a popular referendum should be held.

The situation was extremely delicate: the Colonial Office officials were strongly opposed to early independence, and still insisted that Mauritius was not 'viable'. It was fortunate that Dr. Ramgoolam was so very obviously a man of moderation and goodwill, and that he was able to call upon old associations with veteran British Labour politicians. This time the 'Labour' label could not be interpreted as extremist, Communist, racist. Ramgoolam announced his willingness to accept safeguards for the minorities, including the appointment of an Ombudsman who would not be a Mauritian. Greenwood rejected the suggestion of a referendum as a foreign device; he also rejected the 'association' formula. Independence would be conceded if another election produced a majority demand. But in order to appease the minorities he ruled that the single-constituency system must be scrapped and replaced by an elective system which would give the minorities a greater share of representation.

It seemed that the 'minority' game was now the winner.

Previously administrative practice had been to recognize a 'General' population and an 'Indian' population. Now, the total was subdivided into 'General', Sino-Mauritian, Hindu, and Muslim components. The P.M.S.D. and other opposition groups tried to push this fragmentation process further until there was no identifiable racial—or political—majority in Mauritius.[1] If the Forward Bloc and the Muslim Committee of Action and other Indian dissidents could be prised away from Labour, the way was open to create an anti-Ramgoolam power base (as Jagan had been beaten in Guiana).

An expert constitutional commission, led by a colonial administrator, Sir Harold Banwell, and advised by a political scientist, Colin Leys, came up with an ingenious redistribution of constituencies to favour the urban Creoles. This produced a crisis: Ramgoolam refused to accept what he regarded as a formula for division. A hasty visit by the Colonial Under-Secretary, John Stonehouse, led to a modified 'corrective' device. There were to be 20 three-member constituencies; a two-member constituency for the island of Rodriguez; and eight seats, not competed for, which would be awarded to the eight 'best losers' of those of the four groups which were under-represented in the main election. This 'corrective' device was designed to counteract the over-representation of the Hindu community.

The election was scheduled for 1967. Labour was able to make an alliance with the I.F.B. and M.C.A. to fight for complete independence, and they all campaigned as the 'Independence Party'. The P.M.S.D. elected Duval as leader, and pinned most of its hopes on a theatrical, presidential-style campaign. The P.M.S.D. did well—but not well enough; they won 23 seats, but the Independence alliance won 39 seats.[2] When the 'corrective' seats were allocated to the 'best losers', the two opposing forces were awarded four apiece. This time, Ramgoolam had a mandate from 61 per cent of the M.P.s to support him in his

---

[1] The Hindus are actually more than 50 per cent. *1971 Census*: total population 830,606, Hindus 437,365, Muslims 137, 758. Gaëtan Duval attempted to split the Hindu population by encouraging those of South Indian origin (Tamils and Telugus) to make demands for separate representation. After Independence these groups rapidly moved back into the Labour camp.

[2] A team of Commonwealth M.P.s from Britain, Canada, India, Trinidad, and Malta observed the way in which the election was conducted and affirmed its fairness and propriety.

independence demand; this was only one per cent more than in 1961, when he was rebuffed, but this time independence was conceded for March 1968. The newspaper of the White establishment, *Le Mauricien*, tried to have the last word, asserting that independence was being imposed on Mauritius by Britain against the wishes of all communities except the Hindus.[1] It was a fitting last expression of the topsy-turvy attitude which had sought to keep the Indians as the permanent non-belongers.

The Trinidad Indian politicians had competed for power and office and had lost; the Guyana Indian leader, Jagan, rose to power and held on tenaciously but was ousted eventually; only Ramgoolam, the Mauritius Indian leader, was able to resist all efforts to dislodge him. In all three countries there was a vigorous competition between leaders of different races. In Fiji, the Indian political leaders were never in a position to compete for power, and independence was attained on terms in which they could only acquiesce.

The Fijians remained suspicious of the whole conception of competitive politics until the mid-1960s.[2] The demand for fuller self-government came overwhelmingly from the Indian politicians, until—as the procession of Commonwealth territories into independence began to include all and sundry—the younger Fijian leaders realized that the question could not be indefinitely postponed. A constitutional conference met in London in July 1965 and hammered out a formula acceptable to the Fijians, whereby the legislature would become largely elective—on their terms.

The racial membership of the legislature would be predetermined, but in order to avoid the extremes of communalism, certain members were to be elected by cross-voting, from joint electorates. For the Fijian community there would be nine members elected on a communal roll and three members elected by cross-voting. Similarly, nine Indians would be elected by their own community, and three by cross-voting. Seven Euro-

---

[1] Quoted by Louis Favoreu, *L'Île Maurice* (*Encyclopédie Politique et Constitutionelle*), Paris, 1970, p. 29

[2] Once again, the term 'Fijian' is applied only to the autochthonous community, as is common practice. The Fijian Indians have unsuccessfully asked to share the term, but in all the constitutional documents they continue to be described as Indians.

peans, and others, would be elected by 'general' constituencies, confined to the communities other than the Fijians and Indians, and three by cross-voting. In addition, two members would be nominated by the Fijian chiefs, and there would be four official members.

In theory, either of the two main communities could gain a majority, with the support of the Europeans. In reality, everybody knew that the 'general' electorate would never follow an Indian political leader. With this fail-safe device built in, Fiji held its first election based on universal suffrage in 1967. The Fijians formed an Alliance Party, with European adherents, and some Indians, mainly Muslims and Sikhs.[1] The Indians, led by A. D. Patel, formed the National Federation Party. Out of the 34 seats (communal and general) the Alliance won 22 seats, while three Independents were prepared to support the Party. The Federation Party won only nine seats. It now became clear to the Fijians, under the able leadership of Chief Minister Ratu Sir Kamisese Mara, that they had little to fear from parliamentary democracy, played under these rules.

The Federationalists pressed, unavailingly, for a new constitution, with M.P.s elected by a common roll; coldly, Kamisese Mara told them that this would then lead to 'some form of partition' of the Fijian Islands. Indian demands were lowered when Patel died and a more accommodating politician S. M. Koya (a Muslim born in Fiji) became leader of the Federation Party. Government and opposition agreed to invite a British Minister, Lord Shepherd, to visit Fiji in January 1970, to discuss the final transfer of power, within a framework based on the existing constitution. A draft agreement was quickly worked out with Lord Shepherd, and all was ready for the finale.

When everybody gathered at Lancaster House, it was noticeable that two of Mara's Cabinet were Indians belonging to the Alliance: Vijay R. Singh, Minister for Commerce, and K. S. Reddy, Assistant Minister for Social Services. Yet another Indian, Abdul Lateef, was one of the Alliance delegation (along with several Europeans and one Chinese).

[1] The name 'Alliance' was the same as that of the governing party in Malaysia, dominated by Malay leaders, but drawing support from the Chinese and Indian communities. The Fijians appear to be very conscious of the parallels between the two countries. This is not surprising, for several of the Fijian leaders served as officers of the Fiji military forces in Malaya during the Emergency.

The discussions focused on a development of the previous formula. There would be a Parliament with two Houses. The Upper House, the Senate, was heavily weighted towards Fijian interests, by the nomination of Chiefs and of supporters of the Government. Its function is merely to act as a check on the House of Representatives, made up of 52 M.P.s, of which 27 are elected by communal constituencies and 25 by national constituencies. There must be 12 communal Fijian members and 10 national Fijian members, and the same numbers and proportion of Indian members. The general voters elected three members on their communal roll and five on the national roll. The islands were divided into ten national constituencies. There were certain safeguards, including an Ombudsman.[1] Thus, with decorum and dignity, Fiji became independent in October 1970 (though Fijians remained very conscious that Elizabeth of England was still their Queen).

After Independence, the Alliance Government of Fiji was securely confirmed in office by the general election of May 1972; and no new trend is observable. Prime Minister Mara promotes the politics of conciliation, called 'The Pacific Way'. The other three states have witnessed a trend towards tough, even authoritarian government.

Eric Williams faced his first major challenge after Independence at the 1966 elections. The Democratic Labour Party (D.L.P.) remained the chief opposition party, though its character had changed since the 1961 election. Dr. Capildeo was jealous of all possible rivals, and he rejected the strategy of alliance with Black leaders. His strategy paid off, in the sense that the D.L.P. held on to its Indian supporters: all its successful candidates were returned by areas where Indians formed more than half the population. The legislature was now composed of 36 seats, and the D.L.P. gained twelve of them. The People's National Movement (P.N.M.) won all the remaining seats. Although the other opposition parties fielded well-known leaders, both Black and Indian, they failed to win a single seat.

The election seemed to demonstrate a considerable malaise, after the frenzy of Independence. Both the major parties suffered a decline in their support, the P.N.M. fell from 57 per cent in

[1] *Report of the Fiji Constitutional Conference*, Cmd. 4389, 1970.

1961 to 52 per cent, and the D.L.P. from 42 per cent to 34 per cent. A number of small, radical political groups came into being after the election, but the big protest came with the Black Power rising of February-April 1970.

Black Power drove down to the Caribbean from the United States, fuelled by returning West Indian intellectuals such as Stokely Carmichael. Trinidad intellectuals, and trade union leaders like George Weekes, leader of the oilfield workers, eagerly responded. Unemployment was mounting, especially among young people. The Black Power rising escalated out of minor gestures of protest, and culminated in mass marches and demonstrations. Many radicals intended the Black concept to include all Third World peoples, and therefore the East Indians, but this was far from clear to the ordinary demonstrators, predominantly Black, or to the Indians, whether shopkeepers or villagers, who felt threatened by the demonstrations.[1]

However, as the agitation developed, some Indians were drawn in. Certain army units refused to move against the demonstrators, under the influence of two lieutenants, Rex La Salle, and Raffique Shah, an Indian. Strikes spread to sugar workers on one estate, who ignored the call by Maraj to return to work. Mass demonstrations by oilfield and sugar workers were planned for 21 April 1970, but these were forestalled by the imposing of a State of Emergency and the arrest of many of the Black Power leaders.

In the aftermath of the rising, the Indians tried to sort out their ideas. Among the field workers, some saw it all as a confrontation between a Black government and Black militants: 'Let these bloody Niggers kill each other off' was how this was expressed.[2] Middle-class Indians regarded the movement as a direct threat to them, and a small minority only of Indian radicals and intellectuals saw the demonstrations as the inevitable response to Williams's growing authoritarianism: for example, Krishna Gowandan organized 'Freedom Fighters' among the sugar workers.[3]

[1] This account is largely drawn from David Nicholls, 'East Indians and Black Power in Trinidad', *Race*, April 1971. According to Nicholls, less than 1 per cent of the demonstrators were 'of Indian origin'. The National Joint Action Committee actually claimed massive Indian participation in the march on Port of Spain.

[2] Nicholls relates this as a personal experience.

[3] United action by Indian and Black organized labour remains a long-term possible outcome of these events. A United Labour Front was set up in February

When the Emergency was lifted, Trinidad began to prepare for its second post-Independence election. At this moment Dr. Capildeo died, and the leadership of the D.L.P. passed to a lawyer, Vernon Jamadar, whose view of politics was less narrowly communal. In his speeches he urged 'the brothers of slavery and indenture' to close their ranks. A strong ally appeared in A. N. R. Robinson, Deputy Premier until April 1970, when he resigned in protest against Williams's handling of the Emergency. He now launched an Action Committee of Dedicated Citizens (A.C.D.C.) which joined up with Vernon Jamadar and the D.L.P. to contest the election. However, just before nomination day, while addressing an emotional meeting, Robinson suddenly announced that the D.L.P. and A.C.D.C. would boycott the elections. Jamadar considered he was bound by this announcement, so all the D.L.P. candidates stood down.

Maraj attempted to exploit the situation. He had made a comeback into the D.L.P. winning Capildeo's seat, Chaguanas, at a by-election. Now he launched the Democratic Liberation Party, trying to exploit the magic in the D.L.P. initials. On election day his party was destroyed, and Maraj even failed to hold Chaguanas. Although 90 per cent of the voters were Indians in this constituency, they elected a little-known Black P.N.M. candidate. All 36 seats were taken by the P.N.M., but although they received most of the votes only 33 per cent of the electors actually went to the poll; hence Williams received the support of only 28 per cent of the electorate.

The 1971 election virtually finished off the East Indians as a political factor in Trinidad, at least for many years. It was true that some Indians were elected on the P.N.M. ticket, but only two Indians—Kamaluddin Mohammad and Errol Mahabir (a Muslim and a Christian) were included in Williams's 18-man Cabinet. The D.L.P. had surreptitiously issued instructions to its followers to vote P.N.M. rather than let in Maraj's party. The weakness of the D.L.P. had always been the absence of a programme; now it hardly possessed a presence. Possibly, if a strong challenge to Eric Williams were to emerge from among militant

---

1975, bringing together the oilfield workers and the sugar workers. The leader is Basdeo Pandy. It was claimed that the mass demonstration of 18 March 1975 included hundreds of Indian workers.

Blacks, the D.L.P. and Indians generally, would rally to Williams. Meanwhile, they look on uneasily. Conscious that in Guyana the Indian population has been largely disfranchised, they wonder whether they will suffer the same fate.

For in Guyana, Burnham has made himself impregnable. The next election after the crucial contest of 1964 was staged in 1968. Burnham laid careful plans to win a clear victory. The obvious tactic was to get himself a vote-bank by finding more Black voters. Many Black Guyanese had migrated to Britain and the United States. They were now made eligible to vote, and Guyana diplomats zealously recorded their names. According to 'World in Action', many of these names were imaginary.[1] From the overseas voters, the People's National Congress received 34,429 votes, the People's Progressive Party received 1,003 votes, and the United Force, 1,053 votes. Efforts were made to play on the separatist feelings of Muslims, and some switched from the P.P.P. to the P.N.C. Jagan campaigned hard, and support from the sugar workers was reaffirmed. But when the votes were counted and seats apportioned, the P.N.C. was a clear winner, with 30 seats; the P.P.P. received 18 seats; and the U.F. held five seats. Burnham could discard his unwanted right-wing allies, and govern Guyana his way. In 1970 Burnham proclaimed a 'Cooperative Republic'—a change of name, rather than of substance, though the P.N.C. ideology was that of 'cooperative socialism', and in 1971 the Canadian-owned bauxite company was nationalized. Burnham carried out this industrial expropriation with finesse, for he did not upset either the Canadian or the American governments, who continued to maintain aid programmes in Guyana. Burnham possesses one great advantage: he can always suggest that if a foreign power should make things difficult, Guyana will fall back into the clutch of Cheddi Jagan.

Thus Burnham needs Jagan, and does not seek to destroy him. Jagan draws a salary double that of the other M.P.s as Leader of the Opposition, and his own brother is Deputy Speaker of the National Assembly. Opponents of Jagan suggest that he has lost

[1] Independent Television's programme 'World in Action' alleged that they fabricated most of these names: only 4,700 of the 11,750 voters registered in America were found to be genuine, and of the 44,000 registered in Britain less than a quarter could actually be located. The survey was conducted by Opinion Research Centre, a skilled, professional body. The electorate was increased from 247,604 in 1964 to 367,945 in 1968!

his Marxist zeal; certainly, he still controls the Guyana Import-Export Agency (GIMPEX) set up when he was Prime Minister. Many of the Indian middle class have become strong supporters of Burnham, and provide the P.N.C. with financial backing. Leading Indians have received important official posts. Lionel Luckhoo was appointed Guyana's High Commissioner in London, and Shridat Ramphal became Foreign Minister and subsequently (1975) Secretary-General of the Commonwealth Secretariat in succession to Arnold Smith of Canada—the most prestigious position yet attained by an overseas Indian.

Meanwhile, Burnham exudes confidence. When the next election-time came along, in 1973, the victory was even more complete. The P.N.C. gave itself 37 seats; 14 went to the P.P.P.; and only two to the U.F. (d'Aguiar is of no importance to Burnham, but the Amerindians still support the U.F.). Once again 'World in Action' produced scarifying evidence of election malpractices, both in Britain and in Guyana—where many P.P.P. supporters (the loyal Indian sugar workers) were prevented from recording their votes. The reaction from Cheddi Jagan seemed tired and ineffectual. He seemed to recognize that he had met his match, and could do no more than acquiesce.

Resentment at what is seen as a deal between Burnham, Jagan, and other Indians has been voiced by left-wing Black leaders. Sidney King, once an ardent Jaganite, has now become Eusi Kwyana, and leads the African Society for Cultural Relations with Independent Africa (A.S.C.R.I.A.) which is a radical political pressure group. He insists that the essential foundation for a free Guyana is the reconstruction of African Identity, though A.S.C.R.I.A. also campaigns for a revolution on the sugar estates against 'feudal-capitalism'.[1] However, it seems likely that Burnham can outflank Eusi Kwyana and A.S.C.R.I.A., for he subscribes $50,000 of Guyana's money to African liberation movements each year and is a vocal supporter of liberation. Is it possible that, if ever Black Power became strong in Guyana, Burnham might expect support from Jagan and the Indians who have never forgotten the impact of Black violence before Independence?

Lest one should suppose that the Indian role is always to be

[1] Eusi Kwyana, 'Burnhamism and Jaganism: the Politics of the Old Order', *Black Scholar*, May–June 1973.

the victim, Mauritius provides a different story. The advent of Independence on the terms of the 'Hindus' was galling to the Creoles, and especially to the poorer, urban, dark-skinned Creoles, who could not like the 'Francos' retire into their *châteaux* and beach villas and forget about it all. In a run-down suburb of Port Louis, Creoles and Indians—almost all Muslims— lived in close proximity. It was never clear what set them fighting each other in January 1968, but the police were quite inadequate to restore order, and only after several days, and the proclamation of a State of Emergency, were the contestants separated. The Muslims adopted a new militancy; the crescent flag of Pakistan was flown over their settlements. The Creoles also assumed symbols of their separate culture. Sir Seewoosagur Ramgoolam decided he must adopt measures to make Independence secure. In 1969, a member of the French Cabinet, Debré, brought about a rapprochement with Duval and a coalition.[1] Ramgoolam then introduced an act amending the Mauritius Constitution which postponed the date of the next elections (due in 1972) to 1976. Subsequently, under the Emergency Powers Ordinance, the Governor-General directed that the provision for holding by-elections within a stipulated period could be suspended. Thus, Ramgoolam secured himself from a parliamentary upset for the immediate future.

It was vital to retain the adherence of his electoral allies. The coalition with Duval did not last, for he wanted supreme power. The Muslims were held firm by the allocation of important posts in the Government. Bissoondayal and his Forward Bloc split apart. Seven I.F.B. M.P.s joined the opposition, but five remained loyal to the Government and Ramgoolam maintained his hold over Parliament. The separation of the peoples of Mauritius into parties which corresponded with their ethnic origins seemed almost inevitable. Ramgoolam fortified his party by recruiting and employing all the leading professional and university-educated Indians of Mauritius. There was little chance of ambitious Indians being wooed away by non-Indian political bosses, as in Guyana.

[1] France automatically assumes that Mauritius is within the Francophone sphere. In October 1975 a conference of parliamentarians from all the French-speaking countries was convened by France in Mauritius. Huge sums are available for French cultural and educational projects; some Mauritians bitterly observe that if this money were put into economic development their island would be rich.

The P.M.S.D. had its own troubles. Three of their M.P.s changed sides and joined the Government benches. Others repudiated the leadership of Duval, and in 1970 formed the Union Démocratique Mauricien, under Maurice Lesage. Gaëtan Duval has discovered that charisma is not enough, though he continues to talk confidently of the time when he will be President of Mauritius.

The possibility of effective, multi-racial opposition emerged from the extreme left. When, in 1968, the students and workers of Paris seemed about to overthrow de Gaulle, Paul Bérenger, a young Mauritian, was on the barricades. When he returned home, he launched a revolutionary party, the Mouvement Militant Mauricien. Soon, M.M.M. was inscribed upon walls and doors throughout the island.[1] Bérenger scored a dramatic by-election victory at Triolet, but his main thrust was towards capturing the trade union movement, previously a Labour Party stronghold. In December 1971 a strike of the port workers led to a state of emergency. Bérenger preached the revolt of all the masses, whatever their race; but the M.M.M. proved vulnerable to the same fragmentation as other parties, and in 1973 split apart. The Labour Government survived.

Like Burnham, Ramgoolam makes up for the waning of inter-racial support within his own land by bidding for inter-racial recognition on the world stage. Mauritius is a full member of the Organization of African Unity and provided the meeting-place for the O.A.U. in 1976. Because Ramgoolam and his colleagues are bilingual, they are on good terms with the Franco-phone leaders like Senghor as well as Anglophone Africa. But eyes are not only fixed on Africa: increasingly, Mauritius joins in the diplomatic activity of South Asia, with a special warmth pervading relations with India. The Government of India gave strong support in establishing a Mahatma Gandhi Institute in Mauritius, which will play a recognized part in reawakening consciousness of the cultural and philosophical legacy of India to Mauritius.[2]

---

[1] For an interpretation which is both Marxist and Francophone, see Joyce and Jean-Pierre Durand, *l'Île Maurice, quelle indépendance? La reproduction des rapports de production capitaliste dans une formation sociale dominée*, Paris, 1973.

[2] Similarly, in Trinidad, the Government of India has supported a Professor of Indian Studies as a member of the Institute of African and Asian Studies of the University of the West Indies.

Largely because of outside influences the struggle for independence and for political power has taken the form of a struggle
between races, and it is at the political level that the question of
the final form of the group identity of the Indians in these lands
sometimes designated the Third World's Third World will be
decided.[1] But of more immediate importance to the ordinary
Indian workers is the way in which their economic future is
decided.

	Exports			
Export of Products as Percentage of value of total exports	Trinidad	Guyana	Fiji	Mauritius
Sugar	5·1	27·3	51·1	90
Oil Products and Chemicals	71·9	—	—	—
Metal Ores	—	36·2[1]	5·4[2]	—
Other Edible Products	—	7[3]	8·2[4]	4[5]
Recipients, as percentage of value				
United States	49·6	28·5	15·7	5
United Kingdom	9·8	18·8	34·4	71·3
Canada	3	18·3	11·8	5
Others	—	8*	8·8†	2·6‡

Details of products (as above): [1] bauxite, aluminium; [2] gold; [3] rice; [4] coconut oil; [5] tea.

Other major trading recipients: *Trinidad, †Australia, ‡South Africa.

Even in the 1970s, Mauritius remains almost entirely dependent
upon the export of one crop—sugar—and heavily dependent
upon the custom of one country—Britain. If the other countries
display a little more variety, and are gradually overcoming their
dependence on sugar, they are still, in economic terms, colonies.
Trinidad's oil products and chemicals are subordinated to American international companies. Guyana is almost equally dependent
upon Britain, the main customer for sugar, as upon Canada, the

[1] Authorship of this quip has been assigned to Eric Williams, among others, but
the original author seems to be V. S. Naipaul who takes a mordant view of the
society in which he grew up. He was even less enamoured of his ancestral homeland, described as *An Area of Darkness*, but his worst nightmare seems to be
Mauritius, called *The Overcrowded Barracoon*. Why are the India and Mauritius of
Naipaul so much more awful than they seem to the present writer? Is the outlook
of the cosmopolitan overseas Indian disillusioned by an awareness that nowhere is
home?

4

main purchaser of bauxite and aluminium. Fiji is still tied to its former suzerain on the other side of the world, though North American markets are also vital. The link between the growers and the purchasers is provided in every case by metropolitan agency firms which are producers, exporters, and suppliers to the metropolitan markets all in one.

Three foreign firms control, between them, 90 per cent of the economy of Trinidad.[1] Tate and Lyle dominate the Trinidad sugar industry. In Guyana, 40,000 of the country's industrial workers—150,600 in all—are employed by Booker McConnell, which operates a group of over fifty companies, trading in many different products and processes. Of Guyana's 21 sugar plantations, 12 are owned by Booker's, five by Sandbach Parker & Co., and three by S. Dayson & Co. In the old days, people used to say that B.G. stood for Booker's Guiana, and the sour joke is by no means exhausted.

This, then, is the framework of life for the Indians. About 80 per cent of the sugar workers in Guyana are Indians, and in Trinidad, Mauritius, and Fiji the proportion is even higher. Employment on the estates is seasonal, with a plenitude of work at crop time, and little if any work for the rest of the year. Many of the rural Indians are only fully employed for three months in the year. Among the younger men, total unemployment is often the norm: in Trinidad, in the age-group 15–19 it runs at 35 per cent, and in the group 20–24 it runs at 20 per cent. For Mauritius, the unemployment figures for these age-groups are 55 per cent and 26 per cent, respectively. What makes this situation more depressing is that whereas among the older males education was limited, these young men have all completed a primary school course and many have been through the secondary school. It is only because sugar culture remains grossly under-mechanized that unemployment is not even higher!

Guyana's economy has benefited from the growing importance of rice cultivation, which provides the country's third most important export after sugar and bauxite. Whereas sugar depends upon predominantly Indian labour and bauxite employs a mainly Black work-force, rice culture is almost entirely the preserve of Indian farmers. It is the only sector of the economy free of

---

[1] David Lowenthal, *West Indian Societies*, London, 1972, p. 238. This encyclopaedic work has something about everything in the Caribbean.

foreign control, and during the period after 1950 has greatly increased in importance. Jagan gave the rice industry top priority in his development plans, and it received over 40 per cent of the development budget. The boom years came in 1961–3, with sales of rice to Cuba at prices well above world rates.

Then came 'the troubles' of the middle 1960s. One consequence was a social or communal polarization. The Black population all left the Indian villages, and apart from an occasional Chinese shopkeeper these rural settlements became totally Indian in composition. The area under rice no longer expanded, and the cost of production rose to eat into the profits. A major change which occurred was a conversion from agricultural methods based on human and animal motive power to mechanical methods, with widespread introduction of tractors. This 'modernization', which was apparently an advance in development, seems actually to have had adverse effects. Not only were farming costs much higher but also employment was severely cut. However, once converted to mechanization and having acquired outstanding debts thereby, the farmers were 'stuck with it'.

For the Indian villagers put out of work, the only alternatives are to try to obtain urban employment. They find themselves in competition with Black workers who resent their intrusion. Some try to rent a small parcel of land to make a meagre living. With the declining profitability of rice farming and a rapidly rising population, the rural Indians already look back to the era of Cheddi Jagan as a Golden Age.

In Mauritius some effort to ameliorate the effects of unemployment has been made by a public works relief programme, Travail pour Tous. Men have been put on road-building and other projects, being paid Rs. 20 (or £1·50) a week. Numbers have fluctuated around 18,000 relief workers, reaching a high-point of 32,000 in 1967.[1] The programme severely drained the national finances, bringing Mauritius near to bankruptcy in the late 1960s. Another palliative has been the encouragement of emigration, by means of loans and other assistance. Emigration from Mauritius has been mainly concentrated among the lighter-skinned Creoles, who resent the growth of 'Hindu' dominance.

[1] It was alleged that the Labour Party insisted on large numbers being kept on the public pay-roll so as to ensure its electoral position in this, the year of the crucial Independence election.

About 16,500 emigrated during the 1960s; the largest number—4,600—left in 1968, the year of Independence. Subsequently, emigration settled at an annual figure of about 3,000. During the 1960s, 43·5 per cent went to Australia, 38·5 per cent to Britain, and 4·5 per cent, equally, to France and South Africa. It was an interesting aspect of the Francophone fantasies of the light-skinned Creoles of Mauritius that so few actually settled in the France of their dreams.

A smaller number of Indian Mauritians began to join the emigration stream from about 1970. By then, entry into Britain was severely restricted to persons with professional qualifications or a sizeable bank balance, but there were still chinks in the armour of British immigration restrictions. There is a severe shortage of male nurses in Britain, particularly in mental health hospitals, and young Mauritians began to study to acquire the necessary educational qualifications to be accepted as student nurses. By 1975, a high proportion of those recruited as male mental health nurses for British hospitals were Mauritians. There were also certain openings in Zambia and Malawi for typists, mechanics, electricians, and although the Creoles predominated in this largely temporary emigration, the Indians also joined in.

Emigration, as a safety-valve for young work-seekers, is of less importance for the Indians of Trinidad and Guyana, though a few professional and semi-professional workers find openings in North America. In Fiji, where there is less poverty and un-employment, some Indians have followed the lead given by Fijians in moving to New Zealand. However, New Zealand has tightened up its immigration laws, and they are only able to go as temporary workers.

Altogether, the sugar colonies cannot hope to export their problems of surplus population. They have to evolve their own remedies. The most obvious long-term solution is that of family planning, and after a considerable period of hesitation and in-action most of these countries are encouraging birth-control, with significant results. Whereas there were increases of up to 3 per cent per annum in the 1950s, these levels have now been reduced. The subject continues to be of greatest political sensitivity in Fiji, where the two major communities watch each other's performance with almost neurotic fascination. Both may have some cause for relief in comparing trends:

Fiji: Crude Birth Rates (per 1,000 population)

	Fijian	Indian		Fijian	Indian
1960	37·36	43·75	1970	28·95	30·75
1961	37·43	45·54	1971	29·64	31·03
1962	37·84	42·64	1972	27·82	27·60
1963	37·80	40·20	1973	26·80	28·93

However, this has not restrained some Fijian leaders from calling for restrictive measures, usually of a nature that would by-pass the problem. Thus, in a debate on immigration in 1971, a Fijian Senator called for strict control over the admission of Asians, 'The ones who have the highest birth rates in the world.' Indian Senators retorted indignantly that there was no plot to outbreed the Fijians; instead, they argued that the Fijian islands were capable of supporting a much greater population, and this would increase prosperity, as in Singapore.[1]

A strategy of economic growth may be open to Fiji, but it is less accessible to the other sugar colonies.[2] Paradoxically, conservative Fiji has gone furthest in plans to reconstruct the sugar industry. In 1961 the Australian C.S.R. Company transferred its Fiji operations to the South Pacific Sugar Mills. This did not at once affect control and ownership, but at the time of Independence the Fiji Government began to take over the assets of the company. A more dynamic production policy was introduced, and the Indian cane growers were associated with the industry through the Sugar Advisory Council, to which they sent their chosen representatives.

Trinidad has introduced only a small measure of nationalization. There is a National Sugar Company, which has taken over the Orange Grove Sugar Estates, but the biggest companies are not affected. In Guyana Burnham has not touched Booker's and the other big sugar firms. When in 1973 Jagan offered to deliver all the P.P.P. votes in the Assembly to provide the necessary two-thirds majority needed under the constitution for a bill to expropriate the foreign-owned sugar companies, Burnham ignored his offer.

Sugar has enjoyed a boom in the early 1970s, and world prices

[1] T. E. Smith, op. cit., esp. p. 210.
[2] E. K. Fisk, *The Political Economy of Independent Fiji*, Wellington, New Zealand, 1970.

have made their biggest-ever increase. The Caribbean Prime Ministers, with Burnham as chief spokesman, have confronted Britain, Canada, and the United States with a demand for a massive transfer of financial resources. It is much too early to know whether the man with the hoe and the slashing knife, the Indian worker in his torn trousers and tattered straw hat, will derive tangible benefits from this attempt to obtain a share of the wealth of nations.

In this analysis, the Indians of the sugar colonies are seen as people gripped within certain economic and political institutions which impose a pattern on their societies.[1] Where the Indians are now penetrating urban middle-class society and institutions they are largely absorbed into a provincial or colonial form of the Anglo-American values projected at them on the television screen. Some urban middle-class Indians will adopt a form of Christianity (probably Presbyterian in Trinidad and Methodist in Fiji) which accelerates the process of homogenization. They are likely to marry into similar Indian families, whose young women work in offices and shops. No doubt they can assume the full Indian style, whenever this is demanded; but India is increasingly a vague memory, a tradition, rather than a meaningful aspect of life.

It is through politics, with its racialist pressures, that the urban Indians are compelled to identify themselves in fully ethnic terms. Then, they are likely to make claims which are symbolic, rather than literal. The colonial Indian elites call themselves, and are called, Brahmins, though by no means all of them are actually of a Brahmin caste. The Indianness of urban Indians is a reconstructed Indianness, something self-conscious, and partly assumed.

The rural Indians naturally retain much more of their old culture, though a process of culture-shedding is constantly

[1] In this approach, I am taking a parallel course to Raymond T. Smith (University of Chicago) who in a study of Guyana observed that the 'major dimensions of the cultural system' are established by the political and economic system through which they have to move, and not by what is 'colourfully cultural, as religion, marriage customs, or preferences in music'; 'Race and Political Conflict in Guyana', *Race*, April 1971. The 'folkways' approach of the anthropologist assumes too often that communities create their own environment within the Little Society of the village instead of evaluating the impact of the Great Society beyond the village.

happening. V. S. Naipaul recalls the old Indian string-beds, charpoys, lying about in dusty corners in his family home in rural Trinidad. Nobody slept on the charpoy any more; nobody knew how to make them, or even to repair them, but they were not thrown away, because they represented a memory of India. The Indians of the sugar estates hang on to a lot of lumber like this, in their homes and in their minds. Caste is recognized as an Indian attribute, a badge, but its power is weak. Few estate Indians observe all the ritual processes associated with eating or with purification. Caste has no real sanction, as it still has in India, for there are seldom caste councils to enforce observance of the rules.[1] In broad terms, caste governs the choice of a marriage partner, but even this is not complete. From one generation to another, a man may ascend or descend in the scale of caste status, but this has more to do with his economic status than with ancestry. Religious observance is largely confined to a Sunday 'church-attendance' pattern. Here and there, old rituals will be preserved: fire-walking is often staged, and is in danger of becoming a tourist attraction. But the estate Indians are very sensitive to any suggestion that they observe rituals which are antiquated or 'barbaric'.[2]

The separateness of the estate Indians, of which so much is made, is often not a feature of their ancestral Indian culture, but of their plantation life. In Fiji, the Fijians play rugby football and the Indians play association football (soccer). This apartness in sport does help to keep the communities apart; but it cannot be ascribed to the exclusiveness of Indian culture.

In each of these societies, mixed marriages are rare—Indians marry Indians, and Creoles marry Creoles. Where an inter-ethnic marriage occurs, it is usually between an Indian man and a woman of another race. In such cases, Indian men often have a reputation as careful and considerate husbands. Mixed families certainly do not become pariahs, but they are regarded as marginal by both communities, and the children usually marry the offspring of

[1] A balanced discussion of the meaning of caste in a sugar colony is given by Adrian Mayer, *Peasants in the Pacific; a Study of Fiji Indian Rural Society*, 2nd. edn., Berkeley, 1973.

[2] A political storm blew up in Mauritius over a description by Burton Benedict (*Indians in a Plural Society*, London, 1961) of an obscure ritual which was deemed to denigrate the Mauritius Indians. Ten years later, Benedict's book was still a taboo subject in Mauritius.

similar unions. In Trinidad, those born of mixed, Indian-Afro marriages are called *dougla*, which is said to be an Indian word for 'bastard'. Neither for Indians or Blacks is such a marriage a social advantage, as a marriage with a White or light-skinned person is regarded.[1]

Memories go back a long way in the sugar colonies. The wrong done by slavery and indenture is very much part of people's consciousness today. Yet these memories relate to the sugar colonies, and only in a symbolic sense to India—or Africa. The rural Indian knows that his grandfather or great-grandfather came from a particular province, such as Bihar; and perhaps he knows the name of the district and even the village. But there have been few if any contacts since grandfather departed. No letters will have been exchanged, and information is derived from an occasional visit by a descendant, curious to revisit the old home, but usually disillusioned by the reality.

India is also a transcendental experience. It is Gandhi and Nehru and the *Ramayana* and films made in Bombay, depicting luscious, inaccessible heroines and expensively dressed heroes. India is a sense of belonging to a great tradition, of being the heir of a great civilization. India is a compensation for the poverty of everyday life.

The dream of India, the memories of their forbears' sufferings on the plantations, and their view of the contemporary scene all come together in the work songs which the labourers sing. In Guyana they still sing songs of the past in Bhojpuri, the language (a dialect of Hindi) which was spoken by the first indentured immigrants. But their own, topical work songs are sung in a mixture of Creolized Hindi and *taki-taki* (talky-talky) the lingua-franca of the Guyana plantations: 'Some of the songs are almost entirely in *taki-taki* or have Creole English verses with a "Creole" Hindi chorus.'[2]

The older songs tell of the breakdown of traditional Indian values:

---

[1] In the Second World War, African soldiers fought in Burma, and went on leave to India. They regarded all North Indians as bastards, the mixing of European and Black unions. To them, the dark Tamil people were the only 'pure' Indians. Was this a very early declaration that Black is Beautiful?

[2] Ved Prakash Vatuk, *Thieves in My House: Four Studies in Indian Folklore of Protest and Change*, Banaras, 1969, p. 42.

Sisters wear long dresses, pressing them under their heels,
Gentlemen wear short skirts, showing half their legs,
  Oh these women!
Tying Madras *kortif* on the head, parting hair on the side,
Right in the middle of the market, pushing people with their shoulders,
  No shame is left,
Cigarettes they press between their lips, they sit on chairs,
With no shame before their father-in-law or brother-in-law,
  They giggle, laugh, and talk.

The version given above is, of course, a translation, which loses the cadence of the original. But a rendering of a modern Creole song into standard English keeps much of the original verve: this is a song of election-time:

> D'Aguiar is the fool,
> Burnham is the mule,
> The man Jagan is born to rule.
>
> Play the mandolin, *bhai*,
> Play the mandolin,
> All the young girls drink *palmalin*.[1]

The song was recorded in 1962, when it was possible for East Indians in Guyana to believe that after Independence a better time was coming. The work-song of 1977 evokes a more disillusioned, sadder note. The conclusion to it all may be summed up in the words of a veteran Trinidadian politician and writer: 'There is no neo-colonialism. . . . It is the same old colonialism which has existed since the beginning and continues, independence or no independence.'[2]

---

[1] Both songs recorded by Ved Prakash Vatuk and taken from his work, op. cit., pp. 51, 57. *Palmalin* is toddy.
[2] Lowenthal, op. cit., p. 245, citing C. L. R. James.

4

An Auxiliary Minority

Between the two diametrically opposed situations already considered—in one of which overseas Indians were treated as perpetual outsiders, non-belongers, and in the other where the Indians were active competitors for political power—there is an intermediate situation in which the Indians form a recognized community, distinct and apart, within the political arena. Yet because of limited numbers they can never aspire to a role other than that of a minority, required to conform to the norms of the majority of the Sons of the Soil.

In comparing Malaysia and East Africa there are sizeable differences to record, for in Malaysia the Indian community comprises 11 per cent of the total population, whereas in East Africa Indians now form less than one per cent. However, both examples reveal the Indians as having to adapt to the emergence of a strongly felt nationalism, whereby the majority community has suddenly acquired a very positive sense of national pride. The transition from an imperial system, under which the Sons of the Soil had little or no part in the superordinate political process, into a national, democratic system, in which they are the Lords of the Land has had its impact on the Indians both in Malaysia and East Africa. However, in Malaysia the Indians have always been a subordinate community, while in East Africa they acquired some of the opprobrium connected with colonialism (though missing any of its prestige). So in one situation they have to get away from the 'pariah' image, and in the other to try to shake off the image of 'exploiter'.

Another feature common to both the Indian communities in Malaysia and East Africa was their record of political miscalculation in the crucial period immediately before Independence when the conception of the nation was being shaped. The Indians lagged behind; they were reluctant to identify with the new nations—which, indeed, seemed to have no very great future ahead when they came to birth. This Indian reluctance to become citizens of the new nations served to emphasize their continuing minority status. Their share in the politics of nation-building did not develop; it contracted. The best they could expect was to be co-opted as very junior partners of the real nation-makers. Perhaps they might have contributed a little more, but by their own hesitation they excluded themselves from the central arena of the political contest.

The key to understanding Malaya or West Malaysia is the paradox that both the major communities, the Malays and the Chinese, have a minority complex. The Malays, the Sons of the Soil, regard the Chinese as the intruders who have taken over, and exploited the Malays' own country to their exclusive advantage. The Malays believe that all economic power—which is the real power—is in Chinese hands. A Malay politician who is also an intellectual, Mahathir bin Mohammad, has compared his own people with the Amerindians. He writes: 'It is not enough to be legally [equally] privileged, it is also necessary for equality to be real. It is clearly necessary for the [Red] Indians to have their fair share of the economic prosperity which characterises the America of the whites. . . . In Malaysia there can be no denying that the status of the Malays differs from that of the non-Malays. *The Malays and the Red Indians of America are more or less in the same category.*'[1] For their part, the Chinese hold that they are excluded from supreme policy-making and even from full citizenship-rights by the Malays, who retain complete control over Government, the army, and the police, and who may (they believe) at any time deny all rights to the Chinese and deport those who earn their special enmity. Tension between the two major communities is so acute that in the struggle for what each regards as its due, the case of the Indians is never properly considered. The third community, which is a minority by any definition, is often simply ignored by both big brothers.

Before the Second World War, the Indians were a community of helots in Malaya. More than half of them were workers on the rubber estates, and almost one-third worked for the railways and in public works departments (highways, etc.) and on public cleansing and conservancy. The great majority were Tamils

[1] Mahathir bin Mohammad, *The Malay Dilemma*, Singapore, 1970, pp. 68–9 (italics added). The author became deputy premier.

from Madras, and because immigration was easy—and free passages were available to labourers—many were transients, until the Government of India halted labour migration in 1938 and the population began to stabilize. During this migratory phase, the proportion of males was more than double that of females, and there were other features of impermanence.

During the 1930s, the Indians were about 15 per cent of the total population of Malaya (including Singapore), with Malays 44 per cent, and Chinese 39 per cent.[1] They were concentrated in the rubber districts around Kuala Lumpur and Ipoh, which were also areas of Chinese concentration. The Indians were much less 'visible' than the Chinese, who imparted their own cultural identity to the commercial centres of all the towns. Chinese noise and colour seemed so much more evident than the unobtrusive presence of the Indians, even where they congregated. The rubber industry employed 300,000 Indians and 200,000 Chinese, together with 30,000 Malays and 15,000 Javanese (1937). However, the races were not intermixed, as these figures may seem to imply. Many of the Chinese workers were employed on Chinese-owned estates, while the Malays were almost all employed on small, private plantations, though some were truck-drivers on the big estates. The Indians, living on the mainly British-owned estates, received lower wages than the Chinese or Malays, though their hours of work were also less onerous. They were regarded by the British managers as 'industrious' and 'docile'. The manager was *Mai-Bap* ('Mother-Father') and the ruler of the plantation Indians' little world.[2] In this situation, industrial relations were paternalistic: wages were negotiated not by trade unions (which did not exist) but between the organization of the employers, U.P.A.M. (the United Planters' Association of Malaya), the Labour Department of the Government, and the Agent of the Government of India, appointed to keep guard over the workers' interests. The pay of the Indians

[1] The remaining 2 per cent being Europeans and the aboriginal and proto-Malay people of the jungle interior. If Singapore is excluded from the calculation then the Indian percentage is unaffected, but Malays rise to 49 per cent and Chinese drop to 34 per cent. This illustrates why the Malays and their patrons constantly called for the exclusion of the port city from any new political grouping.

[2] The enclosed world of the Indian rubber worker, before and after the Second World War, is depicted in animated detail by R. K. Jain, *South Indians on the Plantation in Malaya*, New Haven, 1970.

was small, but their demands were small also. They lived simply, and saved frugally, against the day when they would return as big men to their village in South India.

The Indians' passive acceptance of wage-rates determined by others was upset by the wartime rise in prices—particularly in rubber prices—when their own wages remained unchanged. In the Klang district, some 8,000 Indian workers went on strike in April 1941. Troops were called in (and it was an Indian battalion, sent to Malaya to defend the country against Japanese attack) to put down the strike of the Indians; three men were killed.

The Klang strike produced a temporary realization that the Malayan Indians were a neglected community, without representation, largely without rights; but though the Colonial Office worried a little, the Malayan Government, under pressure from U.P.A.M., was concerned only to get rid of the 'agitators' who were responsible for the unrest. Over 360 Indian labourers were held in detention, and those identified as leaders were deported to India.

The weary retreat of the British, Australian, and Indian forces in the face of the Japanese was watched by the estate Indians only as spectators. There were hasty evacuation operations to get some civilians out of Penang, and later Singapore. The Indians were brushed aside. Only about 4,500 were able to get away; the rest of Malaya's 630,000 Indians passed under Japanese rule, as did the 70,000 Indian soldiers who became captives.

The Japanese interregnum produced a reversal of roles for almost everybody in Malaya. The Chinese were regarded as enemies, and subjected to cruel retaliation; many Chinese (mainly led by Communists) took to the jungle and created a resistance movement. The Malays acquiesced in the changeover, and Malay officials and police worked for the Japanese. The lowly Indians were galvanized by the arrival of Subhas Chandra Bose, the militant Bengali leader, after a perilous journey by submarine. Bose now became *Netaji*, their great leader.[1] An army was raised—the Azad Hind Fauj, or Indian National Army (I.N.A.). Some military prisoners were persuaded or coerced into joining, though many refused. More recruits were found among the Malayan Indians, especially from Sikhs in the local police forces. For the Indians in the I.N.A., these were years of pride.

[1] From Sanskrit, *Nayaka*, 'leader, chief, general'.

But other estate Indians were recruited for what was little more than a slave army, condemned to work alongside British, Australian, and Dutch prisoners of war on the 'Death Railway' to link Burma with Thailand. The total number of Indians who died is unknown; one estimate puts the figure at over 60,000.[1] For those who remained on the estates, things were not much better; there were no supplies of rice, and they had to subsist on tapioca and other ground-up roots. When the Japanese surrendered in August 1945, the Indian population in Malaya had sunk to less than 590,000, or just 10 per cent of the total population. It was never to recover its former numerical significance.

The sudden end of the war brought another reversal of roles. The Chinese emerged from the jungle believing that they were about to take over the country. They exacted bloody reprisals from those Malays who had cooperated with their enemies. This Chinese blood-bath was never forgotten by the Malays. For the Indians, the intoxication of the I.N.A. and *Chalo Dehli* ('We March on Delhi') was overtaken by the news of the death of *Netaji* in an aeroplane crash and their own dismissal and humiliation.[2] Everything was in a mess. The rubber estates were run down. Their community organizations were scattered. Their future was in jeopardy; in 1946 there were only 16,000 Indian children at school in Malaya, compared to 26,000 in 1941 (and that was an unsatisfactory total). By contrast, 128,000 children were in Chinese-language schools and 125,000 in Malay-language schools. The other communities were better placed to face the new, post-war world.

On the estates, the Indians resisted efforts to push them back into the docile acceptance of the managers' regime of pre-war days. There were bitter strikes, and Indians took part in the formation of trade unions which were organized across the whole industry and organized on militant, semi-political lines.

---

[1] S. Arasaratnam, *Indians in Malayisa and Singapore*, London, 1970, p. 30.

[2] The subject of *Netaji* and the I.N.A. rapidly shifted from the level of fact to that of myth; many still believe that Bose is alive, and will return in triumph. For a sympathetic but not uncritical picture of Bose, see Hugh Toye, *The Springing Tiger*, London, 1959. For a similar kind of assessment of the I.N.A., see Philip Mason, *A Matter of Honour*, London, 1974. To many Malayan Indians, including serious scholars, these works will appear coldly inadequate; but are they seeking some form of psychological compensation?

Also, in 1946, the Malayan Indian Congress (M.I.C.) was founded as an avowedly activist political organization. The first president was John Thivy, son of a Malayan Indian planter.

Taking their line from the mother Congress in India, the M.I.C. was opposed to British imperial policy. When in 1948 the British bowed to the unexpected political protest of the Malays against the proposal for a Malayan Union, expressing a multi-racial philosophy, and substituted a Malayan Federation in which the Malays would be politically pre-eminent, the M.I.C. joined forces with Chinese organizations to oppose the federation. They organized a *hartal*, a shut-down of business and trade; but the British went ahead, and the Indians found their protest was ineffective.

After the Malay political resistance came the Chinese armed revolt: the Communist rising designed to destroy the British colonial regime. An offensive against the forces of the Government was launched which concentrated on destroying the rubber industry. During the long years of underground jungle warfare —the 'Emergency', as it was euphemistically called—the estate Indians were caught in the crossfire between the Communist Chinese and British authority. A few militant Indian labour leaders joined the revolt. P. Veeraseenam, President of the Communist Singapore Federation of Trade Unions went underground, and was killed in a jungle foray. Ganapathy, also a trade union organizer, was captured in a jungle raid and hanged. Sambasivam, another Indian political worker was also caught by a jungle patrol, but had his death sentence commuted after his case had aroused strong protests in the Indian Parliament. Such examples are few, however, compared to the hundreds of Chinese guerrillas hunted and killed. In addition, about a hundred Indian rubber tappers were killed by the guerrillas, along with 27 Indian policemen.[1]

During the twelve Emergency years, 1948–60, Malaya took a political leap from forms of government which were feudal and medieval into the full experience of independence. The

[1] Mention should be made of the Gurkha battalions of the British army which provided the permanent element in the counter-insurgency operations. When the Emergency was over, Tun Razak, then Deputy Premier of Malaysia, visited Nepal to convey his country's thanks to the Gurkhas. With rare magnanimity he announced that Malaysian citizenship would be extended to any Gurkha veteran of the Emergency who wished to settle in Malaysia.

political style was set by the emergence of the Alliance in 1953, bringing together moderate Malay and Chinese leaders in partnership.

The Alliance was exactly what its name indicated: an alliance of two separate communal bodies, the United Malay National Organization (U.M.N.O.) and the Malayan Chinese Association (M.C.A.). U.M.N.O. was first formed to fight the Malayan Union scheme and to defend the rights of the Malays—or more precisely, the privileges of the Malay aristocracy. The M.C.A. was an organization of moderate Chinese, with strong business backing, concerned to demonstrate the Chinese rejection of Communism, and also—though this emerged only gradually—to demonstrate a commitment to Malaya, overriding any loyalty to the China of Chiang Kai-shek. Within the Alliance, U.M.N.O. and M.C.A. remained separate, distinct organizations, and their respective audiences, the Malays and the Chinese, were identified in communal not national terms.

The equivalent Indian organization was the M.I.C., which at first assumed a distinctly ambivalent stance, oscillating between emphasizing the divergent Malayan and Indian facets of their community, as well as oscillating between the politics of opposition and the politics of cooperation and participation in government. When the new Federal citizenship was first created, the Indians were slow to register, and when they became liable to conscription in 1952 under a National Service Bill, there was a rush by young Indians to leave Malaya. Similarly, the Indians looked on the formation of the Alliance as a threat to their interests. Perhaps still thinking with nostalgia of the days of the I.N.A., they over-calculated the importance of their community in Malayan politics. After 1948, there was a Federal legislature, with fifty non-official members, and five Indians were nominated to the legislative council, a number equivalent to the population strength of the community. However, two of the Indians were selected to represent organized labour, being the sole trade union representatives in the legislature. In 1953 a Federal Cabinet was appointed by the High Commissioner, and no Indian was selected; the five Indian legislators thereupon staged a walkout from the Council. Non-Indian trade unionists asked why their representatives should have placed communal considerations above their responsibilities to the working class.

In part, the trouble lay in the remoteness of the Indian leadership from the mass of the community. The early leaders of the M.I.C. were all urban intellectuals, with a high proportion of lawyers; moreover they were not Tamils, like the mass of the community. The first leader, Thivy, was a Christian Indian, and his successors, Budh Singh, R. Ramani, and others, were northern Indians. Not until 1955 did the M.I.C. elect a president who was a Tamil and a trade union organizer, V. T. Sambanthan. He endeavoured to persuade his community to demonstrate their commitment to Malaya by acquiring citizenship and registering as voters. He also steered the M.I.C. into the Alliance, and just before the first country-wide elections of 1955, the consortium was expanded to include all three community organizations.

The 1955 election was expected to provide a test: the British needed confirmation that the Alliance (led by Tungku Abdul Rahman) could demonstrate effective strength, before conceding independence. Malaya was divided into 52 territorial constituencies. There were no seats specially reserved for any community or interest; the electorate was composed of undifferentiated Malayan citizens. Yet, because of the restrictive citizenship law, and the reluctance of Chinese and Indians to register, the vast majority of electors were Malays.[1] The Alliance had to fit a multi-communal party platform on to a uni-communal electoral system, and try to persuade Malay voters to vote for non-Malay candidates in the teeth of a challenge from other parties emphasizing Malay interests exclusively. The Alliance ticket was awarded to candidates on the basis of an overall deal between U.M.N.O., the M.C.A., and M.I.C., whereby 35 Malays were nominated alongside 15 Chinese and two Indians.[2]

The main challenge to the Alliance came from the Party Negara which remained, virtually, a Malay party. Ramani, the disappointed contender for president of the M.I.C., spoke on behalf of the Party, advising Indians not to support the Alliance, but he was not offered a Party Negara nomination. When the vote was counted, the Alliance was found to have taken 51 out of the 52 seats. Sambanthan was among those elected, and he

---

[1] In 1955 the Indians represented 4 per cent of the electorate and the Chinese 11 per cent, 84 per cent being Malay voters.
[2] One 'Indian' was actually Ceylonese.

was appointed a Minister by the Tungku. The Alliance policy seemed to offer the Indians a small dividend.

The Alliance victory cleared the ground for independence, and an elaborate constitution was drafted, with the help of Commonwealth experts (including jurists from India and Pakistan). The keystone was the recognition of special Malay privileges. Islam was accorded a special status; Malay became the official language; the Malays were guaranteed an entrenched majority of positions in the administration; and Malay rights in landownership were carefully safeguarded.[1]

In the final negotiations leading to Independence the citizenship law was revised. Anyone born in Malaya after Independence acquired citizenship automatically, though on attaining the age of twenty-one it was necessary to make a specific renunciation of any other claim to citizenship (e.g. Indian or Chinese citizenship). The qualifying period of residence for all others was fixed at eight years, as a concession. However, there was also a definite tightening-up on immigration. The Immigration Ordinance 1952, and Immigration (Prohibition of Entry) Ordinance 1953, had already abolished all immigration except for those with 'special qualifications'. From 1959, only persons arriving in Malaya with appointments carrying a salary of $1,200 per month or above were admitted to residence—a provision which only allowed entry, in reality, to senior European staff. There was a ban on entry for all dependants except wives and children under six years. Effectively, Indian (and other Asian) immigration was entirely closed off. The policy of compulsorily sending undesirable Indians back to India still persisted, even after Independence. In the Indian Parliament Nehru was urged to stop the practice, but he replied 'We cannot object to these Indians being sent back' (23 April 1959). It appeared to be Indian Government policy to accept all unwanted or ejected persons of Indian origin into the mother country.

Year by year, the elections for the M.I.C. presidency formed the occasion for a challenge to Sambanthan's leadership, and also to his policy of associating the Indians with a Malaya in which the special position of the Malays was accepted. Ramani

---

[1] The Constitution gives a definition of a Malay as 'One who practises the Muslim religion, speaks Malay, and adopts Malay dress and custom'. This is an exclusive definition—one which many Malays breach, in practice.

remaiend the main contestant, and also advocate of a different attitude. At Independence-time he announced: 'My advice to Indians in Malaya, even after they become Malayan citizens, is to remain Indians at heart.'[1] Yet each time, Sambanthan repulsed his challenge and scored a convincing victory.

After Independence, the legislature was expanded; all the members were now elected from territorial constituencies, numbering 104 altogether. The first post-Independence election was held in 1959, and after protracted dealings between U.M.N.O., M.C.A., and M.I.C., the Alliance fielded a team of candidates composed of 69 U.M.N.O. nominees, with 31 from M.C.A., and 4 for M.I.C. The M.C.A. was in a strong position to increase its demands because, under the more liberal citizenship rules, there were 41 out of the 104 constituencies in which Chinese formed the majority of the electorate. By contrast, there was no constituency in which Indians were more than a quarter of the voters.

The estate Indians remained loyal to Sambanthan and the M.I.C., but there was evidence that the urban Indians tended to support the left-wing parties which now challenged the Alliance, as much as the right-wing Malay parties. The Socialist Front (incorporating the Labour Party) included 7 Indians among its 38 candidates. However, the Alliance fought off the challenge, capturing 74 of the 104 seats; the only other party to make any impact was the Pan-Malayan Islamic Party (P.M.I.P.) with 13 seats.

For twelve years, the Tungku ran Malaya according to the Alliance formula, with every sign of success. The 1964 election brought an even more resounding Alliance victory.[2] The main event of these years was the enlargement of Malaya into Malaysia. At first, Singapore was a constituent part, but only for eighteen months. Thereafter, Malaysia consisted of the peninsula, West Malaysia, the predominant partner, and East Malaysia, the Borneo territories. The whole question was deeply enmeshed in the comparative arithmetic of the populations of the different territories.

---

[1] *Hindu* (Madras), 1 September 1957.
[2] For details, see K. J. Ratnam and R. S. Milne, *The Malayan Parliamentary Election of 1964* (Singapore, 1967). This includes a section on the Singapore election of 1963.

The Banyan Tree

Ethnic Composition of Different Political Combinations (%)

	Malaya (without Singapore)	Singapore	Malaysia(1) (with Singapore)	Malaysia(2) (without Singapore)
Malays	50·1	15	40·6	45·9
Chinese	36·8	76·2	42·2	35·7
Indians	11·1	7	9·4	9·6
Others	2	1·8	7·8	8·8

The ratio between Malays and Chinese was significantly affected by whether Singapore was in or out of Malaysia, whereas the importance (or unimportance) of the Indians was not much affected by whichever form Malaysia should take, though they were a smaller proportion of either form of Malaysia than they were in Malaya. From the Tungku's standpoint, they did not affect the issue, which he saw in terms of his unsatisfactory relationship with the Singapore Prime Minister, Lee Kuan Yew, and in terms of acquiring allies among the tribal peoples of Borneo: Dusuns, Dayaks, etc., with whom the Tungku perceived a 'natural affinity'.

Before and after the merger, the Indians held only a minor position in the arena of national politics. Tun Sambanthan (as he was honorifically called) was regarded as a worthy, but somewhat pedestrian member of the Tungku's team. He managed to restrain unrest among the Indian community, but the leading Chinese Minister, Tan Siew Sin, was much less successful in satisfying the younger Chinese, while the young Malay intellectuals openly denounced the Tungku's Alliance policy as a betrayal of the Sons of the Soil. S. Arasaratnam, a shrewd observer of the dilemma of the Indians summed up the overall situation as follows: Alliance rule had 'produced two decades of communal harmony and rapid economic development, but there was something lacking. The nation was searching for an identity. . . . It lived on for twelve years as a nation without a history, without common symbols and inheritances that its citizens could look back on.'

The general election of 1969 saw a heightened atmosphere of racial suspicion, and even hatred. The Alliance launched the campaign under the slogan 'Vote Alliance for Racial Harmony', but this was not reflected in subsequent events. One of the opposition strongholds was Ipoh, centre of tin-mining, where two Ceylonese brothers, the Seenivasagams, had a mass following. Their People's Progressive Party (P.P.P.) made a particular issue of the injustice of special Malay rights. Said D. R. Seenivasagam: 'Alliance leaders have said that if we don't like it here we can go back to China or India. We're not going anywhere. We're sticking here in Malaysia, the country that we've helped to build with our sweat and blood.'[1] This sort of speech was regarded by the Tungku and his friends as evidence that the Chinese and Indians intended to 'take over'.

The moment of truth came when the results were announced. Once again, the Alliance was a clear winner, retaining 66 of the 104 seats in West Malaysia. However, this represented a decline of more than 20 per cent from the 1964 results, and both Government and Opposition grossly exaggerated its significance. U.M.N.O. retained 51 of the 58 seats it had held previous to the election; but its share of the Malay vote was calculated at only 41 per cent, while the Malay chauvinists of the P.M.I.P. received 40 per cent of the Malay vote. The major disaster was for the M.C.A., which kept only 13 of its previous 27 seats. The M.I.C. suffered its own little setback, being reduced to two representatives in the new legislature.

On the opposition benches, the Democratic Action Party (D.A.P.) captured 13 seats, P.P.P. had four seats, and Gerakan Ra'ayat Malaysia ('Movement of the Peoples of Malaysia') secured eight seats.[2] These parties proclaimed the 'Malaysian Malaysia' concept first propounded by Lee Kuan Yew of Singapore, and their supporters came largely from the tin and rubber districts of the west-coast states where a working class of Chinese and Indians was numerous and increasingly well organized. The left-wing opposition, totalling 25, was made up of 15 Chinese, eight Indians, and two Malays. Thus, the Malayan Indians had swung right back to their former oppositional politics.

The Alliance was still in power at the Federal level, but it had lost the city-state of Penang to Gerakan, while the P.P.P. was able to form a coalition to take over Perak. Much, much too quickly, the opposition parties celebrated their 'victory' by a big parade through Kuala Lumpur. On 13 May 1969 (a day never

---

[1] *Straits Times*, 11 April 1969.
[2] *Ra'ayat* means 'peasant' or 'son of the soil', but it is used here more broadly.

to be forgotten) the Malays retaliated. Those who know only one Malay word, know the word *amok*, or amuck. For three days, Malay bully-boys (many brought in from the countryside by lorry) ran amok through the Chinese quarters of Kuala Lumpur, burning, killing, and looting.[1] The police—mainly Malay, but including some Chinese and Indians—attempted to exert control, but martial law was declared and the Royal Malay Regiment took over. It is widely alleged that the Malay soldiers joined in the killing.

Tungku Abdul Rahman and most of his Ministers acted as though paralysed by the sequence of events. However, the two Indian Ministers, V. T. Sambanthan and V. Manickasavavasagam, offered to go round the streets, appealing for calm, and this offer was accepted. There was no other gesture of reconciliation from the Alliance leaders, and on 15 May, Tun Razak, then Deputy Premier, became Director of Operations and head of a National Operations Council, such as General Templer had set up to fight the guerrillas. The Alliance had opted for a military solution.

Almost all the fighting in May was between Malays and Chinese; the Indians kept behind closed doors. However, as the Malays paraded triumphantly in the wake of the riot, the cry was heard: 'We have finished off the pigs: now for the goats!' (Just as the Chinese are fond of pork, so Indians are supposed to favour curried goat.) On 28 June there was an attack upon a group of Indians in the Malay kampong-suburb of Sentul; fifteen were slashed to death, and others wounded. In the evening several Indian huts were burned, and about seventy Indians moved into a refugee centre. The incident was minor, compared to the holocaust of May; but it was bad enough to convince the Indians that they, like the Chinese, were marked out for revenge.

The period which followed was sinister and strange. People soon went back to work, and Indian and Chinese doctors worked alongside Malays in the hospitals; Indian clerks worked alongside Malay officials in the public departments; but although they transacted business with each other, no one really communicated

[1] A restrained though appalling account is given by a former British police officer who witnessed these events: John Slimming, *Malaysia: Death of a Democracy*, London, 1969. This book is banned in Malaysia.

with a member of another community, and many refrained from saying much to others in their own community. The visitor to Kuala Lumpur who went along to the campus of the University of Malaysia at Petaling Jaya found that friends and acquaintances, normally loquacious in their conversation, were not saying anything at all.

It seemed the end of a 'Malaysian Malaysia'. In September 1970, the Tungku handed over the premiership to Tun Razak, and nine months later the State of Emergency was lifted. Very gingerly, Malaysia returned to parliamentary government. The new pattern was that of a very tight Malay regime, and tough Malay administrators were carefully installed in key political posts. Recognizing that the towns provided the Chinese—and to a lesser extent, the Indians—with a political power base, Tun Razak abolished all municipal institutions in 1971, turning Penang, Ipoh, and other opposition centres over to the central administration. Under the Constitutional (Amendment) Act 1971, any person who publicly questions the Malay special privileges can be convicted of sedition.[1] This last provision is an apt illustration of the two faces of Alliance multi-racialism. Tun Razak can insist that by prohibiting debate about Malay special privileges he is eliminating an issue which provokes people to react on racial lines. His opponents, of course, assert that by further bolstering up the Malay position *vis-à-vis* the other communities he is accentuating racial grievance and hostility.

Having neutralized his opponents, Tun Razak invited some of them to join him. Elections were due in 1974, and the Prime Minister decided to extend his political support by bringing part of the Opposition into the Government. The offer was made to the P.M.I.P. (now P.A.S.) on the Right, and to Gerakan on the Left. The carrot was accompanied by a suggestion of stick: if they did not join, their respective power bases, Penang and Kelantan, need expect no Federal money in future for development. Both parties joined, and the new coalition was named Barisan Nasional, 'National Front'. When the elections came in August 1974, Tun Razak's strategy was amply justified. The political arithmetic involved in handing out the National Front ticket to the different groups, and matching parties against

[1] Alvin Rabushka, *Race and Politics in Urban Malaya*, Stanford, 1973, p. 52.

constituencies, must have been enormously complicated. The calculation was very nearly correct. From the 110 constituencies of West Malaysia, the Barisan Nasional obtained 103 electoral victories. The Malays gave Tun Razak total support; U.M.N.O. won all 62 seats contested, and P.A.S. won all its 13 seats. The M.I.C. was allotted four seats, and won them. Only the Chinese voters refused to give a total endorsement to the Government: M.C.A. won 19 of the 23 seats it fought, and Gerakan won five out of eight seats fought. Just seven opposition (D.A.P.) M.P.s survived, to demonstrate that a Government victory was not always completely inevitable.

The 1974 election confirmed that the Malay hegemony in politics was now absolute; the new umbrella organization, the National Front, is three-quarters Malay in composition. Not only the Indians, but the Chinese also, have been cut down to size.

The election was followed by a reaction from the students. The campus of the University of Malaysia became the arena of protest, but the students were dispersed and many were arrested and the campus was closed until the atmosphere had quietened. The ongoing open political debate will be between young, 'radical' Malay intellectuals, and the Malays who are in power. Chinese frustration is likely to be expressed, as once before, through support for the guerrillas in the jungle; and the Thai–Malaysian border is more and more a No Man's Land disputed between Government and Communists. For the Indians, there is only silence, and the patient hope that maybe, one day, things might change.

The stasis which affects the Indians in Malaysian politics also affects them in economic terms. From among the Chinese, the former coolies and *towkays* (labourers and merchants) have developed into artisans, technicians, industrialists, financiers, capable of confronting their counterparts from Japan or the West. Indeed, their success is a major reason why the Malays continue to see them as the exploiters of Malaya. A few Indians are beginning to adjust to modernization, but most of the shopkeeper class remain shopkeepers, unable to change into entrepreneurs and industrialists. One means of illustrating this *immobilisme* is to offer a number of comparative statistics.

Rural and Urban Population
(expressed as percentages by different communities)

		Malay	Chinese	Indian	Other	Total
1947	Rural	59·7	29·8	9·7	0·8	100
	Urban	21·1	62·3	13·8	1·8	100
1970	Rural	63·5	26·2	9·7	0·6	100
	Urban	27·6	58·5	12·8	1·1	100

This table does not bring out the overall urban growth from about 20 per cent of total population (1947) to nearly 29 per cent (1970); it also obscures the significant increase of the Malays from 49 to 53 per cent of the overall total. What the table does show clearly is the extent to which the Malays are a rural people while the Chinese are predominantly urban and the Indians are balanced between. In 1947–70, more Chinese moved into towns, while the Indian rural population remained more or less constant. The Malays became a higher proportion of town-dwellers; but they became a higher proportion of the rural population also!

Workers on rubber estates, by different communities (%)

	Malays	Chinese	Indians
1947	39	33	28
1967	27	29	44

This table demonstrates that the dependence of the Indian population upon estate employment has actually increased, while both the other major communities have been moving into alternative forms of employment.

Employment by Race and Sector, 1970 (%)[1]

	Malays	Chinese	Indians
Agriculture, forestry, fisheries	67·6	21·4	10·1
Mining & quarrying	24·8	66	8·4
Manufacturing	28·9	65·4	5·3
Construction	21·7	72·1	6
Electricity, water, sanitation	48·5	18	32·3
Transport	42·6	39·6	17·1
Commerce	23·5	65·3	10·7
Government services	48·5	35·7	14

[1] Source: *Mid-term Review of the Second Malaysia Plan 1971–5*, Government of Malaysia, 1973.

The decline in the Indian share in Government service from 35 per cent in 1947—especially in the police, subordinate services (e.g. office messengers), and technical branches—has been accompanied by a massive Malay recruitment into expanding services, especially the army. The Indian decline is not quite so damaging as the figures suggest, but it does demonstrate that Malay substitution has gone a long way.

Wealth can be expressed by two kinds of figures: by how much the different communities can be said to own, and by how much they are required to contribute to the state. By either kind of measurement it can be demonstrated that those who are really wealthy in Malaysia do not belong to any of the groups we have been discussing; Malaysia's wealth is still, overwhelmingly, controlled by multi-national (mainly British) capitalists. Among the domestic groups, the Chinese are far ahead in their dominance over, and contribution to, the overall economy.

Share capital in Malayan enterprises is still mainly in foreign hands: 61 per cent is foreign-owned, while 22 per cent of Malayan share capital is Chinese-owned. Only 2 per cent of the capital is held by Malays and 1 per cent by Indians. For the rubber industry, the inequality is even more striking: 77·7 per cent of the rubber estates are still in foreign ownership; 13·2 per cent are Chinese-owned; while Indians have a 1·3 per cent holding; and the Malays own a mere 0·3 per cent of their country's premier industry. Against this background it is not surprising that those who pay income tax in Malaya contribute in the proportion of 31 per cent expatriates, 51·6 per cent Chinese, 11 per cent Indians, and 6·4 per cent Malays. Figures for annual income, *per capita*, show an average of $837 for the Chinese, $669 for Indians, and $367 for Malays.[1]

As early as 1960, Sambanthan told the Indian estate workers: 'Our fathers came to Malaya as coolies, like the Chinese, without any money. But look at the Chinese today. They have made tremendous economic progress. But we are still the same—penniless.'[2] He urged the importance of social reform—of giving

[1] These figures are largely taken from David Lim, *Economic Growth and Development in Western Malaysia, 1947–1970*, Kuala Lumpur, 1974. See also C. T. Edwards, *Public Finance in Malaya and Singapore*, Canberra, 1970, V. Kanapathy, *The Malaysian Economy; Problems and Prospects*, Singapore, 1970. Pran Chopra, 'Malaysia's Strategy for Survival', *Pacific Affairs*, Winter, 1974–5, provides a more recent account of economic and political developments.

[2] *Straits Times*, 13 December 1960.

up gambling and drinking—but he also devised a positive strategy for improvement. The Indians were encouraged to invest their savings in a National Land Finance Cooperative Society, in order to purchase rubber estates, dividing these up into smallholdings on which Indians were installed as petty rubber producers. The scheme was good, but it lacked large-scale capital, and it was in competition with other Government projects to clear jungle-land for planting with rubber for cultivation by Malay producers. This enjoyed a much higher Government priority than Sambanthan's scheme, and ten years after Independence the proportion of rubber smallholders were 89 per cent Malays, 8 per cent Chinese, and 3 per cent Indian.[1]

In the 1970s the Indians in Malaya are certainly not a depressed community, like the estate Indians in Ceylon, but they remain vulnerable, exposed to economic and political vicissitudes. Dependent as they are on employment on the largely foreign-owned rubber estates, they are apprehensive of the present Government strategy—the 'New Economic Policy'—which aims to transfer two-thirds of rubber production to the smallholders (predominantly Malay) by 1980. The N.E.P. aims to transfer control over 30 per cent of the economy to the Malays. This transformation presumes a growing industry, so that there will still be a share for the Indians in an estate sector, but it will be a dwindling share.

Some estate Indians are moving on to work in the small, secondary industries springing up everywhere under Chinese ownership. They will be employed as labourers and semi-skilled workers. The main alternative for the Indian working class remains the public utilities sector and public transport (private enterprise transport has long been assigned exclusively to Malay operators). Indian living standards may be supported by growing trade union demands, and the Indians remain the most highly unionized community, though their share of membership has declined from 60 per cent to about 50 per cent. The unions know that if they push their demands too far they are likely to incur Government disfavour.[2]

[1] David Lim, op. cit.
[2] Alvin Rabushka (op. cit., p. 24) observes rather cryptically: 'Trade unions have not played an important political role in Malaya because Indians have dominated them since their inception.'

The one ladder for social and economic advancement which the Indians can ascend is that of education and professional training. In the education explosion which followed the Second World War the Indians enjoyed the biggest acceleration. Starting from a miserable third position, they took fullest advantage of the new opportunities. In particular, Indian leaders were the first to discern that the traditional form of education through the vernaculars was, under prevailing conditions, a blind alley in terms of job opportunities. They realized the potential offered by English education, and at the secondary-school level they all transferred from vernacular (Tamil) education to the English medium even before the Chinese also grasped its importance in job-competition.

School Enrolment, Malaya

	Malay Schools	Chinese Schools	Indian Schools*	English Schools
1949	239,000	203,000	39,000	91,000
1959	460,000	416,000	55,000	276,000
1968	743,000	392,000	82,000	644,000

*There are no Indian secondary schools

The advantage gained by the Indians proved only temporary. In 1970 the Government matched its New Economic Policy by a New Education Policy which made it compulsory to use Malay as the medium of instruction in all the primary schools of Malaysia. Henceforward, the Indians and Chinese went on to secondary education on a par with the Malays, or even at a disadvantage to them. However, the previous lead in secondary education had given Indians entry into the University of Singapore and later into the University of Malaya where they gained qualifications which helped them to secure a large proportion of posts in secondary schools and colleges, and in medicine and public health. The best-qualified observer of this process declared: 'The English-educated Indians attained their maximum influence and prosperity in the 1950s and early 1960s.'[1] They were not able to sustain this position. During the 1960s, the basic Indian weakness—the immobility of the mass of estate workers—was reflected

---

[1] Arasaratnam, op. cit. p. 195. The author was Professor of History in the University of Malaysia.

in their inability to match the challenge of the two major communities at the university level.

University of Malaya Enrolment

	1962	1964	1967
Chinese	786	1,330	2,159
Malays	174	443	1,395
Indians	161	211	377
Others	120	141	423
Total	1,241	2,125	4,354

It is often asserted that the effect of English education on the Indians has been to 'colonize' their minds, cutting them off from their own ancestral culture. Sensitive to this charge, some educated Indians have consciously returned to Tamil language and literature and also to the Tamil forms of Hindu religious observance. *Thai Poosam*, the Tamil festival of the New Year, is celebrated almost as an Indian national holiday. Although *Thai Poosam* is not a festival of pilgrimage it has become identified with the Batu Caves, set in a gorge of Malaya's mountain spine, east of Kuala Lumpur. Indians from all over the country gather for the occasion, and there is the same intensity of feeling as at a celebration in the temple-cities of Madura or Tanjore in South India. Some devotees mortify themselves and enter into a state of trance, and the vast crowds of dark-faced Tamils in freshly laundered white robes exult with them.

The ordinary Indians of Malaya determinedly retain their traditional customs and modes of life and despite their isolation from the motherland (few now return, even to visit) they rejuvenate the ancestral culture with garnishings from the Tamil Nadu of today. India remains the land of their dreams. A few very modern Malayan Indians think of escaping from a Malay-dominated polity by emigrating to Australia or North America. The remainder recognize that they could not rebuild their lives in the India of reality. But this alternative remains in the minds of Malay leaders who question the 'umbrella' solution, like Dr. Mahathir, who insists that 'In Malaysia we have three major races which have practically nothing in common.' For him the Malays are the only true Malaysians: 'Should a Malay and an Indian be forced to leave Malaya, the Indian can settle down in

India and be an Indian whilst the Malay cannot. . . . We have no knowledge of Indians from Malaya being refused citizenship of India.'[1]

The Singapore Indians are not similarly placed in a separate compartment and reminded that they are different. Prime Minister Lee Kuan Yew has always included Indians in important positions in his People's Action Party. When the P.A.P. split, between the radical Marxists and the more moderate socialists, several radical young Indians went along with the Marxists. notably James Puthucheary, a leading ideologue.[2] Others supported Lee Kuan Yew, and S. Rajaratnam, Foreign Minister of Singapore, is one of his closest advisers. Nevertheless, looking at the Indian contribution to Singapore politics in perspective, it seems that (as in Malaya) when opposition was replaced by government as the main function of politics, the Indian share began to dwindle.

Beneath a bland exterior, Prime Minister Lee conceals a relentless dedication to *his* conception of Singapore, and anyone getting in the way is pushed aside. Chinese revolutionaries, born in the island, have lost their citizenship and been deported back to China. Some Indians have been threatened with this fate, but so far the threat has been enough to cool their ardour. A separate problem is that of the many Indians formerly employed on the Singapore naval base who are now redundant with the final British withdrawal from east of Suez. Most of these Indian dockyard workers kept their British status, and Lee told the British Government that their future was a British problem. Some were accepted into Britain during the period of a Conservative Government ostensibly committed to stopping immigration. Others still remain, in a post-colonial limbo.

But for most of the Singapore Indians, their future is bound up with that of the island-republic. They have their own special quarter on Serangoon Road, which seems more like Tamil Nadu than South-East Asia. They have their broader place in the multi-racial society, though that conception is sometimes challenged. To promote the growth of multi-racialism, the Ministry of

[1] Mahathir bin Mohammad, op. cit., pp. 132, 175 for quotations.

[2] J. J. Puthucheary is a distinguished jail graduate, gaining his honours both from colonial and independent regimes. While in jail he wrote *Ownership and Control in the Malayan Economy* (Singapore, 1960), a work highly regarded by development economists.

Education sponsored a project for a series of history textbooks in which the early days of the settlement would be presented through portraits of the pioneers—fictional, though supposedly also factually based—representing each of Singapore's ethnic groups: a Chinese, an Indian, a Malay, a European, and an Arab. This project had to be abandoned under pressure from Malays who insisted that Singapore did not just emerge from a swamp but was part of the historic Malay world. 'An ugly situation developed,' recalls Arasaratnam, which was cooled by a swift ministerial decision to cancel the project. It was thought that the Indians might imitate the Malays and claim that *Singapura*, the Lion City, was originally Indian! And so multi-racialism survives in Singapore—by never being tested out too rigorously.

Prem Bhatia, who was India's High Commissioner first in Kenya and then in Singapore, writes of 'Multi-Racialism—a Myth?'[1] He sees an acceptance of multi-racialism in Malaysia as a political necessity, dictated by demographic and economic facts, and he adds: 'A vastly different example is the practice of multi-racialism in Singapore.' Singapore will make a positive achievement of the concept, he believes, because it has succeeded —where so many Third World countries have failed—in transforming economic development from a slogan into a reality with shares for all (or for most). But when he turns to Africa, Prem Bhatia speaks of 'the dying multi-racial concept': 'As for multi-racialism as a desirable goal for socio-political evolution, it is either not considered essential in Africa or is mostly suffered as an evil for which there is no immediate remedy.' Bhatia foresees the 'gradual elimination' of all the Asians from East and Central Africa, except a few who are prepared to identify themselves completely with Africa to the exclusion of all ties with South Asia. Bhatia includes in his assessment the acceptance of marriage between Asians and Africans—something which in the India and Pakistan of the 1970s is almost never accepted between different castes or religions. The formula he suggests for survival, then, is a formula to which the East African Asians will not agree. They are prepared to adapt, but not to the point of assimilation.

It would be strange if the Indians did finally leave East Africa,

[1] Prem Bhatia, *Indian Ordeal in Africa*, Delhi, 1973, Ch. 4.

for this, more than any other area has been the focus of Indian interests and Indian aspirations overseas. In 1923 Srinivasa Sastri addressed his countrymen with the cry: 'Kenya Lost, Everything Lost'. In those days, Indian aspirations alternated between proposals for planting an Indian colony in East Africa for full Indian settlement, and claims pressed on the British Government, and the Colonial Office especially, for parity between the White settlers and the Indian settlers. They demanded civic and political rights and also the right to hold land in the coveted White Highlands around Nairobi.[1]

The contest was effectively lost in 1923, though the Kenya Indians—well-organized through their own Congress set-up—fought on into the 1930s. Both in strategy and tactics they could not decide upon the most effective course. Sometimes they adopted Gandhian methods, and tried to move the colonial government by non-cooperation, no-tax campaigns, and boycotts. When these did not succeed, they fell back upon appeals to the British Government of India and the Home Government. They were no match for the White settlers, who had the measure of their own colonial administration as well as of Whitehall. Some of the Whites still believed that they could make a second Rhodesia in Kenya; and all were determined not to share power with the Indians. As yet, the possibility of African participation seemed unthinkable.

A prominent White settler objective was to restrict Indian immigration, and they were able to take advantage of the critical conditions of the Second World War, when Kenya was the base for operations against Italian East Africa, to introduce restrictions. When the Kenya Indians tried to make a stand, the split which was to open between the Congress and Muslim League in India was reproduced in Kenya. The moderate leader, A. B. Patel, was unable to hold the organization together. One instrument for restricting Indian entry was the Immigration (Control) Ordinance of 1948 which regulated all immigration according to whether the newcomer would contribute to the wealth of East Africa or would compete with 'the existing working population.'

[1] This struggle for civil rights is a leading theme of the present writer's book *Separate and Unequal; India and the Indians in the British Commonwealth, 1920–1950,* London, 1976.

The controls restricted the entry of new, single Asians, arriving for employment. During the first seven years after the restrictions began, 6,452 Asians were admitted, and 926 were refused entry, while 6,580 Europeans were admitted and only 71 refused. However, Asians continued to arrive in large numbers as dependants, and over 26,000 Indian family members were admitted during this period (compared to about 13,000 Whites).[1]

There was a massive increase in all the racial groups of Kenya after the Second World War, with the Asians and Europeans both expanding fast.

Kenya: Population by Race (Census years)

	1931	1948	1962
African	3,000,000 (?)	5,251,120	8,365,942
Asian	43,623	97,687	176,613
European	16,812	29,660	55,759

Although both the Whites and the Africans regarded the Kenya Asians as a monolithic community, they remained perhaps the most widely differentiated people anywhere, among those who went overseas from South Asia. The continuance of immigration, the stream of visitors from the sub-continent, and the constant return of the East African people to India and Pakistan for visits, for study, and for business, meant that caste did not become a memory, a dimly remembered tradition, but remained an active principle, applied more literally, perhaps, than in India itself. For the East African Asians, although modern and materialistic in many ways, are also conservative in their social attitudes towards each other.[2]

---

[1] 'Immigration Policy', Sessional Paper no. 78 of 1956 of the Kenya Legislative Council. Among the White immigrants taking up employment the second largest group after the British (2,504) were Italians (489) who were engaged to take over artisan and technical jobs from Indians on the lines of South African White skilled labour practices.

[2] For a detailed and highly sophisticated account of this society, see Agehananda Bharati, *The Asians in East Africa; Jayhind and Uhuru*, Chicago, 1972. It is not easy to place the author. He was born in Austria, but 'embraced Hinduism at an early age', being accepted by Hindus as a species of holy man. He visited East Africa in 1964, and penetrated fully into the domestic life of the Asians. He deliberately adopts the detached viewpoint of a marginal man, and writes as a professional social anthropologist. His view of the East African Asians has nothing in common with their own self-view; he rejects the 'victims of injustice' version which they almost all cultivate. His book is certainly most stimulating.

5

The most marginal group are the Goans, from the former Portuguese colony on India's west coast: their gaze is fixed upon Catholic, Latin Europe, and some hardly regard themselves as Indians at all. They were important in the pioneer days, when Goan clerks, overseers, station-masters (as well as cooks, tailors, artisans) were at the right hand of the isolated British district officers. They have never achieved much success in commerce, and survive as a somewhat withdrawn ultra-respectable urban group.

The Gujaratis are the largest in number, representing 80 per cent or more of all the Asians. They all speak Gujarati, though some still speak the variant form of the area of Kutch, bordering Pakistan. Apart from a common language and a common occupational association across trade and industry they are not united. About three-quarters of the Gujaratis are Hindu, and the rest are Muslims. The Hindus are broadly separated between the trading elite—the Patels, Shahs, and Lohanas—and the 'small castes', *choti jati*, who came to Kenya as artisans and craftsmen, and many of whom are still in these occupations and are known in East Africa as the *fundi*, from the Swahili term for artisan. The Muslim Gujaratis are all business people, belonging to small communities originally converted from Hinduism—the Bohras, Khojas, and Ismailis.

The remainder almost all come from the Punjab, and speak Punjabi, with Hindi or Urdu, for they are also divided between Muslims, Hindus, and Sikhs—the last being the most numerous. The later immigration accounted for some change in the population mix: after the Second World War the most numerous immigrants were Gujarati Hindus and Punjabi Hindus and Sikhs. Thus, the importance of Muslims and Christians was lessened, and by 1962 the Kenya Hindus had established a clear majority: Hindu 55 per cent, Muslim 23 per cent, Sikh 12 per cent, Christian 9 per cent. In an atmosphere of growing communalism among the Kenya Asians this led to a demand for separate representation in the legislature and to a proliferation of associations and clubs organized on communal lines.

In neighbouring Tanganyika the Gujarati element was even more dominant, and the Ismailis were of outstanding importance. At the 1948 Census, there were 46,254 Asians in Tanganyika, of whom about 27,000 were Muslims, 16,000 were Hindus, about

2,000 Sikhs, and the rest mainly Goans. By 1962, the total had risen to 88,700, with a slight fall in the proportion of Muslims.

The 1948 Census established that 49 per cent of the Kenya Asians were born in the colony, while the proportion for Tanganyika was even higher. Despite the heavy immigration of the following years, the percentage increased, and by 1962, the local-born—the true Kenya Asians—formed 62 per cent of the community. Another strong trend was towards the increasing urbanization of the community. About 1950, 70 per cent of the Kenya Asians were town-dwellers, and the proportion increased thereafter to 93 per cent.

Agehananda Bharati observes: 'We must never forget that East-African India is *not* village India; it is a segment of the urban or marginally urban population of two regions [Gujarat and Punjab] transplanted into another land—not into another milieu, for the Asians accepted little of the interpersonal freedom of the British whom they morally despised, and nothing from the African whose cultural existence they ignored.'[1]

This vigorously critical comment is demonstrably accurate—the Indians have done their best to recreate a more modern, more affluent version of Ahmedabad or Lahore in Nairobi and Dar-es-Salaam, with their gilded temples and mosques, their own clubs, their own schools, their roads—named after Gandhi, Nehru, Vallabhbhai Patel, Jinnah, and other giants of the 'Freedom Struggle'—and, above all, their offices, factories, garages, and shops, all staffed by Asians and purveying Asian goods and services. At their peak, the Asians formed no more than 2 per cent of the total population of Kenya, yet in Nairobi they were one-third of the population.

If the town-centre of Nairobi, and some of its suburbs, like Eastleigh, were nothing more than Asian bazaars and settlements, the basic reason was, however, that the Whites had insisted upon this city, and others, being rigidly segregated according to racial occupation—long before laws in South Africa imposed a similar ghetto policy upon Indians and Africans. During the 1920s and 1930s, the Whites (who formed 10 per cent of the Nairobi population) reserved for their own exclusive occupation 2,700 acres out of the total 6,400 acres within the municipal limits. The Asians (30 per cent of the municipal population) were allotted

[1] Agehananda Bharati, op. cit., p. 135.

300 acres for their own separate housing.[1] The Africans were restricted to outlying areas and were required to observe a nightly curfew. In 1948 the Africans formed 54 per cent of the city population, but the phenomenal growth in population (from 119,000 in 1948 to 344,000 in 1962) was partly a reflection of their growing numbers: by 1962, Africans had become 59 per cent of total city population. Until then, the 'colonial' character of Nairobi had been preserved almost intact. Only after Independence did the Africans begin to supplant Europeans —and Asians—in the better-quality housing and in the better-paid jobs.

The middle-layer position which the Asians had acquired within the social and economic pyramid was consolidated during these last years before Independence. The contrast is perhaps most sharply illustrated by a comparison of incomes in Kenya.[2]

Income Groups, by Race: 1962 (annual incomes)

	Under £120	£120–399	£400 and above	Total
	%	%	%	
Africans	91·4	8·1	0·5	100
Asians	11	20·6	68·4	100
Europeans	1·5	6·3	92·2	100

These figures demonstrate that the Asians did include a group who were very poor (for urban poverty is more harsh than rural poverty) and who lived in slum conditions as casual labourers. But these were the exceptions. Before Independence, over 30 per cent of the Asians were in commerce, mainly retail trading; the rest were clerks, transport and construction operatives, with about 20 per cent as the elite, in professional and administrative posts. Thus, the majority were in middle-level occupations, while a growing elite minority were in top-level occupations.[3]

---

[1] H. H. Werlin, *Governing an African City: a Study of Nairobi*, New York, 1974, p. 53.

[2] Figures from Dharam P. Ghai, ed., *Portrait of a Minority: Asians in East Africa*, Nairobi, 1965, p. 97. This work provides probably the best general survey of the subject. It was compiled just before anti-Indian measures began to be introduced, and it does not therefore reflect the overriding sense of victimization which colours most later studies by East African Asians. It is interesting to compare the above with Yash Ghai and Dharam Ghai, *The Asian Minorities of East and Central Africa*, Minority Rights Group Report, 1971.

[3] In 1963 there were 750 doctors in Kenya: 695 were Indians.

Noticeably absent from the economic chart was an Asian agricultural sector. While a sizeable proportion of the White population were owners or managers of farm estates in the White Highlands, only a handful of Asians had managed to resist the White monopoly of upland, commercial farming. Near Muhoroni, on the edge of the White Highlands, there remained a block of farmland alienated to Asian owners in 1906 to which they tenaciously clung. Otherwise, the 16,700 square miles of Kenya's best farmland remained a European preserve right down to 1960, when an Order in Council at last abolished the White monopoly.

The key to Asian advancement was the early advantage gained in education after the Second World War. The numbers of secondary school leavers increased dramatically.

Kenya: School Leavers, up to School Certificate Standard

	Africans	Asians	Europeans
1948	186	760	135
1949	219	1,150	145
1950	220	1,520	160
1951	228	1,380	170
1952	299	1,670	205
1953	434	2,000	220
1954	240	2,200	270
1955	280	2,500	330

During the 1950s, the tripartite colonial school system continued, with the schools for White children entirely reserved for Whites and controlled by White management committees. Similarly, Indian schools were for Indian children and were Indian-managed, though the great majority of schools for the Africans were missionary schools. The largest secondary school in East Africa was the Mahatma Gandhi School at Nairobi. When university education started in Kenya in 1956, of the 157 students first admitted, 6 were White, 57 were African, and 94 were Asian.

Change was less dramatic in Tanganyika, where the Indian school system was itself divided between schools specially established and controlled by the Ismailis (half the total) and schools for the rest of the Asian population. The Ismaili community was greatly affected by the decision of the Aga Khan to summon a conference at Evian in the French Alps in August 1952 to consider the future of East Africa. The Aga Khan directed his people to give up education in Gujarati and to make English and Swahili the main media of education. He also urged the Ismailis to adopt Western dress and to regard East Africa as their permanent home. His directive was welcomed by the Europeans, who had become almost morbidly sensitive to the 'threat' posed by the Asians.

The truth was that the Asian view of themselves and their future was highly ambiguous, but this did not come across to their White critics. First, there was the official policy of independent India, directed to playing a part in bringing Africa out of colonial bondage, and which emphasized that the local Indians should not be neo-colonialists, exploiting the Africans and claiming superior privileges. The first Indian Commissioner in East Africa, Apa B. Pant, insisted that the Indians must identify themselves with East Africa, and to this end he told them it was 'urgent and essential for Indians to acquire British nationality in order to integrate themselves fully' into the colonial territory.[1] But during the early 1950s, the East African Indians were intensely proud of the new status of independent India; they did not wish to remain colonial subjects. Under the Indian Constitution they could easily obtain Indian citizenship, and they were not required to surrender existing citizenship rights. Most of them became Indian citizens at the end of 1949, as part of their dual nationality.

However, Indian Government policy changed. Mainly in order to prevent certain Indian Muslims from sitting on the fence, the Citizenship Act of 1955 required anyone who had 'voluntarily acquired the citizenship of another country . . . [to] cease to be a citizen of India'. Few Kenya Indians bothered about this, but by claiming British citizenship at the time of Kenya's Independence they lost their rights in the motherland. Yet still they looked to the Indian High Commissioner as *their* representative.

Some politically active Asians did participate in the struggle against British colonial rule in Kenya. The veteran Makhan Singh led the first general strike in 1950—largely confined to the Nairobi area—and he was imprisoned and deported. When the Mau Mau revolt began in 1952, many Kenya Whites believed that this was stimulated by Indian encouragement. Michael

[1] *Hindu*, 24 March 1952.

Blundell, later to emerge as the champion of multi-racialism, declared: 'There are few Europeans in Kenya who do not insist that New Delhi through its official and non-official representatives in East Africa has encouraged and aided the rebellion of the Mau Mau.' They felt a 'burning hostility' to Nehru, he exclaimed.[1] The conservative White settler leader, Group-Captain I. R. Briggs, asserted: 'They want to squeeze us out and make it an Indian colony.'[2] When Kenyatta was brought to trial, an Indian lawyer, P. G. Pinto helped in his defence and was himself placed under detention.

There is no real evidence that the Government of India played any part in supporting the Mau Mau leaders, and certainly it did not aspire to exercise influence after a British withdrawal. Indeed, so determined was Nehru to emphasize African rights to Africa that he almost renounced any Indian participation. In August 1955 he declared that Indians in Africa 'could expect no help from India if they exploited Africans . . . he wanted them to live there only so long as they had the goodwill of the people of Africa.'[3]

The African leaders did not require Indian tutorship. Bold young leaders such as Tom Mboya and Ronald Ngala were forcing their way into the political arena. Their moment came in 1960 when the progressive Colonial Secretary, Iain Macleod, invited the Kenya politicians to their first Lancaster House conference. Some, at any rate, of the White leaders sensed that the Wind of Change was coming; Blundell rapidly jumped upon the multi-racial bandwagon. But most of the Indian leaders remained trapped in the past. An Indian writer observes, 'With a few exceptions, the nationalistic movement completely bypassed the Indian community.'[4] Worse: they got right out of step.

Just before the Lancaster House conference, the standing committee of the Kenya Indian Congress voted by 18 to 2 to retain the communal roll for electoral purposes—that communal roll which they had opposed for nearly forty years. The plan they presented in London was for a complicated representative

[1] *New York Times*, 19 July 1953.
[2] *The Times*, 4 August 1954.
[3] *Johannesburg Star*, 9 August 1955.
[4] Mariyam Harris, *The 'D' Valued Passport* (pamphlet), London, 1971, p. 19.

system which would reserve seats for the different communities, separately, on any common roll, while also retaining communal voting.[1] A few Indian politicians saw the folly of this course; observed Chanan Singh, later a close associate of Jomo Kenyatta: 'When the only political problem in Kenya was that of the Asian versus the European, the Congress sang loud praises of democracy and passed resolutions frequently supporting African aspirations. When, on the occasion of the London Conference, the African community actually needed political support, however, it was not forthcoming.'[2]

The 1960 Constitution followed the kind of pattern demanded by the Indian leaders. Twenty seats in the new legislature were reserved for the minorities (ten Europeans, eight Indians, two Arabs) while twelve of the 'national' seats were elected 'in the same racial proportions'. This lasted only two years, before the African demand for a constitution leading directly to Independence, based on a universal electorate, was conceded. The brief last act of multi-racialism was soon over.

Now that the crunch had come, the African leaders made it clear that the Indians must declare their commitment. Mboya had the most genuine regard for India and its leader Nehru and he took the trouble to alert the Indians to their situation. If they made a genuine commitment to Kenya they could expect equal treatment with Africans, he promised, but, 'If they live in separate compartments it may lead to an explosion.'[3]

When Independence—*Uhuru*—arrived, the Asians continued to linger in the past. Many believed that the African leaders would make such a mess of things that they would call upon the Indians to put them straight. Others, more pessimistic, already argued that there would be no place for Asians in an African Kenya, and made their plans on the assumption that they would soon depart. Immediately before and after Independence there was a massive transfer of capital out of Kenya. Some was European money, but most was remitted by Asians, concerned to safeguard their future. They transferred their funds not to India or Pakistan but to London.

---

[1] Donald Rothchild, *Racial Bargaining in Independent Kenya; a Study of Minorities and Decolonization*, London, 1973, p. 136.

[2] *Hindu*, 5 June 1960.

[3] *Observer*, 10 November 1963.

When the three East African states became independent, there were two major issues over which the Asians appeared to demonstrate an absence of commitment to their host-countries. Throughout East Africa there was a joint network of communications—railways, harbours, posts, tele-communications—known as the East African Common Services Organization, and this very large public corporation employed many Asians. During the colonial period these Asian public servants enjoyed certain special privileges, such as paid leave to India and Pakistan. After Independence, these colonial privileges were withdrawn, and the Asians almost all handed in their notices of resignation in reply. This mass resignation was based on the calculation that the common services would collapse at their departure.

The Secretary-General of E.A.C.S.O. described their action as 'blackmail', but he accepted the resignations and hastily recruited others on short contracts to replace the Asians. At this point, the Asians' negotiator offered to withdraw their notices. The offer was rejected, and arrangements were made to send the Asians home. About 1,500 employees were involved, but with their families the total came to 6,000. When it was clear that they must depart, many chose to go to Britain, where they hoped to match their expertise with suitable jobs. Their bluff had been called: to their surprise (and possibly to the surprise of the Africans) they were not essential.

The second issue took longer to resolve: this was the question of citizenship. Under the new constitutions, persons born in Kenya (or Uganda or Tanganyika), one of whose parents was also born in East Africa, had an automatic right to be citizens. In Kenya, about 40,000 Asians came into this category. All other residents were eligible for citizenship, but were required to register before Independence, or within the 'grace period'— permitted as a concession—up to two years after Independence.

During the months before *Uhuru*, virtually no Asians claimed local citizenship, though the sight of queues of hundreds, even thousands, outside the offices of the U.K. High Commission was registered on the consciousness of all African observers. After *Uhuru*, there was little change. Six months before the grace period expired only 8,174 Asians had registered their names. It should be added that only 844 Whites had registered; their reluctance to identify with the new Kenya was even more marked.

At this moment, Prem Bhatia arrived in Kenya as India's High Commissioner. He toured the country in an effort to persuade Indians to register as citizens of Kenya. He relates that he received a very poor response, for most Indians were determined to claim British nationality: 'A British passport came to represent that very superior status which Nehru had been anxious for the Indians to surrender.'[1] At the eleventh hour, some of the Indians who were still hesitating decided to opt for Kenyan citizenship: during November and December 1965, over 10,000 applications were submitted. Not surprisingly, Africans looked upon these latecomers with some suspicion; rather naively, Indian spokesmen retorted that these applicants were the equals of those who had applied before 1963.

There was a less agonizing transition into Independence in Tanganyika where the Ismailis followed the directive of the Aga Khan and applied for citizenship *en masse*, when they were not automatically qualified, as many were (60,000 fell into the 'automatic' category). By the end of the grace period, 21,557 Tanganyika Indians had been registered for citizenship, leaving only about 6,000 whose status was undefined, or who retained British nationality.[2] An Asian, Amir Jamal, was a Minister in Nyerere's Cabinet, holding the key post of Commerce and Industry.

The first two or three years after *Uhuru* provided a breathing-space in Kenya. In politics, a few Asians remained as M.P.s, elected by a predominantly African electorate. Others played important parts as advisers and organizers. The organizer of the headquarters of K.A.N.U., the Government party, was Joseph Murumbi, son of an Asian-African marriage—though he was identified as an African. Chanan Singh was Parliamentary Secretary to Kenyatta until, in 1964, he was appointed a judge of the Supreme Court. The Treasurer of the Nairobi branch of K.A.N.U. was K. P. Shah. The main role of most sympathetic Asians was to contribute handsomely to party funds and election expenses. The Asians expected gratitude for this support, but most Africans saw it merely as an attempt to buy security.

[1] Prem Bhatia, op. cit., p. 32.

[2] These figures are taken from official statistics, but it must be admitted that astonishing discrepancies emerge as between different statistics compiled for different purposes. Mariyam Harris, op. cit., produces quite different figures—also supplied by official sources.

As qualified Africans returned from American and British universities they took up the top posts formerly filled by Europeans and Asians. The number of Asians in the Kenya public services declined from 12,200 in 1961 to 8,000 in 1968, though this was in a time of rapid expansion. The Nairobi municipality had relied heavily upon Asian officers in middle and top administration; by 1965 the number employed was just over half the 1963 total, even though 30 per cent of the Nairobi officers with annual salaries over £800 were still Asians—some indication of their former predominance. From 1967, all those in the public services who were not Kenyan citizens were dismissed. The African head of the Kenya civil service, G. K. Kariithi, announced: 'Most of the controlling positions are now occupied by our own people. . . . We must concentrate on improving the quality of our service. For this is a national imperative to prove that Njuguna, Okello and Mwakio are as capable as Smith, Patel and de Souza.'[1]

It was the 1967 Immigration Act which was instrumental in prising the Indians out of the public services and also out of many positions in commerce. The Act controlled not only entry into Kenya but also the economic activities of all the existing population of non-citizens. All existing resident's permits were withdrawn, and non-citizens had to acquire passes, for which fees were charged. Different classes of employment were defined, designed to make things smooth for persons with the expertise which Kenya needed, while excluding those in occupations which Africans might readily take up.

The new measures persuaded many Kenya Asians to get out while they could, and the number of applications for permits was smaller than expected. By September 1969, the Government had issued 18,500 permits to non-citizens, rejecting only 1,621 applications. The employment situation in 1968 found the Asians still well ahead of the Africans: 87 per cent of Asians were earning over £750 per annum (a major rise since 1962) while only 2 per cent of Africans had attained this income bracket; by contrast 80 per cent of the Whites earned £1,800 per annum and above. The occupational pattern of the three communities reflected these gross disparities.

[1] Werlin, op. cit., p. 155.

Kenya: Occupational Distribution of the Different Races, 1968[1] *(percentage)*

	Africans	Asians	Europeans
Unskilled labourers	55	1·3	1
Semi-skilled workers	23·3	13	3·3
Office workers & shop assistants	8·5	35·1	12·7
Supervisors & teachers	10·8	21·8	22·5
Administrators, managers, professional staff	2·4	28·8	60·5
Total	100	100	100

The Kenya Government equipped itself with another instrument for Africanizing those parts of the economy which were dominated by the Asians: the Trade Licensing Act 1967. Under this act, certain geographical areas—especially the centres of towns—were reserved for commercial activity by citizens, and non-citizens were permitted to trade only if granted an annual licence. The measure was specially aimed at the concentrations of Asian business and trade in Nairobi and Mombasa.

When the measure was introduced, the Minister responsible said that his target was to eliminate 3,000 non-citizen traders within the first six months. The actual working of the act was less onerous: in Nairobi, 320 traders received notices to quit, or were refused licences during the year 1969, while it was reported that throughout Kenya nearly 3,000 Indian traders lost their right to trade, but this may have been exaggerated.[2]

The effect of the two measures—the Immigration Act and the Licensing Act—was to introduce a mood of near-panic in the Kenya Asian community. Many feared that they would actually be deported. Emigration had been rising, and increasingly it was to Britain that the Kenya Asians went. Each year, more arrived in Britain: in 1965 about 5,000 arrived, and in 1966 about 6,000. During 1967 some 12,000 Asians were reported as landing from Kenya in Britain, and the exodus included many who were in no way threatened by the new regulations. Rumours that the British Government intended to introduce ·harsh restrictions accelerated the movement and special charter flights were improvised by enterprising Asian travel agents. During January-

---

[1] Figures adapted from Yash Tandon, *Problems of a Displaced Minority: the New Position of East Africa's Asians* (Minority Rights Group Report, 1973). Tandon took his figures from the Kenya Government's *Employment and Earnings in the Modern Sector, 1968–1970* (1972).

[2] Yash Ghai and Dharam Ghai, op. cit., p. 21: 'It was reported', they say.

February 1968, a further 12,000 were reported as arriving in Britain. From 1 March 1968, a ban on entry by British passport-holders without 'patrial' links with Britain was imposed. The flood was halted, and only then did many Kenya Asians begin to calculate why they had acted so impetuously.

As a result of the exodus of 1967–8, the next census showed that, though the total population had risen sharply, from 8,636,000 in 1962 to 10,943,000 in 1969, the Asian total fell from 176,613 to 139,593. European numbers underwent the same kind of shrinkage from 55,759 to 40,593. The city of Nairobi showed an even more dramatic transformation: the total population rose from 344,000 to 509,000 within these seven years and the non-African element fell from 138,000 (41 per cent of the total) to 66,000 (13 per cent).

From the late 1960s there was a considerable shift in the Asian occupational pattern, following the policy of Africanization in administration and commerce. When the former White Highlands were opened to non-White settlement, many of the White settlers began to move out. As part of Britain's independence deal, they were guaranteed a fair price for their land (with British Government backing) and most moved on to the more congenial climate of South Africa. A number of Sikhs bought estates from the departing Whites; a wealthy Sikh contractor, Indra Singh Gill, acquired several farms, each up to 3,000 acres in extent. These Sikhs were performing a kind of full circle; they were Jats (farmers) by caste, but had acquired their wealth in business and light industry before moving back into farming, which they now managed on modern, mechanized lines.

The Asian farmers were only a handful, but a large number of Asians moved into the construction industry, which was booming as Kenya became a major field for international tourism. Bidding for building contracts against established British firms, the Indians secured a substantial share of new construction by means of highly competitive tenders. The Indian firms were managed by experienced foremen-craftsmen or *maistries* with capital provided by former traders, eliminated under the Trade Licensing Act. The combination of technical and business skill and experience gave these firms the capacity to take on large projects.

Unlike the British builders, who employed a large permanent workforce, the Indians retained only a nucleus of key personnel, recruiting casual labour as required. In addition, the Indians sub-contracted as much as possible of the operation; for example, concreting, electrical work, joinery, would be let out—often to Africans who were rising from the labouring class into the category of *maistries*. In time, some of these African sub-contractors (often Kikuyu) went on to become competitors in the building market, frequently relying on credit provided by the Indians.

The development in this field seemed to afford a model of how the Asians might adapt to changed circumstances, and also make their role acceptable to Africans. But this pattern of an Indian penetration of a European monopoly, leading to African participation, was not followed in other directions. Prem Bhatia constantly urged Indian businessmen to associate Africans with their firms; but most Indian firms were under single proprietors, or were a family business, and the owners professed themselves unable to adapt to accommodate Africans as partners or share-holders. Those who took in Africans complained that they expected to receive profits without first making any contribution to earnings.[1]

The continuing Asian presence in the commercial sector was a major source of African resentment, whereas their role in other sectors of the economy was accepted. As one well-known African publicist saw the question: 'If the Asians in Kenya produced things instead of squatting in their dukas [shops] to sell at what look like disproportionately high prices, if they scratched the soil themselves to produce, if they worked to produce, instead of juggling with merchandise and exploiting opportunities in the consumer market they would be much more acceptable. . . . If the Asians were just farmers, doctors, teachers, lawyers, skilled technicians, craftsmen and other "productive" workers, African attitudes towards them would change.'[2]

Meanwhile, an economic transformation was under way in Tanzania on much more radical lines than in Kenya, and there

---

[1] Prem Bhatia, op. cit., p. 88. Perhaps the Kenya Asians were right to be sceptical. In Malaysia, many Chinese entrepreneurs have taken Malays into partnership to gain advantage of Government concessions designed to stimulate new Malay enterprise. This is known as an 'Ali Baba' business, and excites the derision of other Malays. See Mahathir bin Mohammad, op. cit., p. 46.

[2] Ben Bogi, 'Anti-Asian sentiments: it's still not too late to undo the harm', *Nairobi Sunday Post*, 8 October 1972.

the Asian community did not become demoralized. Nyerere's programme of African Socialism involved large-scale nationalization of foreign firms, including all the banks, insurance companies, import-export agencies, flour mills, etc. The programme affected Western capital as much as, or more than, Asian big business; moreover, many Asians were retained as managers and executives in the new national corporations. The main thrust of Nyerere's programme was to rejuvenate the rural economy which accounted for more than 90 per cent of the population. This had little impact upon the Asians, except that there was a steady pressure to Africanize the rural retail trading sector, formerly an Asian monopoly. By 1970 about three-quarters of the rural shopkeepers were African.

Although there was no drama and no cause for panic, the Asians of Tanzania started to move on. From about 88,700 in 1961 their numbers had fallen to 85,000 by 1969. Dar-es-Salaam, formerly an Asian-dominated capital, like Nairobi, saw its Asian population fall from 29 per cent of the total in 1960 to 11 per cent (43,600 out of 396,700) in 1969.

By about 1970, the East African Asians were caught in the situation known to those who watch racial problems as that of the 'self-fulfilling prophecy'. This means that people precipitate the situation they most dread by taking action to forestall that situation. By 1970, almost all the Asians were convinced that time was running out for them. Some might calculate that they had only five years left in which to continue their occupations before Africanization deprived them of a livelihood; others might expect ten, or even twenty, years before they were made redundant. Meanwhile, in the lands where they might re-establish themselves, the doors were being closed, and back-entrances sealed off. The strong instinct for self-preservation which all the East African Asians possess, as individuals and families, impelled them to take pre-emptive action.

For most of them, the best form of insurance was to get their money into safe places. The East African countries, like most new states, were making it as difficult as possible for expatriate capital to be remitted abroad. Before the net was drawn tighter, the Asians acted to get their money out of Kenya or Tanzania. For retailers and wholesalers the process was easy: by means of double-invoicing they paid for goods imported from abroad at inflated prices, being credited with a proportion of the inflated price in England or Japan. As one channel was stopped up by Government regulation, so another was discovered. To Africans all this was blatant fraud; to Asians it was the legitimate protection of their interests.[1]

The other main form of insurance was to place a member of one's own kin-group in all the countries regarded as safe havens for the future. The mostly highly skilled would try to go to North America; the other working family members would head for Britain; while the old, the retired, and the wealthy would probably decide to return to India or Pakistan. Entry into Britain now required patience or ingenuity. There was an annual quota of 1,500 vouchers for Britain, specially allocated to the East African Asian British passport holders (those who after 1967 were given the special 'D' passports which restricted entry into Britain). Even though the 1,500 vouchers would admit families, so that 6,000 to 10,000 Asians could enter Britain annually, this number was insufficient to dissolve the queues waiting every day outside the U.K. High Commission.

Many found ways to 'jump the queue' which made holes in the regulations. An increasing number simply got on a plane at Nairobi, knowing that the Kenya immigration authorities would not allow them back, and relied upon Britain having to let them in. There followed the ignominious era of the 'shuttlecock' flights, in which Britain sent the Asians off to Karachi or Delhi, only to have them returned to London. British immigration policy amounted to making things as unpleasant as possible for the shuttlecocks, but to allow them entry at last. By then they had usually exhausted their funds on pointless air journeys, and entered Britain as paupers.

The endless drain of Asian money out of Kenya, and the spectacle of the Asians themselves trying hard to get away, convinced many Africans that no Asians genuinely intended to

---

[1] In July 1975 two English teenagers were arrested at Nairobi airport. Having been invited by Indian friends to spend a holiday in Kenya, they were sent back to Britain with parcels which contained currency to be illegally smuggled out, of which they were totally ignorant. This appeared to be no isolated incident but part of a large-scale operation. Spokesmen for the Kenya Asian community in Britain gave no sign that they regarded this operation as immoral, but dwelt exclusively upon the difficulties of their community. The victimization syndrome seems to be all-enveloping.

identify themselves with Kenya. Complaints about the Asians' lack of commitment were sounded in the Press and in Parliament, and apart from a continuing concern about economic exploitation the main emphasis was upon the Asians' social exclusiveness. Tom Mboya, one of the most candid friends of the Asians, summed it up by declaring: 'Cocktail integration is not enough.'[1] By the 1960s, the conservatism of the Gujarati Hindu business community was able to adapt to inviting Africans to have drinks with them, on the lawns of their houses, or at their clubs, but it went no further. Many Africans insisted that real integration would mean marriage between African men and Asian women.

In making this an issue, the Africans appeared to be demanding more from Indians than from Europeans. White businessmen in Kenya also accepted Africans in their clubs and on their golf courses, but there was no move towards intermarriage. Yet somehow their continuing exclusiveness was not a subject of controversy.

In the pioneer days, many Indians took African wives, though without the ritual of marriage. Their offspring were known by the Indian term *jotawa* which (like *dougla* in Trinidad) is said to mean 'bastard'. These *jotawa* are regarded as outsiders by other Indians. The practice of taking African wives now seems to have died out, though there are still Sikhs, up country, who live in this style, and are held in good repute by their African neighbours; indeed, the Sikhs, with their reputation as hunters and warriors, and now their holdings on the land, are probably the Asian people most acceptable to Africans.

There are no known examples of Asian women marrying Africans.[2] After the revolution in Zanzibar, President Karume ordered girls of Iranian ancestry to be married to Africans, and a *frisson* of horror overcame the Asians. This sensitive subject comes up in all discussion of Asian integration and has a quite disproportionate symbolic importance, both positively and negatively; for Africans it is the unattainable goal, and for Asians the unacceptable price.

The Asian exodus continued. It was estimated that by 1972 only 105,000 remained in Kenya, and only 52,000 in Tanzania.

---

[1] Tom Mboya, *Freedom and After*, London, 1963, p. 109.
[2] Both Prem Bhatia (op. cit., p. 144) and Agehananda Bharati (op. cit., p. 38) state categorically that no Asian woman has married an African.

The unresolved question was whether the outflow would continue steadily, without undue tension and drama, or whether—as in Uganda—the process would suddenly escalate into a mass, enforced departure. Those who speculate on the future of Kenya after Kenyatta have often fitted a mass expulsion of the Asians into their scenario.

All this is very hard upon those Asians who genuinely do have a commitment to East Africa and who plan to remain. It is most hard upon the poorer section of Asians, the rural shopkeepers, the *duka-walas*, so often dismissed with contempt, yet fulfilling a useful function, and the artisans and craftsmen who give good service to the economy of Africa with only a meagre return. These people cannot export their way of earning a living: it is inherently part of the East African scene.

For the businessman, it is really a question of making sure his options are not closed off. However attached he may be to life in East Africa, he is more concerned about expanding his business, and when the warning signs are clear enough he will move on. Big business in East Africa has attained a high level of sophistication, and is prepared to move into any sector anywhere that promises growth; one former Indian Dar-es-Salaam import agent is now a successful figure in the international armaments industry. Indian professional people and intellectuals from East Africa have a similar international competence and acceptance. They adapt to the new environment of Berkeley or Bloomsbury without too much stress.

There are many among those Asians who are citizens of Kenya and Tanzania who hold that until all the non-citizens have left there can be no prospect of a settled future for them in East Africa. According to this view, Africa can accommodate a smaller, less visible, less economically salient Asian group as a permanent element in the population. When one recalls that in the past Indian settlers adapted to successive political and racial changes along the East African coast, this analysis seems justified. Probably those who stay will be the descendants of those who arrived long ago; the others, the recent immigrants into East Africa, will move on elsewhere.

In re-establishing a permanent place for the Asians in Africa, it may be hoped that a more effective kind of community leadership may emerge. The Ismailis have all through been guided by a corporate community policy. This has not always succeeded in preserving the community from African pressures, but they have, at any rate, done their best. Other kinds of leadership have too often failed to produce anything but the most short-term policies. On almost every issue the Asians have been divided—upon caste lines, and even more between the rich and the remainder. In times of crisis, Patels have looked after Patels, but there has been no wider sense of community solidarity, such as the Jewish community can call upon, for example. When poor shopkeepers and artisans became unemployed, and in many cases destitute, after the 1967 regulations in Kenya, they received little if any help from the wealthy Asians, whose main concern was to preserve their own interests.

This is not to suggest that the East African Asians could have avoided the trials they have had to endure by better leadership. They were caught in a post-colonial or neo-colonial vortex in which they were almost helpless. They needed time to adjust and adapt to an entirely different age. But as they struggled to adapt, they were confronted with the nightmare of Uganda in September 1972, and the confirmation of their worst fears. Deep in the consciousness of overseas Indians is this fear of ejection, deportation: the fate of the refugee. Why are they unwanted, rejected? The overseas Indians cannot understand. They will all remember Uganda, because the drama was enacted in the full glare of international publicity. But long before September 1972, the Indians were ejected from Burma. The South Asians have been allotted their share in the twentieth century tragedy of the refugee.

5

The Departure Signal

Perhaps more than in any previous century, the refugee has become a familiar and recurring part of the twentieth-century scene. The refugee is forced to quit the land where he has lived for two main reasons: either he finds himself exposed to such extreme danger that he has little option but to depart, or else he is actually expelled by Government order. The first situation is more common, and usually emerges from the ravages of war, though it may be the consequences of Government action, as in the mass flight of refugees from East Bengal during the repression by West Pakistan authority during 1971. Mass deportation has become all too common in Asia and Africa since the Second World War. The expulsion of Eurasians and others who were legally Dutch citizens from Indonesia in 1956 attained the status of an international news item. Because the Netherlands accepted full responsibility for their welfare, this expulsion-story did not have an unhappy ending. Very different was the fate of several thousand Nigerians expelled from Ghana in 1969, followed by the ejection of Ghanaians from Sierra Leone and Liberia, and the enforced departure from Zaïre of 6,000 non-citizens. All these banishments have gone virtually unnoticed by the world's Press. In the same way the most massive ejection of the Indians—that from Burma—attracted little attention in the West, while the much smaller deportation-operation from Uganda was front-page news—mainly because the refugees headed West, to Britain and to a lesser extent to North America.

The enforced exodus of the South Asian population, almost as a whole, from two apparently very different countries harks back to the question which has been underlying so many of the situations discussed in this book: do the Asians create their own difficulties by their own way of life, and by remaining separate from the host society; or do their troubles arise mainly from excess of chauvinism or racism in the country of their adoption?

Do they offend because they are, visibly, both pariahs and exploiters in alien societies? Or are they scapegoats, singled out for victimization because their adopted country (or its Government) needs an alibi for poor performance in the national sphere?

On the face of it, the Indian communities of Burma and Uganda were very different. Burma had experienced a massive influx of Indians for more than sixty years, and during the 120 years during which portions of Burma were under British rule (the annexation of the whole country finally came in 1886) the Burmese territories were administered as an integral part of Britain's Indian Empire for 110 years. The relationship between India and Burma might be compared to that between England and Ireland. By contrast, the arrival of the Asians in Uganda came in the second, third, and fourth decades of the twentieth century; Uganda retained its African character, with a strong and living tradition of African rulership; the Asians remained a marginal, migrant community of outsiders.

However, in both countries, the Indians were, to a hostile eye, very 'visible'. Both in Kampala, a capital that was little more than a village, and in Rangoon, a major international port, the Indian presence was the dominant element. This Indian dominance of the nation's capital was a most obnoxious aspect of the fight for national renascence to the Ugandan and Burmese leaders.

National feeling seemed to be aroused by the presence of the Indians with an almost tidal regularity, usually as economic conditions were good or bad. Perhaps the Indians might have survived, except that in both countries a military dictator came to power, with no very clear political or economic programme but with a need to demonstrate that he was more effective than his parliamentary predecessors. Both General Ne Win and General Idi Amin decided to exhibit a 'show of strength' to their countrymen by playing upon the forces of xenophobia. Very publicly and noisily the agents of neo-colonialism were rejected. In Burma neo-colonialism was mainly symbolized by the United States; in Uganda it was symbolized by Britain, but others were also picked upon; in both countries, the Israelis as international scapegoats and whipping-boys were summarily despatched. But the most visible, the most accessible of all the foreigners were the Indians; and they felt the main force of military tyranny, they were chosen for the most crude persecution.

Although Burma was ruled from 1826 to 1937 as an outlying province of India, the British rulers treated Burma as 'different' from the rest of the Indian Empire. In international terms, it was viewed as a buffer-zone between South Asia, firmly under British control, and China—still regarded as the 'sleeping giant' of the world—and also as against French activities in Indo-China and Thailand. It was partly to preserve this buffer role that the British quite deliberately did not develop land communications between Burma and India. There was no great difficulty in extending the Indian railway system from East Bengal into Arakan, and thence via the Taungup Pass to the banks of the Irrawaddy River, but plans for this extension were always shelved. Similarly, there was no attempt to build effective road links, and right down to 1942 the only route between Manipur in India and the Chindwin Valley in Burma was a little-used mule track.

In part this deliberate isolation of Burma from India was because in domestic terms it was deemed to be free of the infection of political agitation. When the last Mughal Emperor was removed from his shadowy throne at Delhi he was exiled to Rangoon, and subsequently a number of the more troublesome Indian political leaders, such as Bal Ganghadhar Tilak, were banished to the political neutrality of Burma for a while. When India obtained its first major instalment of political reform in 1919, Burma was excluded, as showing no demand for political institutions. The Burmese promptly demonstrated the inaccuracy of British assessments by launching a nationwide boycott campaign. Similarly, when a second major political leap forward was envisaged for India, with a series of Round Table Conferences in London (1930–1932) Burma was set aside for separate treatment. The Indian National Congress believed that the British Government was pursuing a deliberate policy of *divide et impera*, reserving a separated Burma for 'Crown Colony' status. The Burmese leaders similarly suspected that they were going to receive unequal treatment, but they also resented Congress efforts to gather them into the Congress camp when they felt no identity of interest. The separation issue simmered on, a cause of bad feeling and misunderstanding between Indian and Burmese political leaders, until the link was completely severed under the Government of Burma Act 1935.

During the constitutional debates of the 1920s and 1930s the leaders of the Burma Indians demanded and obtained separate representation for their community in the new elected legislature by means of special Indian constituencies in Rangoon and elsewhere. They might, perhaps, have relied upon the numerical strength of their community to ensure that an effective Indian voice was heard in the political debate; Indians formed more than half the population of Rangoon. According to the 1931 Census there were 212,929 Indians out of a city population of 400,415. But the Indian leaders adopted a minority approach to politics, and the Burmese identified them as a minority.

Although a proportion of the Burma Indians were birds of passage, coming to Burma to earn better money, and then returning after a season to India, many others were born in the country, regarding it as home. There was a good deal of intermarriage, mainly between Indian men and Burmese women, because of the relative scarcity of Indian women. Sometimes the Indian husband returned home, leaving his Burmese wife inadequately provided for, but most of these unions were permanent, and produced stable homes for the children of the marriage. These Indo-Burmans were often called *Zerbadis*, though the term became unacceptable to them.[1] In many cases the Indian father was a Muslim, and then the child was brought up as a Muslim, thereby causing affront to the Buddhist Burmese.

Feeling against intermarriage seems to have existed from earliest days: it was expressed in a traditional jingle, 'Do not take foreigners, oh ye Burmese women.' But the feeling became sharper in the atmosphere of political competition in the 1920s and 1930s. One Burmese member of the legislature declared: 'Besides taking our country and our property they take our sisters. The Burmese nation will become extinct. What use will Home Rule be to us ... when the Burmese nation has become half-caste by gradual extinction?'[2] This attitude provides a striking contrast to that professed by Kenyan Africans who call insistently for intermarriage. The Indians seem to give offence whether they

---

[1] The derivation of *Zerbadi* is obscure, but it may imply 'Child of Gold', i.e. the offspring of a woman bought by her man. *Zar* in Persian and Urdu means gold.

[2] Both quotations are taken from N. R. Chakravarti, *The Indian Minority in Burma; the Rise and Decline of an Immigrant Community*, London, 1971, pp. 11, 125-6. This work provides the most complete account of the subject and is especially thorough in the discussion of economic issues.

keep apart or whether they assimilate. It was noticeable in Burma that the offspring of the many marriages between British men and Burmese ladies did not seem to arouse the hostility of the Burmese, while the even more numerous Sino-Burmans were accepted as full members of Burmese society.

The dual image of the Indian overseas as both pariah and exploiter was explicitly held by most Burmese, and it was in the deteriorating economic conditions of the late 1920s and 1930s that radical feeling moved from a latent into an active phase. Enumeration of the Indians according to their employment showed the great majority—about 66 per cent—in unskilled or semi-skilled occupations. These included workers in manufacturing industry, public transport, public services (e.g. cleansing and public works), seasonal agriculture, mining, and the oilfields. About 10 per cent of the Indians were craftsmen and technicians of every kind (posts and telegraphs, printing, etc.), while about 16 per cent were traders and shop assistants. Four per cent were clerks, many in the public offices, and 4 per cent were professional people, landlords, and others with higher levels of income.

It has been calculated that in the 1930s the Indians formed no more than 8 per cent of the total workforce in Burma; yet their importance in certain key occupations made them appear much more conspicuous than they were in reality.

Percentage of Indians in Key Occupations, 1941[1]

	%		%
Railways	70	Medical doctors	58
Port workers	70	Business, banking	58
Water transport	51	Public administration	30
Armed forces	41	Oilfields and refineries	50
Police	46	Rice-mills	26

As we have seen from the figures cited previously, the great majority of the Indians in Burma were engaged in work of an unskilled and even menial nature: work which, until the onset of the world depression, the Burmese despised and rejected. Rangoon had a sewage system adequate only for a limited section of the

[1] Figures adapted from N. R. Chakravarti, op. cit., Ch. 3, 'Occupations of Indians in Burma'. These are taken from *Report on the Immigration of Indians into Burma*, by James Baxter, Rangoon, 1941.

city; the task of removing the night-soil and keeping the streets clean fell to an army of Indian scavengers. The Rangoon port—through which 85 per cent of the country's imports and exports passed—was mechanized only to the most basic extent, and the loading of cargoes was mainly by hand—the hands of Indian dockers. Similarly, the harsh and dirty work in the rice-mills and saw-mills was undertaken by Indian labour, and the harvesting of the paddy in the rich farmlands of the Irrawaddy Delta was dependent partly on the availability of Indian harvest-gangs. The Indian that most Burmese actually saw was an almost naked, sweating, grimy Tamil or Ooriya labourer, straining like an animal at some heavy load. Yet, paradoxically, the Indian that came into their mind's eye was very different: it was, in the words of U Nu, Prime Minister of Burma, 'the Chettyar with the bloated abdomen called Allagappa'.[1]

The Burma Chettyars were organized in a fraternal business network, the Nattukkottai Chettyar Association (N.C.A.). The N.C.A. had about 1,500 member banks in Burma in the 1920s, though after the Depression the number fell to about 1,300. The largest Chettyar firm was the Bank of Chetinad, with over forty branches throughout the agricultural districts of Burma. The N.C.A. decided rates of interest and other terms of trade, and it was most unusual for a member firm to go against its directives, though these had no mandatory effect. The main Chettyar business was to give credit to the paddy farmers. The Burmese peasant seldom had the instincts of a capitalist. When he harvested the paddy and sold his crop he liked to have a good time, make a contribution to a pagoda, buy clothes and jewels for his wife—and then just hang on till the next harvest. Chettyar credit ensured that he could hang on. The interest levied upon loans against the next crop was not excessive, and the banker was just as interested as the farmer in a good harvest. The Chettyar had no desire to become a landlord: that was not his business. He flourished when the farmer flourished, and all went well until the Depression years when the world price of food-grains collapsed. In 1930 the market price fell from Rs.200 per hundred baskets to Rs.50 (in present-day equivalents, from £15·30 to £3·70). The peasants were unable to pay their taxes and their debts. Unable to collect their

[1] Hugh Tinker, *The Union of Burma; a Study of the First Years of Independence*, London, 1957, 4th edn., 1967, p. 96 n.1.

dues, the Chettyars foreclosed and took the land. In Lower Burma almost 48 per cent of farmland became the property of non-agriculturalist landlords, and two-thirds of this total was owned by the Chettyars.

Not surprisingly, to the Burmese peasant the explanation of his appalling change of fortune was that the Chettyars had stolen his land. The issue of absentee landlordism became a major political question for Burmese politicians in the late 1930s. Two measures were introduced in the legislature to fix fair rents and to buy back agricultural land for distribution to farmers. Neither came into operation on account of the Japanese invasion.

Though the Chettyars were the main focus of anti-Indian feeling in Burma, as so often happens, the impact of racist feeling was felt elsewhere. In 1930 the Indian dockers of Rangoon went on strike for higher wages. The employers engaged Burmese workers instead, but when the Indians capitulated they discharged the Burmese and reinstated the Indians. The resentment of the Burmese was not vented upon the European employers, who had made use of them, but upon the Indians. The rickshaw pullers were the first target, and about 2,000 of their vehicles were destroyed by Burmese bullies. Some 7,000 Indians were scared out of their homes, and in June 1930, 33,000 Indians left Rangoon for their ancestral land.

The next major anti-Indian outbreak came in July 1938, and this time the attack was triggered off by a book criticizing Buddhism, written by a Muslim. The author was a Burmese Muslim, but a rabble-rousing Burmese politician saw this as a means of toppling a political rival, and incited attacks upon the Indian community, first in Rangoon and then in Mandalay. About £140,000 damage to Indian property was inflicted, and 11,000 Indians were repatriated to India as destitutes. Then there were riots in April 1940 in which 26 Indians were killed; others were deported to India.

This was the unpromising background to the negotiation of an immigration agreement between India and Burma in 1941, when the transitional arrangements after the separation of 1937 expired. The Burmese Ministers insisted on restricting new entries, and imposed conditions upon existing Indian residents, including the power to deport anyone 'cohabiting' with a Burmese woman who then deserted her. A satisfactory compromise was effected, but when the agreement was published in India there was a storm of protest, especially against the cohabitation clause. Gandhi lent his authority to the protest, and the Government of India decided to cancel the agreement. Just at this moment, in December 1941, the Japanese army invaded Burma.

Relentlessly, the Japanese advanced upon the capital, Rangoon. Because the capital, and especially the port, depended so completely upon Indian labour, the British authorities encouraged them to stay. The avenues of departure were sealed off, with the promise that the Indians would be evacuated when the time came to leave, under official arrangements. Before Rangoon was abandoned, 70,000 Indians were evacuated by sea; subsequently, 4,801 Indians left Burma by air. The great majority had to make their own way on foot through uninhabited jungle country, over mountain passes into the eastern borderlands of India. They received only a bare minimum of support by the way, and many failed to reach journey's end. Between 400,000 and 450,000 trekked out on foot and from 10,000 to 50,000 died on the way. From the Burmese they received little help and much hindrance.[1]

The 1931 Census of Burma had enumerated 1,017,825 Indians among the population, of whom 617,521 had been born in India. After the 1942 exodus the Indian population was almost halved, and it seems probable that the great majority of those born in India returned to the motherland. As they took with them only what they could carry, they left their possessions behind. The wealth of the Chettyars has been assessed at £60 million, while the total wealth of the Indians in Burma was not less than £150 million.[2] (This compared to a United Kingdom investment in Burma of £40–£50 million.) Most of these assets were never recovered.

The three years 1942–5 were (according to a Burma Indian) 'the darkest in the history of Burma' which 'impoverished or practically denuded both Burmans and the Indians who could

---

[1] For a detailed account of this episode, based upon contemporary, on-the-spot narratives, see Hugh Tinker, 'A Forgotten Long March; the Indian Exodus from Burma, 1942', *Journal of Southeast Asian Studies* (Singapore), vol. VI, no. 1, March 1975.

[2] N. R. Chakravarti, op. cit., p. 95 (Ch. 7, 'An Estimate of the Wealth of Indians in Burma'). Dr. Chakravarti actually assesses the total as 'somewhere between £150 and £375 millions'.

not escape'.[1] As in Malaya, the Indians had to hand over their wealth or their labour for the use of the Japanese. The Indians who greeted the returning British-Indian forces in 1944 and 1945 were sadly depleted in numbers and reduced in circumstances, though a few had enjoyed a little power and prestige in the Indian Independence League or the I.N.A.

As war-ravaged Burma set about the task of restoring peace-time conditions, it became obvious that neither British administrators nor Burmese politicians wanted a massive return of the Indians, though some returned under military control to rehabilitate the Rangoon port facilities and public transport services.

The British Government intended to impose a period of waiting before handing back to the politicians, but their hand was forced by the new, militant mass-political power of the Anti-Fascist Peoples Freedom League (A.F.P.F.L.) led by the dynamic young Japanese-trained *Bogyoke* ('generalissimo') Aung San. Aung San precipitated a trial of strength with the British Governor, inducing him to accept A.F.P.F.L. claims to govern the country. The new A.F.P.F.L. Government soon took action to stop further Indian immigration. From the end of hostilities up to April 1947, 245,773 Indians entered Burma (mostly those who had fled in 1942) against 141,728 who departed. The new Minister for Labour and Industries decided that this movement must stop, and in June 1947 an Emergency Immigration Act imposed strict controls on all persons seeking entry from any country. Nehru protested to Aung San—who was in some senses his disciple—but the ban remained.

A Constituent Assembly was elected, including a few Indian members, notably Abdul Razak, the political mentor of Aung San. When a Committee was formed to draft a constitution, two Indians were included. One, Zora Singh, was a former I.N.A. leader; the other, M. A. Raschid, had been a student activist with Aung San and his lieutenant, U Nu, and was to become a Cabinet Minister after Independence. The Constitution was not ungenerous to those domiciled Indians who wished to be citizens of independent Burma: all who had lived for eight out of the ten years before Independence in Burma were eligible. However, there was the same hesitation about taking out local citizenship as among overseas Indians in general. Between 35,000 and 40,000

[1] Chakravarti, op. cit., p. 174.

Indians actually made application after Independence, and of these 10,000 were accepted as citizens. As Burma elected to leave the Commonwealth, the rest became foreigners, required to register under the Foreigners' Registration Act. The procedure was cumbersome and slow, and many without certificates became liable to deportation.

After Independence, there were still about 750,000 to 800,000 Indians living in Burma, although the official figures (1954) showed only 226,743 Indians and 96,000 Pakistanis as resident aliens. The 1953 Census enumerated 140,346 Indians and Pakistanis living in Rangoon, out of a total city population of 737,079.[1] Indians were rapidly eliminated from the public services, such as the posts and telegraphs and the railways, where they had formerly predominated; these services suffered severely in loss of efficiency thereby. Indians were partly excluded from commerce by various restrictions: thus the former Indian market in Rangoon, the Sooratee Burra Bazaar, was renamed Bogyoke Market, and its stalls were transferred to Burmese traders.

The greatest blow to Indian interests in the early post-Independence years was the elimination of the Chettyars from agriculture and its credit-financing. A series of legislative measures between 1948 and 1953 brought agricultural land into state ownership. After a good deal of Chettyar complaint to the Government of India, a delegation arrived from Delhi to hold conversations with the Government of Burma. Compensation provisions were then introduced into the legislation, but in actuality the Chettyars had to write off their surrendered land as a dead loss.[2]

Throughout the 1950s there was a steady movement of Indians out of Burma and back to their homeland. Even before Independence, the authority of the A.F.P.F.L. Government was challenged by armed rebels, and during 1949 the revolts spread to embrace many of the minority peoples. A majority of the urban centres throughout Burma—including the second city, Mandalay —fell into rebel hands. In these conditions of chaos, the Indians suffered more than most. The Indian Parliament was informed in December 1949 that over 50,000 Indian nationals had left Burma, including 12,000 who were brought back at Indian Government

[1] Hugh Tinker, *The Union of Burma*, p. 188.
[2] Chakravarti, op. cit., p. 178, and Tinker, op. cit., pp. 238-40.

expense as being totally destitute. During the next two years a similar number decided to leave, salvaging what they could.

Even at this period, the Indians could take out only very limited assets. The law required them to sell their property to citizens of Burma, who, being in a strong position, bought the Indians' houses and lands for a tithe of their real worth. The Indians were forbidden to take out most of their savings by severe exchange regulations. Doubtless the traders managed to evade these regulations, but those who had worked in industry or Government service had to abandon their savings.

During the mid-1950s the scene brightened a little for a small number of Indians with academic qualifications. Before 1942 the majority of medical doctors in Burma were Indians; partly because many departed, but also because training was seriously interrupted, there were only 400 Government doctors in 1951 compared to 650 before 1942. As a temporary measure, 300 doctors were engaged from India and Pakistan on short-term contracts. In addition Burma applied to the United Nations for medical and scientific assistance, and many of the U.N. personnel were Indians. A large U.N.I.C.E.F. programme was directed by John Barnabas from India, while an important mission from the U.N. Technical Assistance Administration was led by an Indian, Dr. J. F. Bulsara.

However, these demonstrations of the benefits of the Indian connection did little to ameliorate the lot of the majority of Burma Indians; nor did the close relations at Government level between India and Burma do anything to help them. The Prime Minister from 1947 to 1958 was U Nu, a great admirer of Gandhi and Nehru, and a notable example of Buddhist tolerance and charity. Jawaharlal Nehru was a frequent and welcome visitor. His arrival was always the signal for a mass demonstration by the Indian population of Rangoon, but Nehru often appeared put out by these demonstrations, obviously preferring to concentrate upon his relations with the Burmese leaders.

At the time of separation in 1937, Burma was required to assume part of the Indian public debt, on account of the railways and other installations acquired by means of Government loans and grants. This debt stood at Rs.60 crores (£45 million) in the mid-1950s, and was a source of much irritation to the Burmese. After protracted negotiations India virtually wrote off this debt, only exacting a supply of rice to the amount of Rs.15·6 crores (£12 million), and even this was at a price far higher than Burma could have obtained in the world market. As in most creditor-debtor relationships, generosity by the creditor did little to appease the resentment of the debtor.

Because India rated good relations with Burma much higher than the fate of the Burma Indians, they could expect no real support if a crisis came, as it did when General Ne Win seized power in 1962. During U Nu's regime, the Indians might have seen their overall condition deteriorate, and their opportunities shrink and wither, but the worst they had to suffer from the Government was a degree of bureaucratic and police harassment. Under Ne Win, they became the target of a sustained Government campaign to drive them out.

Ne Win came to power after Burma had experienced about fifteen years of abortive 'development' out of which the country had achieved very little. The American-inspired programme of industrialization had produced nothing except a number of expensive installations, working at half or quarter capacity. When alternative technical aid was sought from Yugoslavia, Israel, and other sources, this also failed to satisfy. Ne Win therefore enunciated a new programme, the 'Burmese Way to Socialism'. By definition this excluded all foreign aid or advice, and very rapidly the foreign experts were sent packing. The 'Burmese Way' also had no room for private enterprise and private profit: it was argued that a few had enjoyed advantages while the mass of the people had gained nothing. Steadily and swiftly, Ne Win acted to implement his programme.

Nationalization had two imperatives: to remove the last vestiges of foreign control, and to restrict capitalist enterprise to the petty huckstering of the vegetable market. Both these objectives hit the Indians hard. As private trading was replaced by state marketing, the Indian shops were forced out of business, except in remote areas where the Government writ did not run. Such non-commercial Indian institutions as remained were—like all other foreign institutions—taken over by the state. The take-over affected Indian schools, orphanages, and the Ramakrishna mission hospital. Where Indians still survived, as teachers or doctors in Government institutions, they received notice of dismissal, even when there were no qualified Burmese to take their place.

Having been made redundant, the Indians were ordered to leave. By May 1964 the Government of India had classified over 300,000 recent arrivals as refugees.[1] Special ships were chartered to run between Rangoon and Madras, and air services were extended. The enforced repatriation, or deportation, of the Indians continued down to about 1969. No exceptions were permitted. Among those expelled were Indians noted for charitable and philanthropic work among the general population, and others who had made a recognized cultural or scientific contribution to the advancement of Burma. The ruthless manner in which these honoured servants of Burma were forced out seemed designed to emphasize that the new Burma would not be indebted to any except its own people.

The actual circumstances of departure were humiliating. Customs and Immigration officials searched everyone, and confiscated anything valuable they discovered, such as jewellery, cameras, or watches. There were even stories of gold teeth being extracted at the dockside. Women were searched as thoroughly as the men. All currency notes of Rs.50 and above were sequestrated, and people left the land in which many had spent a lifetime with only a few rupees in their pockets.

When the expulsions were completed there still remained an estimated 250,000 Indians in Burma.[2] These folk were mainly stateless persons: very few were citizens of Burma, but they were left alone because they were virtually invisible. Some of them belonged to groups who dwelt on the margin of Burmese society. These included Arakanese Indians, Muslims of mixed ancestry, Gurkhas, and Manipuris, living in their own villages very often as agriculturalists or wandering around as pedlars or itinerant craftsmen. In the cities and towns there were still Indians of Untouchable origin, doing the most menial and degraded tasks which no Burman would undertake. Within the mainstream of Burmese society, there still remained a few persons of Indian origin who had adopted Burmese dress, used a Burmese name, spoke the language habitually, and conformed to Buddhist practices. They included a few civil servants and professional people with a very developed instinct for survival. Their children would, in time, deny any connection with India. Throughout

[1] *Hindu*, 27 May 1964.
[2] *Hindu*, 31 March 1969, for estimates of Indians remaining in Burma.

Burma in the most remote corners there are still night-watchmen, servants, cooks, craftsmen, even some shopkeepers, who are recognizably Indian, but who are accepted members of the local community and who have been left alone. They may not be left alone for ever.

And so the Indians in Burma have come to the end of the road, and hardly anyone retains any interest in them or their problems. In little towns in Tamil Nadu and other parts of India, the survivors sometimes gather in coffee-shops or clubs and talk about the Burma they knew—the good old Burma, the Golden Land, where there was so much colour and gaiety. They are like old colonial hands in retirement in Britain or France as they hark back to the good old days that are gone for ever. For the Indians of Burma there are only memories.

At the final official count, the Asian population of Uganda totalled only 74,308 (1969) and was smaller than in either of the two neighbouring East African countries. Yet this represented a phenomenal—probably unequalled—growth rate during the previous five decades. In 1921 the Indians in Uganda numbered a mere 3,518, so that there was a twentyfold increase in the 48 years to 1969: by contrast, the increase of the Kenya Asians over the same period was sevenfold. In the 1920s the East African Indians regarded Uganda as a dismal backwater of jungle and swamp; yet increasingly it beckoned as a land of opportunity, and the amazing Asian growth rate was mainly the result of immigration.[1]

Uganda's principal export crop was cotton, and the main market was India; not surprisingly, therefore, the cotton business was virtually an Indian monopoly. In the 1930s, 187 of the factories in Uganda where the raw cotton was ginned were Indian-owned out of a total of 194. These ginning-factories were owned by a small number of wealthy entrepreneurs, but a much

[1] Perhaps the attractiveness of Uganda to the Asians should not be exaggerated: see Michael Twaddle, ed., *Expulsion of a Minority; Essays on Ugandan Asians,* London, 1975. In his Introduction, 'Was the Expulsion Inevitable?', Twaddle questions the concept of East Africa as 'the America of the Hindu', and makes a critical examination of other generally held views, including views which are repeated in this book. *Expulsion of a Minority* is valuable in bringing together scholars from different disciplines, and their conclusions apply to the Asians overseas beyond Uganda.

larger number of small Indian brokers dominated the purchasing of the cotton from the African farmers and its transport to the factories. The Uganda Government eliminated these middlemen by encouraging the formation of growers' cooperatives, and these provided the seedbed for African business activity. Indians had no great difficulty in discovering new commercial openings.

Indian immigration was now running in large figures, though temporarily halted during the latter years of the Second World War; the 1948 Census recorded 35,215 Indians in Uganda. The increased concentration of Indians in urban centres, especially in Kampala and Jinja, was resented by Africans, and in 1945 there were anti-Indian riots which started in the towns and spread, sporadically, across the country. The traders and purchasing agents were the main target of African animosity. Four years later there were riots again, largely fomented by Ignatius Musuzi, leader of those African farmers who aspired to set themselves up in commerce and who also entertained political ambitions which the paternalistic colonial regime had kept in check.

Apa B. Pant, the newly appointed Indian Commissioner, visited Uganda and preached the message of integration, but this had little meaning to the leaders of the community. Their organization, the Central Council of Indian Associations, dominated by the wealthier businessmen and lawyers, was much more cautious and respectful to the colonial authority than the Congress organization in Kenya.

The business community was overshadowed by two great firms, founded by Gujarati traders who had arrived in Uganda before the First World War: Mulji Madhvani and Nanji Kalidas Mehta. Their business empires operated as a kind of duumvirate. From the cotton business they had moved out into a score of different enterprises; one of the most important being sugar-growing. Although they owned their own plantations, they (and other Indians) alienated only a tiny fraction of the agricultural land of Uganda. Out of 74,748 square miles, only 530 square miles were in non-African ownership. The massive resentment of White land-ownership in Kenya and Chettyar ownership in Burma had no parallel in Uganda. Other Madhvani and Mehta enterprises included breweries, hotels, and glass and textile factories. Their activities spilled over into Kenya. Mulji Madhvani built a palatial residence at Jinja, where he maintained a style of living which was a strange combination of *nouveau-riche* ostentation, tempered by the austerity of his Gujarati ancestral background. He was a millionaire, but estimates of his vast wealth vary from £1½ million to £100 million.[1] Madhvani did not live for himself or his family alone; he employed his wealth for a multitude of good works, endowing schools, hospitals, and other public benefits. When African leaders criticized the Asians in Uganda they usually pointed to Mulji Madhvani as an example of how they ought to behave.

During the 1940s and 1950s, while concern about racial conflict in Kenya and its political implications deepened, there was no worry about a racial problem in Uganda. There, the political debate revolved around the position of the Baganda and their king, Mutesa, within the framework of tribe and nation. When the Kabaka, Mutesa, was exiled by the colonial Government there followed a campaign for his re-instatement that achieved a level of national political demand. Because the Asian leaders kept right out of this campaign, some African statesmen began to view them as people who had no place in the country.[2]

As African political demands mounted—and became increasingly effective—a small group of young Asian intellectuals, with Western university training, pressed the leaders of the community to move away from the communal attitudes of the past into a more overt political identification with African independence demands. They formed the Uganda Action Group in 1959 as a kind of brains-trust to be put at the disposal of the Africans to assist in formulating policies and organizing popular political parties. The Group did not last more than two years, as it became evident that African leaders had their own very positive programme for independence. As in Kenya, the new political parties were glad to receive substantial financial backing from Asian big business, but this did little to enhance the political standing of the Asians.

[1] Prem Bhatia, op. cit., p. 8, gives the figure of £100 million. He stayed with the Madhvanis many times, and ought to know. Agehananda Bharati, op. cit., p. 51, puts the figure at between U.S. $3 million and $20 million. Douglas Tilbe, *The Ugandan Asian Crisis* (pamphlet) 1972, p. 9, estimates Madhvani's wealth at £20 million sterling. The chapter, 'Economic Aspects of the Expulsion of Asians from Uganda', by M. A. Tribe in *Expulsion of a Minority* does not include any assessment of Indian investment in Uganda.

[2] According to Sir Amar Maini, 'Asians and Politics in Late Colonial Uganda', in *Expulsion of a Minority*.

Independence exposed the strains and stresses between the Baganda and other Uganda Africans, but the Asians were in no way involved in the debate. They were able to obtain citizenship upon the same terms as in Kenya, but just as in Kenya there was obvious reluctance to acquire citizenship, except among the 15,000-strong Ismaili community which applied for Ugandan citizenship *en masse*. At Independence (1962) there were altogether 77,400 Asians in Uganda. During the next eighteen months, apart from the Ismailis, there were few candidates for registration as citizens, but as the grace period drew to its end there was the same last-minute rush as in Kenya: 24,212 applications were received, almost all from Asians. By the end of 1964, 7,448 registration applications had been processed, virtually all in respect of Asians. Because Uganda required evidence that applicants had formally renounced other forms of nationality, many applications were held up until proof could be furnished of renunciation. This was often slow in coming; one explanation was that the U.K. High Commission was dilatory in dealing with these cases, another was that some Asians wanted to hedge their bets, and hoped to retain some form of British nationality as insurance.

Most of the Uganda Asians were not British subjects. If they were born in Uganda or in one of the princely states of western India they had the ambivalent status of British protected persons. As two Kenya-born Indians have observed: 'The status of British protected persons is anomalous both under international law and British law. They have no territorial connexion with Britain, are not nationals, and yet . . . they can demand the protection of the British Government in foreign countries.'[1] As part of the Independence deal for Uganda, Britain had undertaken to accept the entry of British East African Asians into the United Kingdom; hence, after 1962, it was easier than before for some Uganda Asians to obtain British passports, and during the next seven years about 3,000 left Uganda for Britain.[2]

The hardening of African nationalism against the Uganda Asians was slower in taking effect than in Kenya. Still, in 1965,

---

[1] Yash Ghai and Dharam Ghai, *The Asian Minorities of East and Central Africa*, p. 24.

[2] The nature of the British undertaking was affirmed by Iain Macleod in a letter to the *Spectator*, 23 February 1968. The undertaking was reaffirmed in a more qualified fashion by his successor as Colonial Secretary, Reginald Maudling, to Parliament (*Hansard*, 25 March 1971).

Yash Ghai could assert that Uganda was 'more tolerant of Asians as a separate community; not many anti-Asian speeches are made, nor much advice handed out to them'.[1] The Asians in Uganda were somewhat ahead of their neighbours in prosperity: the average cash earnings of Asian males (1962) were £592; in Kenya the average was £551, and in Tanganyika, £564. Although there was a broad spread from rich to poor, as in Kenya, the number of poor unskilled workers in Kampala and other towns was smaller than in Nairobi.

About half the Uganda Asians owned their own business; the rest were employees, and of these 11 per cent were people with professional or high technical qualifications, 16 per cent were in administrative, managerial or executive positions, 30 per cent had secretarial or clerical jobs, and 30 per cent were skilled manual workers, such as carpenters, mechanics, or masons. The Asians displayed considerable mobility, and as in Kenya were an urban group, almost exclusively. They observed the anti-Asian legislation of Kenya in 1967, and the British ban of 1968 with alarm, but they were not yet themselves placed in jeopardy.

Although there were no overt measures against the Asians, they were slowly being displaced by administrative action. The most obvious sector for action was that of the civil service: immediately before Independence there were 2,000 Asian civil servants; by 1968 (in a time of bureaucratic expansion) their number had declined to 1,300. The reduction arose partly because Asian civil servants were resigning, voluntarily, to take up positions in commerce or industry or else to emigrate to Britain.[2]

Then, in 1969, Milton Obote followed the Kenyan example and implemented Immigration and Trade Licensing Acts, designed to eliminate non-citizens from the economy and to advance Africanization. All non-citizens, of whatever occupation, were required to obtain work permits. Certain items of trade were not to be handled by non-citizens; the list covered 34 categories, including beer, cigarettes, soft drinks, motor vehicles, and essential foodstuffs. The legal status of the Uganda Asians was given, officially, as comprising 36,593 holders of British passports

[1] Yash Ghai, 'The Future Prospects', p. 143, in Dharam Ghai, ed., *Portrait of a Minority*.

[2] Nizar Motani, 'The Ugandan Civil Service and the Asian Problem, 1894–1972', in *Expulsion of a Minority*, especially pp. 107–10.

(mainly British protected persons), 8,890 Indian citizens, 253 Pakistani citizens, 1,768 (Indian) citizens of Kenya, and 26,657 Uganda citizens.[1] However, the latter category appears to represent all those who had applied for citizenship, and it included 12,000 whose papers had not been finally processed. The 1969 Immigration Act followed legislation in 1965, and the overall effect was to increase the difficulties of acquiring citizenship and to impose restrictions on all classed as foreigners, with severe penalties against those who infringed the law.

The British Government viewed with some alarm the predicament of the 12,000 Asians whose status was still suspended in limbo, and during 1970 discussed the situation with President Obote. The President seemed ready to agree to a trade-off, whereby the British Asians holding 'D' passports would receive an increased number of special vouchers entitling them to enter Britain, and in consideration the case of the 12,000, and others whose Ugandan nationality was in doubt, would receive early attention.

Although the Uganda Asians were under the same disabilities as the Kenya Asians in emigrating, a considerable number appear to have succeeded in getting out between 1969 and 1971. Their total number fell from 74,000 to about 50,000. A few thousand entered Canada, and a few hundred obtained entry into the United States, but most somehow entered Britain, or else returned to India or Pakistan. However, the Government of India adopted a restrictive policy, following the British Immigration Act of 1968, enacted without any prior notification to India. As Anirudha Gupta has noted there was a 'growing estrangement between India and the Asians in East Africa'. Because so many of them claimed British nationality and clearly wanted to emigrate to Britain, and not to return to India, they were treated as no longer the responsibility of the Indian Government. The Asian British passport holders were required to obtain visas before being admitted to India (though other British passport holders were freely admitted without visas). After some time, an agreement was reached whereby the 'D' passports were stamped with an assurance that any holder admitted to India could, as of right, proceed to

[1] Census of August 1969, published in *Statistical Abstract 1971*, Republic of Uganda, 1972.

Britain.[1] On this basis, many Uganda Asians—mainly the elderly, and those who had retired—went to India.

However, nobody appears to have monitored the exodus between 1969 and 1971. When the crisis arrived, the friends of the Uganda Asians were all asserting that there were 80,000 at risk; this figure is cited by Yash and Dharam Ghai (*The Asian Minorities of East and Central Africa*), by Mariyam Harris (*The 'D' Valued Passport*), and by Douglas Tilbe (*The Ugandan Asian Crisis*). Paradoxically, by quoting a total which was 60 per cent above the true figure, the friends of the Asians aroused even greater hostility against admitting them on the part of the National Front and other anti-immigration organizations!

There was now a strong pro-Asian pressure-group in England demanding the speedy admission of the 'D' passport holders, led by an immigrant from Uganda, Praful Patel. The campaign stressed that the Uganda Asians were all educated, middle-class people, fluent in English, and Western in their way of life. As the crisis intensified, so the emphasis upon the 'British' character of the Uganda community intensified, leading even to the statement that they formed 'minorities of Britain, living temporarily outside Britain'.[2] Perhaps this propaganda played its part in inducing the British Government to allow the Uganda community into Britain when the crunch came: but many of the new arrivals suffered because they were quite unable to live up to the stereotype which had been created for them.

Meanwhile, the Uganda Asians arriving after 1969 mainly did conform to the stereotype, for they were the wealthier, more sophisticated members of the community. Most were able to arrange for the transfer of their funds, though the official limit on the export of capital was £5,000, later reduced to £2,500. Many settled in the pleasant London suburb of Harrow, which they whimsically called Kampala (after all, it was also on a hill). The flight of the better-off Asians, withdrawing their funds, at a time when Uganda was passing into a period of financial stringency with an acute shortage of foreign exchange, served to intensify African feeling against those who remained.

[1] This procedure was opened to all East African holders of 'D' passports. William Deedes told the House of Commons (December 1973) that only 8 per cent of those who went to India subsequently demanded entry into Britain.

[2] Yash Tandon, *Problems of a Displaced Minority: the New Position of East Africa's Asians*, p. 24.

When Idi Amin staged his coup against Milton Obote in January 1971, the Asians welcomed the change, and possibly so did the British Government. It was hoped that General Amin would ease off the anti-Asian campaign. The Ismailis must have been pleased to see a Muslim replace a Christian as President; they had given generous support to the building of mosques, and other measures to promote Islam among the Africans. Negotiations were resumed by British representatives concerning the 12,000 whose citizenship applications were pending. There was not much progress. General Amin made speeches exhorting the Uganda Asians to identify more closely with the country, introducing the familiar theme of intermarriage. He indicated that he would be glad to marry the widow of Mulji Madhvani's son, Jayant, after the latter died in 1971; the widow deemed it prudent to depart to the United Kingdom. Affairs came to a head in December 1971, when Amin summoned the Asians to gather in his new International Conference Centre to hear his account of their misdeeds in the past and to reflect on his exhortations to do better in future. It was noticeable that Amin praised the Madhvani and Mehta families as examples of how Indians had benefited Uganda. Amin announced that the 12,000 applications still pending were cancelled.

Thereafter, the atmosphere of crisis intensified, and in August 1972 General Amin issued decrees expelling all the Asians from Uganda, the order to be made effective within ninety days. Amin accused the Asians of 'economic sabotage' and of 'encouraging corruption'. He informed the Governments of Britain, India, Pakistan, and Bangladesh that they would have to take back all their nationals. At first it seemed that the order covered all the Asians, but in response to a protest Amin declared that Uganda citizens would be exempt.

The first reaction of the British Government was one of incredulity. By now they were getting accustomed to Amin's erratic behaviour, and they assessed this move as a ploy to secure additional British aid in the form of arms and other equipment. The Asians took the decrees very seriously, and besieged the U.K. High Commission, demanding certificates to enter Britain. The High Commission dealt with these demands with what must have appeared to the Asians to be deliberate lack of urgency. A Cabinet Minister, Geoffrey Rippon, journeyed to Kampala to negotiate.

He was reported to have hinted that Britain might expel its Ugandan residents in retaliation, and also terminate its programme of aid, worth £4½ million. Mr. Rippon returned empty-handed to London. Local authorities in Britain responded to the possible arrival of the Asians by insisting that their schools and housing were already filled to capacity. Leicester City Council took space in Kampala newspapers to advertise its inability to accept any more newcomers.

However, if the crisis showed up the worst side of the Britain of the 1970s, it also revealed that there was still a better side. A number of Christian and other voluntary organizations began to plan for the arrival of the Ugandan refugees, and soon afterwards the Government announced the formation of a Resettlement Board, headed by a former under-secretary at the Home Office, Sir Charles Cunningham, which would assume responsibility for the reception and care of the refugees. Sir Alec Douglas-Home appeared on television to make it clear that the British Government accepted full responsibility for all the British Asians, and although this was announced without much warmth there were, at any rate, no reservations about this acceptance.

When the first planeload of refugees arrived on 18 September 1972, they were rapidly accommodated in housing at a former R.A.F. base, and all subsequent arrivals were provided with Government accommodation, if wanted. However, many of the new arrivals retained their spirit. They had been permitted to bring with them only £50 in cash and up to £500 of their possessions. But many had relatives and friends prepared to help them. Although the Government had designated 'red' areas from which the Ugandans ought to be excluded, they made for these places where work was available and looked for jobs. These were the enterprising ones, the fortunate ones.

Meanwhile, under General Amin's orders, the status of all the Asians in Uganda was being ruthlessly investigated. Even those whose Uganda citizenship had appeared to be fully established found that they were required to produce fresh evidence, which was then often rejected. The Ismaili community had believed that the decrees would not affect them. As hundreds of Ismailis found themselves denied citizenship, their morale began to crack. Believing that they were vulnerable, they too joined the exodus. Amin's fury grew, and even the Madhvani and Mehta families were deprived of their citizenship and, after a spell in jail, were deported.

The Resettlement Board expected to have to cope with more than 50,000 British passport holders; when the last party had arrived, it was found that slightly more than 29,000 people had entered Britain. In addition, 10,000 returned to India, and these were said to include 6,000 British passport holders. When it became clear that Britain intended to honour its obligations, the Indian Government made a reciprocal gesture: any British Asian could opt to settle in India, providing that claims to British citizenship were renounced. A mass return was expected, but relatively few wanted to go to the ancestral motherland in preference to settling in Britain.

Other countries offered to receive the refugees as a humanitarian act. Canada took 6,000, of whom the majority were Ismailis; the United States accepted less than 1,000, and 2,000 returned to Pakistan. The most unfortunate victims were the stateless people, of whom 4,000 ended up in camps organized by the United Nations, the largest number (1,500) in Austria. Then followed a long period of agonizing searches for family members. Because of the chaos of the last weeks, there were many instances in which mothers and children arrived in Britain, and were accepted as British, when the father was confined to a U.N. camp in Europe, denied entry into Britain. Only when Roy Jenkins became Home Secretary in March 1974 were these cases of separation resolved by permitting fathers to join their families in Britain; the last 250 divided families were reunited during 1974.

On Home Office instructions, the Resettlement Board gave top priority to finding accommodation for the camp-dwellers, and as a result the last refugees were shifted, and the last camp closed, one year after the expulsion.[1] Finding employment was a more difficult task. The refugees were almost pathetically grateful for the help they received, and most were prepared to accept any job, however different from their previous occupation or however menial. However, the refugees inevitably included the poor and the elderly and the uneducated—those categories of people who the apologists had pretended did not exist. For a man over forty, who could speak no English, and whose previous experience was

[1] This did not mean that all the refugees were provided with houses or flats; some were placed in old people's homes, orphanages, etc.

that of a pedlar or small shopkeeper there could be little hope. There were proposals for providing small loans to such people. In previous cases where British subjects had left a country under duress, abandoning their property, the British Government had awarded compensation, whether or not it could claim this back from the country whence they came. The former *duka-walas* hoped that they might receive a few hundred pounds to start a tobacconist's shop or a newspaper stand, but the objections to giving loans to the Asians from certain politicians put an end to such a move. One of the first statements Jenkins made to Parliament as Home Secretary was to announce that 20 per cent of the Uganda Asians were still unemployed. Reports by Community Relations Councils revealed that approximately 25 per cent of them were, at the same time, existing below the poverty line. For these people there is only a twilight world: they may be refugees for the remainder of their days. But for others—the 80 per cent—there has been a new start, and for the young people the possibility of moving into the world of the West with fewer traumatic reservations than were felt by other South Asian youngsters in Britain.

The fate of the Asians who were allowed to remain behind in Uganda is obscure. It is asserted that 1,000 remain, of whom 250 are British Asians, but the total may well be higher. Part of Amin's programme was to disperse the Asians into the countryside, and there may be a considerable number who, like the remaining Indians in Burma, have found a kind of safety by making themselves invisible. A small number of doctors and technical specialists were exempted by Amin, and remained at work in Kampala and other towns. But as Amin proves himself to be as unpredictable as ever, these professional people are likely to move on as soon as openings occur.

For all the overseas Asians, the Uganda experience inflicted a wound which not even time may heal. Except in the Caribbean and in Mauritius, where they are an ineluctable part of society, there is a haunting fear that the Uganda story could at any time produce a sequel elsewhere.[1] For Britain too, the Uganda experi-

[1] In 1975 an exodus began from Malawi to Britain which is on a smaller scale but which bears all the marks of the Uganda expulsion. It remained unobserved until a sensational report about Malawi immigrants being given luxurious accommodation at the public expense focused attention on President Banda's expulsion policy in spring 1976.

ence was a searching episode, exposing the limitations of all the preconceptions about a multi-racial society. However, the British muddled through the Uganda experience, as they have muddled through so much else, without creating a disaster. The future remains open; it is for native Britons, and Brown and Black Britons, to determine what that future will be.

6

The Hope of Integration

From the time when the Race Relations Board was established under the 1965 Race Relations Act there was an acknowledgment that the old conception of Britain as a tolerant, colour-blind society must be replaced by an acceptance of racial prejudice as a component of British life. However, there remained a belief among liberal people—reaffirmed by public and official pronouncements—that Britain could attain a state of tolerance and recognition of other people's values by a process of educative experience. The goal was never defined, as in the United States, as that of assimilation or 'melting pot'; the goal was said to be that of integration.

This term is frequently employed as though it were self-explanatory, but like many other terms (for example 'democracy', 'community', 'Commonwealth') it does not retain any very precise meaning if it is examined closely. The idea of integration seems to comprise many different states. On one side, it implies a looser form of assimilation, in which all share the ability to operate as equal citizens of an open society (though retaining private concepts of religion and culture). On the other side, integration is not much more than willing acceptance of a plural society in which the different groups are associated in the factory or the shop but otherwise go their own ways.

Despite its vagueness, integration is still pursued by people of goodwill because the other alternatives suggest open conflict or confrontation within British society. The alternatives are either a partition on racial lines, which might crystallize round a Black Power movement, but more probably would lead to Caribbean separatism, Sikh separatism, Punjabi Muslim separatism, Bangladeshi separatism, etc., etc. (as well as reinforcing present-day tendencies within native British society to emphasize Welsh separatism, Tyneside separatism, Orkney separatism, etc.). The other alternative would be a much more acute consciousness of class conflict. This might emerge as a broad working-class solidarity, but would more probably emphasize the solidarity of the coalfields or the railways—in which some Black and Brown people might have a place—and would also bring out the isolation and alienation of so many of the impoverished immigrants from the more affluent White workers—the stark fact of an 'under-class' whose main hope lies in revolt rather than in extracting concessions from the prevailing system.

Hence, integration survives as a goal and as a strategy for most of those involved in what is called the 'race relations industry'. It forms the background to any examination of the realities of the situation of Asians in Britain.

The Asians of Britain are still in a transitional phase. They have not shed the outlook of new immigrants, and they have not yet come to regard Britain as their home. There is actually an enormous volume of movement among all Commonwealth immigrants: in 1962–73 there were 6,425,662 arrivals of Commonwealth citizens in Britain and 6,207,683 departures of Commonwealth citizens from Britain. The composition of the Asian population reflects this transitional quality.

The total population of the United Kingdom in 1971 was 55,347,000, of whom about 750,000 could be categorized as Indians and Pakistanis (then including Bangladeshis). All except a few thousand actually resided in England, whose total population numbered 46,719,000, so that the Asians formed less than 1·5 per cent of the population of England, and a minute fraction in Scotland and Wales.

The estimate of 750,000 as the total number of Asians living in Britain is reached after a number of calculations have been made. The 1971 Census of Great Britain required a declaration of a person's place of birth and also of his parents' place of birth. If we take the simple numbers of persons born in the sub-continent, 321,995 declared they were born in what is now the Republic of India and 139,935 as born in what was (until December 1971) united Pakistan. This appears to provide a total of 461,930 born in India and Pakistan (with Bangladesh) and domiciled in Great Britain.[1]

[1] *Census 1971, Great Britain: Country of Birth Tables* (Stationery Office, 1974). Many of the Sikhs in Britain were born in the canal colonies of undivided Punjab which are now part of Pakistan. Did they correctly record their place of birth as 'Pakistan' or did their loyalty to India make them insert 'India' as their place of birth (which, of course, it was then)? It is anyone's guess.

However, in the days of the Raj, many children of United Kingdom parentage were born in India while the father was serving in the army or the civil service or working as a missionary or in business. All those born in India both of whose parents were born in Britain may reasonably be excluded as 'White Indians' (as some demographers call them). By this reckoning the totals are reduced, and the Indians of Britain are numbered as 282,680 and the Pakistanis as 134,615: total 417,295.[1]

However, there is also the problem of the children born to persons from South Asia in Britain. While Britain was passing through its 'Liberal Hour' in adjusting to these newcomers, it was the practice of the Ministry of Education and other public bodies to regard such children as no different from anyone else born in Britain, and no separate statistics were kept for them. However, the South Asians who are born in Britain (especially the Pakistanis), their parents, and the population at large all continue to view the British-born as Indians and Pakistanis, and it is therefore intended to add them to the total.

When the immigrant totals are reduced to their component elements by sex and date of arrival it is found that there are striking differences between the Indians and Pakistanis. The Indians (born in India) comprise 155,745 males and 126,935 females, and although during the earlier years of the immigration there were significantly greater numbers of males arriving, this was of the order of 3:2 or 5:3, and during the latter years (from 1965) the numbers were more or less equal. Hence, most of the Indian immigrants enjoyed the same kind of family life as at home, with the same opportunities for having children.

The Pakistani total (born in Pakistan) for 1971 is made up of 98,040 males and only 36,575 females. Moreover, the arrival of women as an element in the Pakistani emigration was delayed until long after Indian women were arriving in numbers comparable to men. Down to 1962–3, the Pakistani female immigrants numbered only a few hundreds every year, and thereafter the ratio was still 3:1 against the women. Only in the late 1960s did sizeable numbers begin to arrive to make family life possible.

[1] Most calculations also eliminate persons born in India, *one* of whose parents was born in Britain, but the difference is not great and we have chosen to regard such people as Indians. For a full discussion of this question, see A. M. Field, *et al.*, *1971 Census Data on London's Overseas Born Population and their Children*, G.L.C. Intelligence Unit, Research Memorandum 425.

Hence, when the Indian and Pakistani totals are supplemented by the addition of British-born children there is a dramatic disparity between them: for the Indians, there are 230,000 British-born, increasing their total to 513,000, while there are only 42,000 children born in Britain to Pakistani parents, making a total of 177,000.[1]

In 1971 the number of Pakistanis also included those who were already claiming to be Bangladeshis, and from December 1971 the new state was accorded international recognition. How many Bangladeshis were living in Britain? Reputable journalists logged a figure of 140,000.[2] But the actual total was probably half that number: 70,000. The majority of Bangladeshis in Britain were single men, living away from their families.

However, the combined total of 690,000 does not represent the entire South Asian population in Britain as there are still the immigrants from East Africa to be reckoned with. It is frequently stated that one out of every four of the Indians and Pakistanis in Britain have arrived via East Africa. One writer estimates that there are 200,000 Asians from East Africa in Britain.[3] Even if we are to accept these large numbers as accurate, it is necessary to recall that some of them were born in India or Pakistan and therefore show up in the Indian and Pakistani totals. However, the 1971 Census shows that 59,500 persons born in Kenya are now settled in England. How many of these are Asians?

The Census does not attempt to answer this question, but remembering that in the period 1920–60 the Kenya Asian community was between three and four times larger than the European community (most of whom eventually moved on to Rhodesia, and South Africa), it is reasonable to take 40,000 as the minimum number of Asians born in Kenya now domiciled in Britain. The Census does not identify arrivals from Uganda and Tanzania separately from persons arriving from other parts of Africa; we may assume that a figure of 40,000 for the Asians born in Uganda and Tanzania is certainly not excessive. Finally, among the Caribbean immigrants to Britain there is a small proportion who are East Indians and who are marginal to both the West

[1] G. B. G. Lomas, *Census 1971, Coloured Population of Great Britain*, Runnymede Trust report, 1973, works over the same materials and computes a total of 483,100 Indians (226,800 born in Britain) and 169,700 Pakistanis (41,400 born in Britain).

[2] For example, Peter Hazelhurst: see *The Times*, 19 July 1971.

[3] Yash Tandon, op. cit., p. 31.

Indian and Asian communities; there are also a number of political refugees from South Africa, and there are small but growing numbers of Mauritian Indians in Britain.

These additions take the total of Asians in Britain beyond the suggested total of 750,000. Moreover, many of the officials who participated in the 1971 Census more or less openly admit that in areas of multi-occupation their enumeration was not necessarily accurate. It is possible that the total of Asians in Britain in 1971 was as high as 800,000. But the question is of burning interest only to those who see the Asians as a 'threat' to the British way of life. For the rest of us, it is enough to establish that they are a substantial minority; smaller than the Irish immigrant community (one million), about equal to the West Indian, and more numerous than the Jewish community (half a million).

After the Second World War there were about 7,000 Asians living in Britain, so there has been an increase of more than a hundredfold during the period of less than thirty years. The main increase actually occurred in the decade 1960–70. The immigration of the 1950s was on a minor scale; there were about 47,500 settlers from India (30,500 males and 17,000 females) and 14,500 from Pakistan (12,800 males and 1,700 females).[1] The Indian pioneers were mainly Sikhs, many being ex-soldiers; some had been ejected from their villages when the Punjab was partitioned. The ex-soldiers had often kept in touch with former British officers of the Indian army, and in at least one instance it was a former officer, now personnel manager of a factory, who offered jobs to former Sikh soldiers. The new arrivals turned up in ones and twos. Legend has it that at first all put up at one house in Gravesend, owned by a Sikh, with a local wife who looked after them. The more successful purchased their own houses, and in turn provided staging posts for those who followed, who now pursued job opportunities in Greater London and the Midlands. By the late 1950s, many were bringing their families along with

[1] The Census tables list dates of arrival. There were also 69,600 from India (32,300 males and 37,300 females) and 9,000 from the area which became Pakistan (5,200 males and 3,800 females) who had arrived before 1950: the majority before 1940. It seems reasonable to ignore most of these, as most were returning to the land of their parents (note the large proportion of women) or else they were Eurasians, identifying themselves as British. We are excluding the Eurasians from consideration in this study, though they emigrated in large numbers after Independence.

them (1958: 3,600 males and 2,140 females arrived) and identifiable Sikh communities were being formed.

The migration of the Muslims followed a pattern established
long before. British steamship companies, like P & O, operating
to the Far East, drew the greater proportion of their crews from
India. These men were brought to Calcutta by *sirdars*, who ranked
as bos'ns or cox'ns. They naturally brought the men of their own
village or neighbourhood: all were country-dwellers, men without education. Some steamship companies favoured the tall, up-
standing hawkfaced men of the districts bordering the Punjab and
the North-West Frontier: men from Campbellpur, Nowshera
(Peshawar District), Rawalpindi, and Jhelum. Other companies
took their seamen from the lithe seafaring folk of East Bengal,
especially from Chittagong, but also from inland Sylhet (whose
inhabitants were great travellers). The advantage of having a crew
who all spoke the same tongue and followed the same habits and
customs was obvious.

The companies discharged their crews at the end of several
voyages at Calcutta, but some seamen discharged themselves in
the port of London. They could get shelter for a time with the
Imam of the Seamen's Mosque in east London, and he advised
them on jobs and lodging houses. In the Britain of the 1950s
there were many job vacancies in the south-east and Midlands for
men prepared to do rough, dirty work, and the Pakistanis increasingly brought in their kin to take these on. Besides the
Pakistan districts already mentioned, there were a number of
arrivals from Mirpur, formerly part of princely Kashmir, but
attached to Pakistan as Azad Kashmir after 1949. These people
had also undergone the disruption of their former way of life as a
result of partition, and they grasped the opportunity of emigration. The Pakistanis established themselves in east London, from
Aldgate to East Ham, the traditional reception area for new
arrivals, like the Huguenots, onward to the Jews from Poland.
Gradually, the Pakistanis also moved out to areas where they
could get work; many went into the textile mills of the West
Riding of Yorkshire.

It was in the 1950s that this new pattern developed, but numbers
were still few, and were totally overshadowed by the massive
movement of West Indians into Britain. It was to stem the
Caribbean tide that the 1962 Commonwealth Immigration Act

was passed, imposing limitation upon free entry, and the Act had a dramatic impact upon Caribbean immigration.

Paradoxically, it seems to have given a stimulus to the Asian immigration. There was still a demand for labour in many industries, and in certain locations, which could not be met from local sources. Employers were still trying to get recruits. In the early years, the restrictions left many avenues open: for example, all who had served in the armed forces of the Crown received special consideration, and two million Indians and Pakistanis came into this category.

Settlers from India, Pakistan, Kenya, 1960–1971

	INDIA		PAKISTAN		KENYA	
	M	F	M	F	M	F
1960	6,515	3,750	3,335	430	650	590
1961	11,765	5,545	10,210	635	835	615
1962	10,945	5,420	9,400	920	1,065	820
1963	11,090	5,110	9,800	1,350	900	810
1964	9,055	6,740	6,190	2,080	1,950	1,395
1965	10,885	9,945	5,215	2,460	2,850	1,785
1966	10,615	10,595	6,420	3,315	2,860	2,245
1967	11,910	11,230	9,580	4,100	4,300	3,520
1968	11,525	12,525	5,480	4,420	6,255	5,600
1969	5,830	8,295	6,400	5,350	2,955	2,955
1970–71	7,055	10,050	7,785	7,115	4,280	4,600

Figures taken from Census, Country of Birth Tables.

NB: These figures are *net*. They indicate the numbers settled in Britain in 1971. They do not represent the numbers arriving, of whom a proportion returned to India or Pakistan or moved on to North America or elsewhere. The Kenya figures are not exclusively those of Asian settlers, though it is reasonable to assume that they account very largely for the totals; certainly from 1967 onwards.

New arrivals rose to unprecedented figures, and it was largely to stop Asian immigration that the Labour Government imposed a new set of regulations. The category of unskilled work vouchers was dropped in 1964. The White Paper of 1965 fixed an annual maximum of 8,500 work vouchers, except for professional immigrants, particularly doctors. At this point, the 'primary' immigration was virtually stopped, but was replaced in almost

equal numbers by a 'secondary' immigration. The rules still permitted dependants to join the head of a family in England, and the
majority of those arriving after 1965 presented themselves as
dependants. Of course, a large number were the bona fide wives
and children of men who had arrived alone, but the joint family
system (still almost universal among rural farming families)
encouraged the augmentation of the two-parent or nuclear
family by members of the extended, joint family. Nephews
arrived, being named as sons, and uncles arrived, claiming to be
fathers.

To the Asians, it was part of the great game of getting the
better of the bureaucracy which they and their forefathers had
been perfecting for centuries. The British immigration authorities
took a more severe view of these practices, and did their utmost to
close the loopholes. The 1968 Act not only stopped the free entry
of the British Asians from East Africa but also tightened up the
controls on the entry of dependants. According to the most
authoritative observer of Pakistani immigration, even the 1968
restrictions were frequently evaded. Only children under 18
could enter as dependants, and only if both parents were resident
in Britain. It became the practice for the wife of a Pakistani
immigrant to bring over her 'sons' (really the nephews and
cousins), and having 'dumped' these boys to return home after a
few weeks in Britain to the ancestral family household.[1]

During the later 1960s, the issue of Asian immigration was
taken up in a sensational manner in British party politics. In
particular, it was alleged that large numbers of Asians were getting
into the country illegally, and occasional discoveries of smuggling
operations, organized from France, Belgium, and the Netherlands,
gave credence to this belief. A movement developed to encourage
the Asians to return to their countries of origin, and some politicians even advocated compulsory repatriation. This political
emotion found a legislative outlet in one of the first measures of a
new Conservative Government in 1971.

[1] Badr Dahya, 'Pakistanis in Britain; Transients or Settlers?', *Race*, January
1973, p. 253 fn. This study is the most thorough and detailed account of the
immigration from (West) Pakistan and its impact upon social conditions in the
'sending' areas. There are very few studies of Asians in Britain of any value,
partly, perhaps, because many of the Asian community have come to regard
investigations into their circumstances as 'spying', but also because British social
scientists have such a superficial acquaintance with the cultures of South Asia.

The preamble to the 1971 Act mentions provisions for repatriation, but this is not directly implemented in the Act which is mainly intended to impose upon later arrivals from the 'New' Commonwealth the condition of being migrant workers instead of being immigrants with the prospect of becoming citizens. Under the 1971 Act, a worker is admitted only for twelve months in the first instance, and is liable to deportation if he infringes his conditions of admission (for example, if he changes his job, in certain circumstances). The Act also tightened up the penalties against anyone attempting to smuggle people in illegally, and—perhaps the most contentious provision of all—empowered the Home Secretary to deport any illegal immigrant who was discovered, including those who entered Britain before the passing of the Act.

One last legislative amendment came about as the result of President Bhutto's decision to take Pakistan out of the Commonwealth in 1972. Britain's Pakistan Act was not vindictive, and those who had arrived before the ending of the Commonwealth connection were not penalized. But certain difficulties arose; for example, Pakistani citizens could no longer be British civil servants or members of the armed forces. About 50,000 Pakistanis responded to this situation by making application for United Kingdom citizenship, and 15,896 Pakistanis became U.K. citizens in 1973.[1]

There followed a period during which there was strong political pressure to reduce all immigration to a trickle and to get rid of all illegal immigrants. The 1971 Act came into operation on 1 January 1973. The hunt for illegal immigrants was intensified, and seventy were deported in 1973. During 1973 only 1,053 persons were admitted from the 'New' Commonwealth with work permits, compared to 3,124 admitted during 1970 with work vouchers. Whereas 53,000 dependants entered Britain in 1967, the reassuringly low figure of 18,000 was announced as the number of admissions during 1973.[2] On 21 February 1973 Robert Carr, the Conservative Home Secretary, gave a warning that if

[1] The new Bangladesh was accepted as a member of the Commonwealth.

[2] Subsequently, a Home Office announcement surreptitiously amended this total to 86,000 (*Hansard*, 7 November 1975). There had been a 'clerical error'. Not surprisingly, Enoch Powell made this the subject of another denunciation of bureaucratic deception of the British people (5 January 1976). It was another reminder that migration figures are almost always suspect.

any other African rulers tried to follow Amin of Uganda in expelling British Asians 'they could not assume there was an easy option—which perhaps President Amin was able to assume.' Next time Britain would not accept the Asians as a British obligation. 'Having accepted the burden of the Uganda Asians it would not be right for any [British] Government to accept a similar load.'

David Lane, the Minister responsible for immigration, was convinced that there was a well established 'immigration industry' [sic] at Islamabad and Dacca, where applications for entry certificates had to be obtained from the U.K. High Commission.[1] The British officials processing applications were therefore instructed to make the most rigorous inquiries before sanctioning entry. At the end of 1973, there were 8,069 applications for entry to Britain on file at Islamabad and 5,981 on file at Dacca. During 1973, 11,657 applicants were interviewed at Islamabad, of whom only 4,238 were granted entry certificates, while 643 were refused; the rest were referred back. At Dacca there were 9,544 interviews, and 1,573 certificates granted, with 474 refused. The waiting period was one year at the U.K. High Commission at Delhi, twenty months at Islamabad, and three years at Dacca.[2]

When Roy Jenkins became Home Secretary in March 1974 he reversed this policy. No persons entering Britain illegally before January 1973 would be liable to deportation in future. All who had arrived before that date were offered an amnesty, with 'indefinite leave to remain'. In the three months immediately after this announcement (which was extensively publicized in the Urdu, Punjabi, Bengali, and Gujarati press) 667 illegal immigrants came forward to ask for amnesty—an indication, perhaps, that the size of the illegal population had been grossly exaggerated by the more sensational newspapers.[3] Jenkins sent a junior Minister to meet the officials at the U.K. High Commissions in South Asia and devise means to clear the backlog of applications, particularly in regard to newly married Asians. It was hoped that this might be a 'once-for-all' operation, uniting all who wished to make their homes in Britain. It seems unlikely that the migration from South

[1] These statistics and comments came in a debate on race relations in the House of Commons on 28 November 1973.

[2] Information in *Hansard* (27 March 1974) in reply to a question by Cyril Smith, M.P., and announcements by Roy Jenkins to Parliament, 8 November 1974.

[3] Announcements by Jenkins to Parliament, 11 April 1974 and 2 July 1974.

Asia will actually be mopped up by this humanitarian move. There will always be means whereby resourceful people can enter Britain. Young men betrothed to Asian girls in Britain will demand the right of entry, for example.[1]

The discussion about Black and Brown people in Britain has focused upon immigration as the key issue; this has not assisted promotion of the ideal of integration. The debate can more usefully be directed at the situation of the Asians as they become an accepted feature of the English scene. The distribution of the Asians—and of people from the 'New' Commonwealth in general—is heavily weighted to certain areas, which are mainly the areas where employment opportunities have been brightest.

Persons Born Outside the U.K. as a percentage of Population

	1961	1971		1961	1971
England & Wales	4·6	5·9	South-West	3·3	3·8
Greater London*	—	14·3	Wales	2	2·1
South-East	7·3	9·4	Yorkshire & Humberside	2·7	3·6
West Midlands	4·5	6·2	North-West	3·1	3·9
East Midlands	3·3	4·4	North	1·4	1·6
East Anglia	4·4	4·8			

* The G.L.C. did not exist in 1961

NB: The Greater London total also forms part of the South-East total

The concentration of the people from overseas in the London

[1] After this book was completed the whole question of admission into Britain from South Asia again became heated with the 'leaking' of a confidential report by D. F. Hawley of the Foreign and Commonwealth Office, who studied the procedure at the offices of the High Commissioners and concluded that 'deceit and false documentation' were being carefully organized by travel agents and others. He concluded that the argument that 'the end was in sight' was unrealistic, and he asserted that the pool of applications at Delhi alone totalled 50,000 to 70,000 (*The Times*, 25 May 1976). The Hawley report produced an outburst of fresh demands for a stricter policy. Some immigrant leaders responded to these demands; Dr. Dhani Prem stated that if all the current applications were treated generously the Asians should accept that this was enough. In July 1976, Roy Jenkins announced that a comprehensive register of the relatives of the Asians in Britain eligible for entry would be compiled under the supervision of three M.P.s (who presumably would act as watchdogs). Once again, there was the implication that the question could be resolved for all time. But unless Britain adopts the same ruthless procedure as South Africa, and in future turns away all new arrivals who are married or betrothed to Asians domiciled in Britain, the flow will inevitably continue.

area and in the South-East (which includes more than one-third
of the total population of England and Wales) is the most striking
feature of these figures. The only other area with an overseas
population higher than the national average (in 1971, though not
in 1961) is the West Midlands, which includes the second city,
Birmingham. Within the Greater London area, the Asians are
probably the most widely dispersed group among the immigrant
communities. A survey of every ward in all the boroughs of
Greater London revealed that less than 2 per cent of all the wards
were without Asian residents; Southwark is the borough with the
lowest proportion of Asians. The London boroughs with high
Asian populations are (in descending order) Kensington and
Chelsea, Ealing, Camden, Westminster, Tower Hamlets, and
Brent. The London ward with the highest proportion of Indian
residents (more than 25 per cent) is Northcote in Southall; the
highest proportion of Muslims—mainly Bangladeshis—(over 10
per cent) are in St. Mary's Ward, Tower Hamlets.

Somehow, the impact of Black and Brown people is not so
pervasive in London, with its varied and cosmopolitan population, as it is in provincial towns, with their strong sense of local,
regional identity. It is therefore in places like Coventry, Leicester,
Wolverhampton, Halifax, Bradford, Oldham, Dewsbury,
Nottingham, High Wycombe, Bedford, and Gravesend that
the transformation has been most keenly felt.

The arrival of the Asians coincided with a great shift in urban
living which followed the Second World War. There was something like a social revolt or repudiation of the housing pattern
which had been created during the nineteenth century in the
industrial towns of England. The working class had been housed
in box-like terrace houses, whose front doors opened directly on
to the street, and whose back doors led to drab sheds and privies.
Professional and upper-class people resided in big, double-fronted
town houses with large principal rooms, a labyrinth of passages
and staircases, and poky rooms on the top floors for the servants.
The movement away from this nineteenth-century housing stock
began in the 1930s: the affluent moved out into old country
cottages and new ranch-houses; the working class moved into
new council estates and into new private 'semis'. The movement
accelerated in the 1950s and 1960s, as post-war building boomed
in the more prosperous areas of newer industry; the old folk, and

the more unfortunate and depressed, were left behind. They now became the reluctant neighbours of the 'Coloureds', who moved into the houses which the native English had discarded.

The housing needs of the general population are satisfied according to these proportions: public housing, 27·6 per cent; owner-occupied housing, 46·3 per cent; rented, unfurnished accommodation, 18·7 per cent; rented, furnished accommodation, 2 per cent; other, 5·4 per cent. The Asians did not have access to local authority housing: a local five-years' residence qualification is almost a universal requirement, and most of the Asians were automatically excluded. Hence, only 11·2 per cent of the Indians and 6·3 per cent of Pakistanis have been allocated public housing.[1] Similarly, the Asians find difficulty in renting unfurnished accommodation from native English landlords (the only landlords who are really colour-blind are those letting luxury flats at inflated rents). Thus, only 17·3 per cent of Indians and 15·3 per cent of Pakistanis are in unfurnished rented accommodation, and this is almost invariably rented from an Indian or Pakistani landlord who has bought up an old upper-class house and divided it into units for multi-occupation. Furnished, rented accommodation is considered the least permanent and secure; it is usually expensive, and, until 1975, the tenant had tenure only at the humour of the landlord. A far higher proportion of the Asians than the English live in this type of accommodation—13·2 per cent of Indians and 20 per cent of Pakistanis. For the Pakistanis, this will usually be a doss-house (politely called a dormitory) where six men will share one room with three beds: sleeping in turns, as one or the other goes on shift. The advantage of these places is that they are relatively cheap, and the newly arrived worker is able to save from his pay.

The rest of the Asians—58·1 per cent of Indians and 57·9 per cent of Pakistanis—own (or are buying) their own houses, a far higher proportion than the national average. The middle-class Asians live mainly in semi-detached suburban houses erected in the 1930s, but the working-class Asians live in the old, decaying inner city in Victorian terraces, without modern conveniences. The houses of the Asians can usually be distinguished, because

[1] These statistics, and those following on employment, are taken from a study by Professor Peter Collison based upon the Census returns.

the mortar-courses are picked out in white or yellow, and the window frames are gaily painted, green, orange, or red. The houses are usually well tended inside, even though the plaster may be cracking and the roofs leaking, and even though another family will probably share the house, so that the owner can pay back the purchase-price.

Sophisticated Indians borrow on a mortgage, like their English neighbours, but the more traditional people borrow from their own kinsfolk, and it is usual to put up the purchase money in cash. This mutual self-help characterizes most of the social behaviour of the Asians.

The Asians came to Britain because many of the older labour-intensive industries were unable to obtain workers at the low rates of pay which were traditional. The textile industry, the garment industry, and the steel industry took them on, as did bus companies and the railways in which (until the mid-1970s) rates of pay were also low. The only way to earn a bigger pay-packet in all these industries was to work long hours for overtime; and this the Asians did, often working an eighty-hour week.

In the Indian community, 57 per cent of male workers were on manual work, while 83·3 per cent of the Pakistanis were manual workers, of whom two-thirds were unskilled or semi-skilled. The remainder of the Indians were found in a broad band of occupations: 6·6 per cent being employers or managers, 10·5 per cent being professional people, 18·9 per cent shop assistants and office workers, and 2·4 per cent serving in the armed forces. The Pakistanis included only 2·3 per cent in managerial positions, 3·4 per cent as professional people, and 5·6 per cent in shop and office jobs.[1]

A high proportion of Indian married women also go out to work, a higher proportion than among the general population. The Indian women do assembly-jobs in factories, sew and knit and make clothes, and work in laundries. A few work in market gardens or in other outdoor work. Where they work alongside Englishwomen they are often delegated the lower-paid work; for example, there are often bonus schemes in laundries for those

---

[1] The categories of employment not mentioned include: *Indians*, 1·7 per cent in personal service (hotels, hospitals, etc.) and 2·4 per cent self-employed (hawkers, taxi-drivers, etc.). The *Pakistanis* show 2·3 per cent in personal service and 2·3 per cent self-employed; 0·7 per cent of Pakistanis are in the armed forces.

whose output attains a certain level, but the Indians are usually denied the opportunity for earning bonuses. A smaller number of Pakistani women work, and only where they are not required to mix with men. Because they speak no English, the Pakistani women are often put under a Punjabi-speaking supervisor, often a Sikh woman. Their earnings are lower than those of the Indians.

Overwhelmingly, the Asian men have come from the country-side, though those who have been in East Africa have acquired urban skills. Many of the Sikhs arrive with a general mechanical ability, a kind of native technical wit, which can be refined into the specialized skill required—in a branch of the motor-car industry, for example. Many of the Indians, especially, achieve a significant level of job-mobility, after some years on the bottom rung of the ladder.[1]

Readiness to take a step downwards in the socio-economic scale, in the hope of subsequently moving upwards, is also demonstrated by many professional or middle-class people. The Sikhs especially, but also the Punjabi Muslims and the Gujaratis, come to Britain as members of a village community or an extended kinship network. The village, or the clan, will include some members who have gone a long way in India or Pakistan. From the village they have gone to college and they have become executive civil servants, or lawyers, or college lecturers, or have attained other positions of responsibility. Perhaps they have disappointments or checks in their career; for whatever reason, they resign and come to Britain to join their village brothers, the *biradari*. They find that men who were peasant farmers, yeomen, are working on the factory floor, so they decide that it is not beneath their dignity to become a conductor on a bus, or an assistant in the post office, or a pay clerk. For some time they will

[1] It is a wry paradox that because so many Asians do remain in jobs at the bottom of the economic ladder this has given them a certain immunity as unemployment in Britain topped $1\frac{1}{2}$ million in the mid-1970s. Those made redundant from the better-paid sections of British industry prefer to draw unemployment pay rather than move into the unskilled, menial sectors of industry. Race relations watchers have long dreaded what might happen in a prolonged slump. Tension appears to be greatest among school-leavers who are competitors for scarce jobs and who face the immediate prospect of unemployment. A number of attacks upon young Asians, including the murder of a Sikh student, drew attention to the worsening situation in the spring and summer of 1976.

accept this position, well below their attainments, but within a few years the more enterprising and able get back into professional positions. They may rise again to the level which they had attained in India or Pakistan.[1]

Probably the most significant reduction of racial discrimination in Britain has occurred at the level of professional or semi-professional employment. Until the late 1960s, Asians were not employed in banks or in department stores, on the grounds that 'the customers would object'. Shortage of qualified staff led to the introduction of one or two Asians, when it was discovered that there was no overt negative reaction from customers. Asians were then accepted as bank-clerks, chartered accountants, insurance agents, etc. Acceptance in these positions depends very much on performance, and many of the Indians, particularly Gujaratis, can demonstrate that they are every bit as efficient as their English counterparts.

In positions where an idiomatic command of English is required, acceptance has not been so smooth. Teachers arriving from India and Pakistan discover that their degrees do not admit them to teaching. They are required to obtain a recognized diploma, and even then employment is often denied on the grounds that their form of English is unintelligible to British children. There is an excessive sensitivity on both sides about this issue, with the Asians maintaining that as educated people they do not need to improve their English, and sometimes with British teachers objecting that they cannot understand the Asians when they employ well-known idioms of 'Indian English'. This controversy has also occupied the medical profession.

Doctors arriving in Britain with a Commonwealth medical qualification are accepted (though in Canada and the United States they are rigorously excluded until they have obtained North American qualifications). Many Asian doctors employed

[1] My favourite story concerns a Sikh army officer who served in North Africa, Italy, and the Congo, and who defended his country in Kashmir and on the North-East Frontier. He commanded his battalion, but then he had to retire, and returned to his village. He was still an active man, but there was nothing to do, and he was bored out of his mind by his relatives, and especially by his mother. He made his way to England, and lodged with village relatives. The only job he could find was that of a labourer on a building site. For several months the former lieutenant-colonel swung a pick, and heaved shovel and bucket. Then he met a Sikh who offered him a place in a travel-firm, and he now is a successful businessman.

in hospitals are required to undergo a period of further training, but meanwhile they undertake hospital duties. Their further advancement to the more attractive (and profitable) levels of medicine, such as registrar or specialist, is often blocked, while younger English doctors pass them by on the upward way. The reason often given is that the Asian doctors lack adequate knowledge of English. In 1975 the British Medical Association required all overseas doctors in Britain to undergo a test, which was largely concerned with linguistic capability; 60 per cent of the overseas doctors did not pass, and the incidence was especially heavy among the Pakistanis. In reply, many alleged that they had to work such long hours that they did not have the opportunity to refine their command of English.

In actuality, demands from employing authorities for better English from Asian professional men seem to be adjusted to the scarcity or otherwise of candidates in that particular locality. In the Home Counties, Asians with English which is sub-standard by British reckoning will face appalling difficulties. Yet an Indian teacher, not long arrived from India, will have no trouble in securing a post under the Inner London Education Authority, where the hazards faced by teachers create a permanent staff shortage. Similarly, a Pakistani doctor with speech patterns quite unfamiliar to English ears will be an acceptable addition to a hospital on Tyneside or Teesside, unable to maintain a casualty service for lack of doctors. Aware that they are treated as second-class people, from a professional point of view, the Asians tend to withdraw into their own circle.

However, it is the middle-class Asians who do 'integrate' most into the social life of their English counterparts. Much may depend upon the Asian's wife, for a man who comes to parties leaving his wife at home is often not popular. The situation is likely to vary according to the Asian's profession. A university lecturer or a BBC producer is much more likely to mix with his English peers than a businessman (apart from the inevitable two-hour business lunch). There is a superficially cosmopolitan level of intercourse in which Asian and English intellectuals can participate. A discussion of politics, or economics, finds much common ground. But if, for example, the fundamental subject of sex emerges, both sides find that they start from basically different preconceptions.

For the rest of the Asians, their social contacts with the native British are limited to mixing in pubs, and (to a much lesser extent) on the terraces of football grounds. Drinking is something in which the Asians, especially the Sikhs, can outdo the native British. This is an all-male pastime, conducted with some of that display of masculinity which has traditionally featured in English working-class customs. By now, in almost every town, there are some pubs where the Asians go regularly, and some to which they never go. There is a kind of silent apartheid. Quite a number of public houses in London and the Midlands have Indian landlords. According to a uniquely informed observer, there are actually six Muslim landlords; for a minority of Pakistanis, especially the single men, have taken to alcohol as a regular relaxation, despite the Holy Prophet's abjuration.[1]

The Sikhs in Britain drink more heavily than at home, but in most other respects they keep to their traditional way of life with few concessions to the land of their exile. Almost every Sikh community is a projection of a Sikh village in the Punjab; in some instances, it is said that there are more *gaon-walli* of the village brotherhood living together in England than there are back in the village. Even though some Sikh families have lived in Britain for ten or twenty years, and show no sign of leaving, they regard themselves as full members of the ancestral village. It is probable that they have bought agricultural land with their English savings, and perhaps sent home a tractor. A brother will farm the land, but it is not made over to him. Village politics, with its factions and feuds, is exported unchanged into the English setting, and Punjabi state party politics is more important to the English Sikhs than the municipal or parliamentary politics of their adopted home. Leaders from the Punjab, assuming a religious guise, will be invited to Britain, and their news of home is eagerly taken in. The venerable gentlemen will return with handsome donations and subscriptions for local political and religious purposes.

The focus of Sikh life in Britain is the temple or *gurudwara*. The first was started in Southall in 1962, and now there are fifty throughout the South-East and the Midlands. Every Sikh remains a Sikh, whether or not he displays the full symbols of his faith: the uncut hair and beard, the turban and steel bangle (also the short

---

[1] Badr Dahya, op. cit., p. 272; it is stated that the Pakistanis are the *owners* of six public houses in Bradford, Dewsbury, Leeds, and Cambridgeshire.

drawers and symbolic sword, unseen). About half the Sikh men in Britain are shaven and shorn, but they are still members of the *gurudwara*, and of course the option to return to the full beard and turban is always open to them. Nevertheless, when members are selected for the *gurudwara* committee, and especially for president, only the bearded Sikhs are candidates.[1]

Most of the Sikh temples are housed in former Nonconformist chapels, abandoned with the waning of English Christianity. These buildings are well adapted to the open Sikh congregational worship and to their hospitable *langars* or kitchens where any wayfarer may be fed. The sturdy Sikh women participate in the services, sitting down one side of the temple, and of course play an essential part in the feasting and other celebrations. The temple is not only a place of worship; it is also the centre of community social life, a kind of employment exchange, and a fully functioning organization for political protest or demand. Within the community of almost every *gurudwara* there are at least two factions competing for effective control; but these differences are put aside whenever the Sikhs want to contest some issue outside, in the arena of English public life. Although each *gurudwara* is separate and autonomous, they can cooperate effectively in a common cause. Anyone viewing the great Sikh processions through London to demonstrate against the 1971 Immigration Bill, or against Indira Gandhi's emergency powers in 1975, must be impressed by the display of controlled disciplined passion, not quite unleashed, by the massed Sikhs.

The Sikhs have fought a number of political, legal, and industrial battles over their right to keep the turban. A number of bus companies have been crassly obdurate in denying this right, and demanding that the Sikhs wear peaked caps, like other bus crews. The Sikhs have tried negotiation and they have tried militant action; sometimes they have worn down the opposition, and sometimes they have been defeated. But they have not conceded the right of their employers to dictate to them.[2] Similarly, in their effort to defy the law regarding the wearing of crash-helmets on

[1] The vogue for beards and long hair among young Englishmen in the 1960s and 1970s has given young, sophisticated British-born Sikhs the option of appearing both traditional and Westernized; some young Sikhs have beards, only judiciously trimmed, and long hair, only lightly cut and groomed, giving them a romantic appearance.

[2] D. Beetham, *Transport and Turbans*, London, 1970.

motor-cycles and scooters, the Sikhs have steadily maintained their right and duty to wear the turban, while not pleading for special sympathy, and without claiming to be above the law. And the community demonstrates its solidarity with the resisters with an unflamboyant determination.[1]

The Indian Workers' Association or Hindustan Mazdoor Sabha is also a largely Sikh-inspired institution. The first I.W.A. started at Southall in 1957 with 120 members; the membership of the various I.W.A.s in the 1970s is about 10,000.[2] Although I.W.A. finances are not so well run as those of the temples, they have accumulated considerable resources. They own cinemas showing Indian films, as well as reading-rooms and other facilities. Indeed, the Sikh community increasingly becomes self-sufficient, with its own shops, garages, hire-firms, travel and insurance agents, etc.

The Sikhs in Britain are forward-looking, and their British-born sons and daughters are encouraged to acquire training in fields like engineering and medicine which have a solid value. How exclusive are the Sikhs? Occasionally a man marries an Englishwoman; he remains within the community and the wife is welcomed if she will conform to the values of the Sikh religion. But Sikh girls must marry Sikhs. The accepted doctrine is that any Sikh may marry any other Sikh; but in reality it appears that Jat Sikhs will marry only their own people, and not the Mazbi and Ramdasia Sikhs whose origin is more lowly.

Although the subject is not openly discussed, most Sikhs would prefer to take their brides from the Punjab (marriages are, of course, arranged by the parents). A Punjabi girl is pure, uncontaminated by the decadent ways of the West. It follows that certain inducements are required to make marriage with a British-born Sikh girl attractive. One solution is that of higher education; a lady doctor or scientist or designer is a good match. Another solution is for the father to present a really fabulous dowry. He is not usually expected to provide a house for his newly married daughter, but he is expected to stock up the house with electric gadgets and furniture, and to fill the wardrobe with suits for his new son-in-law.

[1] The crash-helmet question is surely not insoluble. The question has been posed: what headgear do Sikh jet-pilots wear? Something on those lines should be acceptable.

[2] There is an I.W.A., Great Britain, which states on its notepaper that it was founded in 1938.

The Gujaratis retain something of their ancestral austerity, but they have adapted further than other Asians to their Western surroundings. Unlike the Sikhs, they do not openly advertise their presence. The community includes a number of important industrialists as well as professional people, businessmen, and shop-keepers. Yet there are also the working-class Gujaratis, who have tackled the problems of the shop-floor on a broader basis than the Sikhs. Labour leaders from among the Gujaratis have been to the fore in challenging the common factory situation in which the jobs with superior rates of pay are reserved for the White workers, with the Asians relegated to jobs confined to low, basic wages. Gujarati leaders have demanded that their people be regarded as skilled workers, when they have earned this by seniority and merit. Often, White shop stewards and other union officials have declined to act for them, and they have organized on their own behalf, staging strikes when other means have failed. Sometimes they have bitten off too much, as in the disastrous ending to their confrontation with Imperial Typewriters. But gradually they are getting across the lesson that Asian workers cannot always be treated as the helots of the workforce.

The Gujaratis are more insistent than the Sikhs on observing traditional caste rules, and in particular in arranging marriages within the proper circle laid down by caste. Organized religion plays a less central part in the community life of the Gujaratis, though they have their own priests and, increasingly, their own temples.[1] Even when Gujarati men slide away from the conventional practices—perhaps eating meat and drinking liquor—the women cherish the old ways, observing prayer rituals and dietetic laws scrupulously, though they may have just returned from a full day's work in a television factory.[2]

The Pakistanis and Bangladeshis, even more than the Indians, make their religion the central fact of their life in Britain. Wherever there is a Muslim group, someone with a modicum of

---

[1] When a new Gujarati temple was built, mainly through the efforts of Prafu Patel and other East Africa Asians, some critics protested against perpetuating religious forms and observances which emphasize the linguistic and other divisions between the different Indian groups in Britain.

[2] There are few authentic descriptions of life among Indian immigrants. Probably the most revealing is *Rampal and His Family*, recorded by Ursula Sharma (London, 1971). Here an Indian worker tells his experiences to an anthro-pologist who is also a literary artist.

7

Koranic learning is appointed as their religious leader. In the larger communities there will be a full-time religious teacher, supported by his fellow Muslims, and designated to lead their prayers and to drill their boys in the precepts of the Koran. There are very few mosques, in the conventional sense of a special building for prayer, but in most towns the Muslims have purchased a house which is set aside for congregational prayer and religious instruction.

In their own country, the Pakistanis are not, as a whole, especially religious, and their middle class has largely given up religious observance, except upon formal occasions. But rural people are zealous still, and most of the immigrants are simple, rural people. Among the Bangladeshis, the people of Chittagong and Sylhet districts are considered especially pious (though not as pious as those of Noakhali, a neighbouring district). Also, the practice of Islam is one of the few ways in which in England they can, for their own esteem, demonstrate their superiority to those who live around them. Even before the birth of Bangladesh, the Bengalis and Punjabis formed separate congregations wherever they were numerous. The separation is now complete.

Whereas, among the Indians, there is a religious continuum, stretching from the most orthodox and pious all the way to those whose observance is perfunctory and occasional, among Pakistanis and Bangladeshis there are really only two categories—the believers, and the deviants, known as *mawalis* or loafers in Urdu. British Muslims celebrate the fast of Ramadhan with painful rigour, even amid the heat and hectic pace of the production line or the blast-furnace. Most of them insist that if they die in Britain their bodies should be buried in the homeland, Dar-ul-Islam and not Dar-ul-Harb, the land of strife and contention, England, though the Koran insists that the body should be buried immediately after death.

Islamic orthodoxy is most active in ensuring that the women keep to their proper place and do not stray into the man's world (unlike their Sikh sisters, Muslim women are not permitted in the mosque). If Muslim women in Britain do not observe *purdah* in the strictest sense of donning the all-enveloping *burka* when they go out, they are in *purdah* to the extent that their horizons are restricted to their own home, and the homes of close neighbours and relatives. There is great concern about girls preserving a proper modesty, and some Pakistani fathers are so horrified by the idea of having to send daughters to mixed schools that they are prepared to withdraw them and defy any summons that the local authority may serve upon them.

As we have observed, the predominance of men means that many Pakistanis live in all-male dormitories, though sometimes a group of young males will lodge with a senior relative, in which case his wife is permitted to associate with these male relations. Where the woman is senior to them, she may provide a helpful, motherly influence, but when the wife in England is a second wife, many years younger than her husband, her position with the male relatives may be unhappy.

Pakistani spokesmen often seem aggressively defensive about the position of their women, and when there are meetings with local do-gooders to promote 'multi-racial understanding', a Pakistani will usually deliver a lecture on the exalted status which Islam accords to women, contrasting this with the immoral habits of the English girls.[1]

The sex-ratio among the Muslims in England is subject to striking variations according to age. Among the very young (aged 0–9 years) there is something like parity between the sexes, but then there are almost four male teenagers for one female. In the years between 20 and 30 years—the years of early marriage— there are three men to two women, but for all older age-groups— except the ancient—there are far more men than women.[2]

The constant flow of human traffic, back and forth between England and the old home, indicates how far the Pakistanis still are from regarding themselves as settlers in Britain. On the contrary, the steady remittance of a large proportion of workers' wages to

---

[1] Badr Dahya, op. cit., p. 260 observes, 'It seems that these remarks were meant to tell outsiders to leave the migrant women alone, especially with regard to the *purdah* and their lack of English'. The position of Pakistani women is more fully examined by Verity Saifullah Khan, 'Asian Women in Britain; Strategies of Adjustment of Indian and Pakistani Migrants', in Alfred de Souza, ed., *Women in Contemporary India*, Bombay, 1975.

[2] *Sex Ratios by Age*

(*1971 Census: Country of Birth Tables: Pakistanis and Bangladeshis*)

Age			Age		
0–9: males	6,405	females 5,000	40–49: males 16,670	females 3,950
10–19: males 25,800		females 6,980	50–59: males 7,410	females 1,490
20–29: males 15,500		females 10,375	60–69: males 1,743	females 890
30–39: males 28,645		females 9,410	Over 70: males 425	females 555

Pakistan, and their investment in tall, brick-built houses in Pakistan—*pukka* houses, often called 'England houses'—indicates their firm resolve to return. And yet, while they frequently pay visits to their old homes, and are simultaneously admired and fleeced (as Badr Dahya explains so graphically), they usually come back to Bradford or Sparkbrook, to the curious limbo-life endured by many a Pakistani in England.

Of course, some Pakistanis and Bangladeshis deliberately break away from the chain which binds them to the ancestral homeland and firmly make their home in England, with wife and family. They can then link up with a dozen Pakistani associations claiming to represent the community in their area, but few of these have the solid qualities of the Sikh neighbourhood associations. Factionalism is endemic, and there are open antagonisms between the Pakistanis and Bangladeshis which cannot be resolved within the brotherhood of Islam. When a Bangladeshi candidate was nominated by the Labour Party in a Bradford local election, the Pakistanis voted unitedly for the Conservative candidate and helped him to win a safe Labour ward.[1] The Bangladeshis are themselves divided over many issues. When a Bangladesh Relief Fund was launched in Britain in 1971, supported by generous contributions from workers of every sort, thousands of pounds were misappropriated by persons collecting for the fund. The subsequent attempts to investigate the defalcations lasted four years, without arriving at any conclusion.

Badr Dahya, the detached Pakistani assessor of the Pakistani immigration, believes that 'we can expect some sort of cultural erosion, no matter how gradual, with regard to some practices, customs, and beliefs which come to be modified and adapted in a new milieu.' Is there, then, a process of integration at work, despite all the evidence of the Asians' strenuous efforts to preserve their separate identity? What interaction can be discerned between the Asians, and what the race relations experts call 'the Host Community'?

In Britain as in Africa and South-East Asia many people regard the ultimate form of integration as intermarriage. This is more rare in Britain than elsewhere, because it is dreaded on both sides: by the Whites and by the Asians. Unless an Englishman marries the daughter of a maharaja, or an Indian marries a peer's daughter,

[1] Badr Dahya, op. cit., p. 262.

it is regarded as a misalliance. But the immigration is, effectively, still only in its second decade and attitudes may change significantly within two more decades.

Meanwhile the most obvious meeting-point is that of television. Almost every Asian household, however poor and cramped, will possess a large colour-television set, and this is turned on during all the hours of transmission, except when the children are doing their homework. This exposure may do something to familiarize those who already know English with Western or English ways; but for those who cannot understand English—like the vast majority of the wives—it remains a fantastic, barely comprehensible entertainment.

A few educated Asians who aspire to be leaders join the British political parties. So long as they stick to making vague speeches of goodwill, they are welcome enough; occasionally they may be invited to stand as candidates in local elections, though usually only in wards with a sizeable number of their own community. Experience shows that it is more difficult for an immigrant to win, as a proportion of the party stalwarts will decline to turn out for him.[1] The political parties value their visible participation as a token of the multi-racial policies which they profess; but no Indian or Pakistani has been elected to Parliament in the era of immigration, although Shapurji Saklatvala, a Parsi, had been M.P. for North Battersea in 1922-9, when Indian voters numbered a few hundred instead of a quarter of a million.

However, late in 1975 there was a dramatic change. In October 1975 the Community Relations Commission issued a study comparing the two general elections of 1974. This focused upon marginal seats in which the numbers of immigrants were in excess of the majorities attained by the successful candidates. It was calculated that in 59 constituencies the 'immigrant vote' was decisive. At both the 1974 elections the Conservative Party held on to 14 of these seats and Labour held on to 30, but in 15 constituencies Conservatives lost to Labour in October 1974. Sample surveys showed that West Indians and Asians voted

[1] Bashir Maan, a Pakistani Glasgow councillor, stood as Labour candidate in East Fife in February 1974; he was placed fourth among four candidates. The Liberal Party fielded three Asian candidates in 1970 and one (Dr. Dhani Prem) in February 1974. Tariq Ali stood as International Marxist candidate at the same election, and Baldev Singh Chahal contested Southall on the turban ticket (both lost their deposits).

overwhelmingly for Labour candidates.[1] Thus, it might be argued
that the Labour Government owed its tenuous majority to the
'immigrant vote'. The Conservative leadership appeared to take
the report very seriously and a new solicitude for the Asians and
West Indians was manifested. For the first time, an Indian Conservative prospective parliamentary candidate was adopted (a
former cavalry officer).

The arena in which the integration idea is accepted philosophy
is that of community relations: the network of local councils set
up with Government backing to improve the conditions of the
immigrants in relation to 'the Host Community'. The Community Relations Councils employ their own officers, and about
one-quarter of the C.R.O.s are Asians. They and the Asian
members of the councils are, whether they like it or not, brokers,
middle-men, trying very often to stretch meagre resources to
cover massive needs. These 'race relations' Asians are under fire
from their own compatriots when they do not make demands
with sufficient urgency and boldness, and they are under fire from
their White Community Relations colleagues when they do not
damp down militancy and impatience in the Asian community.
Their only tangible satisfaction is that of being treated as important people so that when the Mayor gives a civic reception or the
local M.P. makes a speech, they have their place among the
notables. It is not a reward which satisfies the more large-hearted
and large-minded of the Asian collaborators.

An arena in which the integration concept is sharply tested out
is that of relations with those English who possess power to invoke
sanctions for or against them. We have noted that the trade
unions do not provide a positive force in assisting the immigrants
towards a fuller participation in industrial democracy. Employers,
on the whole, may be regarded as neutral. Because most Asians
are reliable workers who do not make trouble unduly they get on
with employers; indeed, in many factories where round-the-
clock operation is the rule, they are essential: there would be no
night-shift without them.

Relations with the police provide a subject for frequent news-

---

[1] Community Relations Commission, *The Participation of Ethnic Minorities in
the General Election October 1974*, 1975. Whereas 89 per cent of Black voters
voted Labour, and only 2 per cent Conservative, 78 per cent of Asians voted
Labour and 13 per cent Conservative.

paper comment. In most inner-city areas, the police and young West Indians now look upon each other as adversaries, if not enemies. Most Asians, including young Asians, avoid contact with the police; back in India and Pakistan the police are notorious for *zoolm* (cruel tricks) and *zabardasti* (strongarm methods). A few young Asians adopt the idea of Black Power and join up with similar West Indians to challenge police oppression. But these are a tiny minority, and they mostly come from more affluent levels of society. (Tariq Ali, the best-known Pakistani radical, is the scion of a leading West Punjabi family of administrators and judges.) Very few Asians have joined the police since police chiefs first became conscious of the need to attract 'coloured' recruits in about 1970. The first 'coloured' recruit to the Metropolitan Police was a shaven Sikh, a former sub-inspector in the Kenya Police. He did not stay long in the force.

An important element in hastening or impeding the 'cultural erosion' envisaged by Dahya is the way in which the Asians perceive the *Gora Log*, the Whites, the English among whom they work and live. Many arrived in Britain with an image derived from a favourite British Indian Army officer, and their initial impression of the English was good. This view often becomes clouded by experiences with English workmates, and most Sikhs (and less explicitly Pakistanis) now despise the people of England. They are said to be lazy, work-shy, unreliable, given to cheating and dishonesty. The English women are said to be immodest, bold, unwomanly, and often promiscuous. There are exceptions, of course; almost every Asian knows of an individual English person—man or woman—with a reputation for selfless community service, devoted to others, in a way that (so it is said) no Asian would be. But the image of the 'good' individual is not as important as the pervasive image of the 'bad' crowd.[1]

Probably the strongest force making for integration of the Asians is the adoption by Asian families of many features of the English style of suburban living. They go for walks in the park; they grow flowers in the garden; they take the car out into the

[1] This impressionistic picture, derived from casual conversation—often rambling—is largely restated in *Rampal and His Family*. However, it should be noted that Badr Dahya reports a very different image, based on his reading of the Urdu press and letters from immigrants. In particular, he quotes one comment: 'The English are very honest and reliable. . . . Everybody helps you to show you the proper way of doing things.' Op cit., p. 268.

country; they have a family holiday in the summer at the seaside.
They may still have far more obligations to kinsfolk and caste-
fellows than any European, but they see their future as between
themselves and their own children within the environment they
themselves have chosen.

The growth of this quiet integration suffered a considerable
check in the late 1960s when anti-immigrant politics stimulated
immigrant-baiting on an unpleasant scale. The 1971 Act was
interpreted by many Asians as a sign that one day they would be
compelled to follow their Uganda brethren in being forcibly
expelled. This fear—which is never voiced, except secretly—
slowed up the process of applying for British citizenship which
is the most obvious aspect of integration. Many Asians argued
that if the law could be reversed, as it had been since 1962, then
British citizenship provided no guarantee: they could be relegated
to a second-class citizenship, as the East African Asians had been.
In addition, the East African experience demonstrated that the
Government of India would not regard any who had renounced
their Indian citizenship as any longer having a claim on the
motherland. Hence, many have hung on to their Indian citizenship,
even after twenty years' residence in Britain.

In this tug of loyalties, the representatives of the governments
of India, Pakistan, and now Bangladesh in London—the High
Commissioners—have played a role which often appears negative.
Regarding themselves as diplomats, they do not wish to get
involved in labour problems or social issues, so they steer clear of
the immigrant organizations. Yet they are aware that the 750,000
Asians represent some kind of asset—certainly financially for the
remittances they regularly send to the motherland.[1] The High

---

[1] The Pakistan Government offers a favourable rate of exchange for emigrant
remittances and it is stated that £40–50 million per annum is sent back through
official channels. For emigrants from India and Bangladesh, the black-market rate
of exchange is much more favourable than the official rate and the remittances
have 'gone underground' (for India, the 'official' remittances total £10 million
per annum): see M. Lipton and J. Firn, *The Erosion of a Relationship; India and
Britain since 1960*, London, 1975, p. 78. There are many United Kingdom firms in
India who find great difficulty in remitting their profits to Britain because of the
tight exchange controls. They are prepared to offer rupees in India against sterling
in Britain at a very favourable discount rate. The Indian immigrant in Britain pays
in his remittance to an agency and is promptly notified that his family in India
have received payment in rupees at the black-market rate. It is more profitable—
and also much more expeditious—than sending money back through the official
channels.

Commissioners therefore grace the immigrants' social gatherings and deliver speeches extolling Gandhi, Jinnah, Iqbal, and Tagore. But they give no guidance on the vexed question of whether the loyalty of the immigrants should be committed to Britain or to the motherland. By contrast, when Apa B. Pant was High Commissioner, he concerned himself in a practical way with the problems of the Indians in Britain. His public speeches were constructive, and doubtless his private advice was constructive also.

In North America, people from South Asia (or 'East Indians', as they are often called) form tiny fractions of the population: in 1971 there were altogether about 52,000 South Asians in Canada and about 32,000 in the United States.[1] However, a brief consideration of their situation may be useful in the light of the 'melting pot' philosophy in the United States which contrasts sharply with the acceptance of cultural pluralism in Canada.

The East Indians or 'Hindus' of Canada were mainly Sikhs, first attracted to British Columbia by jobs in the lumber industry, on

---

[1] Census statistics in the United States present even more difficulties than the British figures for deciding how many people of South Asian origin there actually are in the population. Under the heading Indian (which, of course, is distinct from the figures for Amerindians) the Census has three headings:

Total Foreign Stock		Foreign Born		Native*	
Total	White	Total	White	Total	White
75,533	63,466	51,000	41,412	24,553	22,054

* Of foreign or mixed parentage.

Sources: Bureau of Census, vol. 1, *1970 Census of Population, Part 1, Characteristics of the Population* (p. 568); *Annual Report of the Immigration and Naturalization Service, 1972* (pp. 51–3).

These figures appear to indicate that the great majority of those who were born in South Asia (or whose parents came from there) were actually 'White Indians', in British demographic jargon. Their parents were American missionaries, or were among the thousands of Americans who spent a few years in India as 'experts' of one sort or another. On this reckoning, only 12,067 persons in the United States in 1970 were 'ethnic' Indians. However, the Census requires all informants to place themselves in a given category, one of which is White or Caucasian or Indo-European. An undetermined number of South Asians categorized themselves as Indo-European. In this connection we may refer to the immigration figures which show that in 1951–69, 20,367 persons entered the United States from South Asia. In 1970 the number of arrivals was 8,795 (in 1971 there were 13,056 arrivals). Of course, many, if not most, of these persons returned to South Asia, but the different statistics do seem to show that the estimated total of 32,000 for 1971 could be approximately correct.

farms, and on the trans-continental railroad. By 1907, there were about 5,000, almost all in the west, but thereafter in response to Canadian, anti-Asian chauvinism they were banned from entry, and in 1941 the total East Indian population numbered only 1,465. They were excluded from all rights of citizenship, including the franchise and service on juries.

With Indian Independence, Canadian policy became more liberal; the East Indians were admitted to the vote, and sizeable numbers came to study, though not to settle. The first major change came with the amendment of the immigration regulations in 1962 which lifted the embargo on immigration from countries outside Europe and the United States. Then, in 1967, the regulations were entirely rewritten so as to remove any racial element. Potential immigrants were assessed on a points system, relating to education and training, occupational skill, and employment opportunities or arrangements. The new points system was closely related to the needs of the Canadian economy and placed a premium upon professional and technical skills.

In the late 1960s the Canadian economy was entering a phase of expansion. More closely related to the potential Asian immigrants, it was also a time when Canadian educational policy was geared to an accelerated programme of development in university and other higher education, to give Canada parity with the United States. All these conditions favoured Asian professional people, but in addition there was a 'special relationship' between Canada and India as the two spokesmen for non-alignment and advocates of cooperation between middle-rank countries in development. Large numbers of Canadian experts and officials worked with their Indian counterparts, and both sides got on well with each other.

In 1961 the total East Indian population of Canada was 6,774, but thereafter it rose rapidly until in the late 1960s between 5,000 and 6,000 Asians were entering Canada every year.[1] Most of these immigrants were professional people, or technicians for Canadian industry. Many arrived as post-graduate students, and by their academic performance gained posts in schools and colleges. Being

---

[1] In relation to Canada's overall absorption of immigrants these numbers were insignificant. Total admissions into Canada in 1966 were 194,743, of whom 4,094 came from South Asia; total admissions for 1969 were 161,531, with 7,059 from South Asia. Numbers rose steadily until 1974, then declined.

widely distributed throughout the country in dozens of colleges, laboratories, hospitals, and offices they preserved their Asian identity simply as their own private possession. Only in British Columbia was there a recognizable Asian population, and the second- or third-generation Sikhs who now formed the back-bone of the community combined their continuing support for their *gurudwaras* with participation in the local Chamber of Commerce and Rotary.

This Asian success story was somewhat dimmed in the mid-1970s by two developments. When Mrs. Gandhi gave the order for the explosion of an Indian nuclear device, the Canadians felt aggrieved. India's nuclear programme had depended heavily upon Canadian support, including the provision of nuclear materials, but there had, supposedly, been a 'gentleman's agreement' that India would never proceed with a nuclear explosion. The Canadians felt that they had been made a party to an act which might easily trigger off decisions in a dozen other countries to 'go nuclear'. The intellectual rapport between Indian and Canadian scientists and other scholars sagged considerably.

More broadly, Canada felt the effects of the oil crisis and the subsequent depression almost as much as the United States. There was unemployment, and cut-backs followed in the higher education programme. Suddenly Asians were viewed as com-petitors for scarce jobs, and in British Columbia, especially, there was a revival of the anti-Asian feeling of earlier decades.[1] Asians began to assert that Canada's supposedly non-racial points system for immigrants seemed, after all, to exclude them. The effect was to curtail the Asian immigration perceptibly. Also, there may be more of a demand upon them to define their position in relation to Canadian society. The effect of new Government policies, following the concessions to French Quebec, does not seem to be a greater tolerance but rather a more conscious effort to create a dual Canadian identity. Discussion ranged round the alternatives of 'assimilation by coercion' and 'participation by consent'. The Asians occupy only a tiny corner in this debate, and it is not even clear whether they desire to be heard.

[1] The South Asian (mainly Sikh) population of South Vancouver increased from 11,000 in 1971 to 22,000 in 1975, and violent attacks upon Sikh people and property followed. The Sikhs were called 'Ragheads' and accused of being disloyal to Canada. See Ted Ferguson, *A White Man's country: an exercise in Canadian Prejudice*, Toronto, 1975, pp. 188–94, 'Aftermath'.

The transformation of the Asian situation in the United States also came about through dramatic changes in immigration policy. The few hundred Asians who had penetrated into America were concentrated on the west coast, and formed an extension of the Canadian Sikh migration. In California, with its cults and sects, there were also many *swamis*, bringers of esoteric tidings. But American immigration policy banned the entry of all who were not eligible to become citizens, and the 'Asiatics' were in this category. When Rabindranath Tagore entered the United States from Canada in 1929 he was subjected to humiliations which caused him to cancel his tour and depart immediately.

After the Second World War there was a symbolic easing of the ban, and India and Pakistan were allocated an entry quota of one hundred per annum, which was rapidly submerged by applications stretching out for years ahead. Under Presidents Kennedy and Johnson the whole quota system was reorganized. In place of the old regulations favouring immigration from Britain and North-West Europe there was substituted an annual entry of 120,000 Western immigrants and 170,000 from countries outside the West. As in Canada, the selection procedure favoured those with skills in short supply in the United States.

The new rules became effective in 1968. The main beneficiaries of the new arrangements were applicants from the Philippines, Korea, and Taiwan, while many also came from the Caribbean. Indians, rather than Pakistanis, gained advantage from the new set-up, even though the Government of India looked with disfavour on emigration to America.[1] Whereas 5,205 Indian nationals entered the United States in 1969, there were 15,589 arrivals in 1972 (when there were also 58,276 arrivals from the Caribbean).

Most of the Indians are professional people—professors, architects, engineers—but some are businessmen. Gujaratis have established capitalistic beginnings, and so have Sindhis—Hindu

[1] The United States suffers from a severe shortage of doctors (by its own uniquely affluent standards), and any outsider who can satisfy the American medical authorities of his professional competence—not an easy task—is sure of employment which can be highly lucrative. For a time, the Pakistan Government permitted its doctors to sit for the American medical examination at a local centre, and every year hundreds of the country's best-qualified medical men competed. Eventually President Bhutto stopped this brain-drain; India never allowed the American exam to be held within its boundaries, though a number of Indian doctors try their luck at the centre in Afghanistan.

traders compelled to leave West Pakistan. There is considerable discussion among well-placed people in Calcutta and Bombay as to how a son or a daughter can obtain employment in America. It is no longer very chic to have a relation working in England, but America. . . . Some get their American jobs because of outstanding ability, and some because their fathers have positions of importance in commerce or banking.

Not many Indian workers join the Sikh farmers of California who toil as their pioneer fathers did. A few of the older men still speak Punjabi, but associations with India have faded and many have married local women who are Roman Catholics. If one happens to look at a Sikh in his check shirt and peaked cap—perhaps on a long-distance bus, or in a diner—there is little to distinguish him from the Mexicans and other brown-skinned, wrinkled men who extract a hard living amid the rich valleys of California. If America is not a melting-pot, it is a kind of shredding machine which leaves nothing exactly as it was.

Indians and Pakistanis in North America are unlikely to make a separate mark upon the continent. The most distinguished, like Dr. Gobind Khorana, the Nobel prize-winning physicist, become part of the top level of the technocracy of America, and there is not much that is distinctively Indian left over. The remainder form an unnoticed minority among all the other minorities.[1]

Back in Britain, if the process of integration is to be a reality it will have to accommodate Asian characteristics as a recognized variant to the accepted pattern. This will not be easy, for Britain has never accepted the idea of cultural absorption and synthesis as America at least has attempted to do. The original American colonies of English Puritans and English Catholics have been transformed by German, Scandinavian, Mediterranean, and other cultural forces, and even the rejected Negro has made a mighty impact with the Blues and the culture of Soul. England has responded hardly at all to the influence of the Fleming, Huguenot, Yiddish and Caribbean immigrations.

English concepts of integration have been founded on the assumption that the immigrants would adapt and adjust to

---

[1] White Australia has many Indian residents (most arriving via Fiji) though most are isolated individuals. There is said to be a sizeable Indian community at Woolgoola, New South Wales.

English standards (and many race relations studies have been based on this assumption). Yet even by the standards of adjustment and adaptation, the process of integration has scarcely begun. In the mid-1960s, race relations experts used to assume that when a generation of Black and Brown teenagers grew up speaking in accents indistinguishable from their White peers—talking like Cockneys, or Geordies, or Brummies, or in the more suburban tones of Hampstead or Edgbaston—then they would be accepted as British, in a way that the speakers of Indian English never could be. Those teenagers are now among us, and their accents are indeed the authentic accents of our cities and regions. But this has not noticeably brought integration nearer.

These teenagers are the incalculable element in the situation. Thus far, very few of them have received the opportunity to say how they feel about themselves and about this England in which they were born and brought up. The choices they make —and the choices which are forced upon them—are vital. But it is not really they who will decide whether Britain in the 1980s is to be Two Nations—one White and the other Black and Brown—or whether the integration idea can be turned into a reality. That question will be answered by the English at large.

Index